STONE CLEANING

and the nature, soiling
and decay mechanisms
of stone

Donhead Publishing specializes in high quality books for building practitioners in the field of building conservation. If you would like further details of our forthcoming titles or if you have a publishing proposal that you would like to discuss with us then please contact Jill Pearce, Donhead Publishing, 28 Southdean Gardens, Wimbledon, London SW19 6NU.

In order to produce this book quickly for the conference delegates, the publishers have used camera ready copy provided by the editors and contributors.

STONE CLEANING

and the nature, soiling
and decay mechanisms
of stone

Proceedings of The International Conference
held in Edinburgh, UK, 14–16 April 1992

SPONSORED BY
Historic Scotland
Scottish Enterprise

ORGANIZED BY
**The Robert Gordon Institute
of Technology, Aberdeen, UK**

EDITED BY
Robin G.M. Webster,
Scott Sutherland School of Architecture,
The Robert Gordon Institute of Technology

© Historic Scotland and The Robert Gordon Institute
of Technology

First published in the
United Kingdom in 1992 by
Donhead Publishing
28 Southdean Gardens
Wimbledon
London SW19 6NU
Tel. 081-789 0138

ISBN 1 873394 09 8

A CIP catalogue record for this book is available from the
British Library.

Printed in Great Britain by The Bath Press, Avon

Contents

SESSION II   CASE STUDIES AND EXPERIMENTAL INVESTIGATION

SESSION III   THE CLEANING OF CARBONATE STONE

SESSION IV   URBAN CONSERVATION ISSUES

SESSION V   CHEMICAL AND
MICROBIOLOGICAL STUDIES

SESSION VI   STONE DECAY, WEATHERING AND FUTURE PROSPECTS

Steering Committee

Professor R. Webster
Professor S. Baxter
Mr I. Maxwell
Mr J. Lindsay
Mr P. Donaldson

Acknowledgements

This conference has come about as a direct result of a joint initiative in 1988 by Historic Scotland and Scottish Enterprise to fund research into the cleaning of sandstone. This research was carried out by an inter-faculty group at The Robert Gordon Institute of Technology in Aberdeen, who formed the Masonry Conservation Research Group there. The first research programme was completed in 1991 and has led to further research and to the perceived need for this conference which will encourage the international exchange of experience and research in stone cleaning and conservation.

The conference organizers are indebted to the commitment of all concerned at Scottish Enterprise and Historic Scotland, to the Royal Incorporation of Architects in Scotland for their support, and to all members of the Masonry Conservation Research Group at RGIT, who have generously helped with advice and by reading papers.

In particular, we wish to record our grateful thanks to Jill Pearce of Donhead Publishing, and to Karen Sage, without whose friendly but vigorous pursuit of contributors, proof reading, typing and self-propelled organization these conference proceedings would not have been published.

Foreword

The intention of this international conference is for the exchange of research findings and experience in the cleaning and conservation of stone buildings and to allow those with different points of view to meet and reach a greater understanding of this quite complex problem.

The background to the issues and the need for research is very ably dealt with by Ingval Maxwell in his overview, and needs no repetition here. The other papers have been loosely grouped into six sessions, to give a structure to the proceedings and to allow some selection by delegates with only specialist interests: it is recognized, however, that the subject matter of some of these sessions inevitably overlaps with others, and we hope that delegates and readers will not complain if the sessions are seen not to be watertight.

The editing of the papers has been carried out sparingly, as an intention of the conference has been to include a wide range of those with different interests in the subject, and it has been decided not to exclude papers which represent rather partial views, as they help to give the context within which the debate and practice of stone cleaning and conservation currently operates. The scientific papers have been read by experts in the field before inclusion.

As can be seen from the contents, the papers range from practical case histories to laboratory experiments, and from historical perspectives to future prospects. Those taking part include architects, planners, contractors, geologists, chemists, biologists, conservators and social psychologists. This represents a considerable range of expertise focusing on a subject that has an important impact on our built environment.

It is intended that these papers are published before the conference, in order that speakers need not concentrate on the detail, which can be found within these pages. More time can then be spent on questions and the exchange of views so that the conference itself will increase our understanding of problems and acceptable solutions, the need for further research and promote the cause of good practice.

The views expressed are not necessarily those of the editor and the sponsors and no responsibility is taken for them.

Professor R.G.M. Webster

OVERVIEW

---

1 Stonecleaning – for better or worse? An overview

INGVAL MAXWELL
DA Dun RIBA FRIAS FSA Scot
Assistant Director Works, Historic Scotland

ABSTRACT

Of all the maintenance and work actions to which a building can be subjected, stonecleaning is probably, the most visually dramatic. It is a process which changes the fundamental appearance of the structure, has tended to be conceived on the basis of the urban regeneration argument, and has generally been determined on superficial aesthetic grounds. Whilst choice of technique by and large centres on the perceived quality of the finished job, it usually lacks a detailed awareness of the consequences. It also risks considerable disappointment for the building owner, and agent, should the emerging results not meet the original expectations. Whilst the visual significance of cleaning should not be under-estimated, neither should the repercussions. Unfortunately, evidence abounds where the detailed results are less than satisfactory, and permanent damage has been caused to buildings.

BACKGROUND

Having been adopted for a number of decades, the processes of cleaning sandstone should be the product of a competent industry. An industry where understanding is paramount, where skills are second to none and where techniques and expected results are fully understood and appreciated. And yet there appears to be no known method of cleaning which safely, and totally, removes established patterns of surface staining and discoloration without creating damage to the stone, its tooling and detail. There also appears to be no reliable system where the longer term consequences can be fully predicted with confidence. To date, numerous Scottish buildings have suffered permanent damage by injudicious or inappropriate cleaning methods being used. (Figure 1). This damage is both visual and physical. In many cases, it is also permanent.

Figure 1   Usher Hall, Edinburgh: with the passage of time since cleaning, efflorescence appears to have increased, leading to the blistering and exfoliation of some cleaned vertical masonry on plain-face work.

In discussing the problem, early in 1988, the British Isles Technical Forum summarised their view that water washing of sandstone was generally inadequate. They considered that abrasive cleaning caused unacceptable damage to the stone surface and was likely to accelerate subsequent deterioration, and that chemical treatments were variable in their immediate efficacy and uncertain in their long term effects. They concluded that no known method of surface cleaning could safely remove established patterns of staining and discoloration, and were of the opinion that no reliable technique of sandstone cleaning existed where the longer term consequences could be predicted with confidence. In the absence of such a system, they suggested that it was probably prudent to forego the cleaning of sandstone, or to confine it to the removal of loose surface deposits of dirt.

The primary purpose of the group is to provide the opportunity to discuss technical matters affecting the repair and conservation of historic buildings. Instigated by English Heritage and consisting of prominent members representing national, official and private conservation interests, the forum's view must be seen as revealing real, and significant, attitudes of considerable concern.

The trigger for such a discussion emerged in 1987 as a result of Historic Scotland's predecessor Historic Buildings and Monuments Directorate (HBMD) being asked to consider the case to clean Glasgow Cathedral; a monument in the care of the Secretary of State for Scotland and thus looked after by HBMD. Although a number of stonecleaning firms offered to carry out site trials free of charge, HBMD took the view that it wished to undertake preliminary tests under controlled and specified conditions. Consequently, a formalised contract for stonecleaning trials was set up and these were undertaken in June 1987.

As part of the assessment, and following preliminary laboratory testing of stone and possible techniques, a detailed specification was drawn up which described the methodology to be adopted (Annex A). In each test category, the least aggressive technique was to be applied first, gradually increasing in strength until visible results could be recorded.

In acknowledging that the soiling was unusually heavy and complex, the emerging report (Annex B) raised many uncertainties about the overall effects and concluded that it would be most inadvisable to proceed with any of the tested techniques (Figure 2). It also suggested that there was insufficient experience of the long term effects of cleaning, and identified the need to explore this further to avoid creating risks on the building which might well accelerate erosion and decay.

STATUTORY AWARENESS

Historic Scotland (HS) has consistently upheld the cautionary line of its predecessors with regard to the cleaning of listed buildings. The 'Memorandum of Guidance on Listed Buildings and Conservation Areas' (1), issued before the Glasgow Cathedral trials, states:

Cleaning is an operation which will change the colour of the stone and may change the quality and character of its surface. Some frequently-adopted methods result in distortion of original detailing and loss of sharpness in the masonry as a whole. Stonecleaning therefore requires listed building consent even if only to ensure that satisfactory methods which respect the qualities of the tooling or polish of the masonry are employed. The necessity and/or desirability of cleaning at all should always be carefully considered: many buildings are pleasantly weathered rather than dirty and the effect of cleaning may be very short-term indeed, perhaps no more than a few years; and where the facade is soot blackened (and may even have been deliberately lamp-blackened) or badly stained, care should be taken to ensure that there are no old plastic repairs which will remain black or grey when the stonework has been cleaned, or any old ill-matched indenting and/or pointing which will be obtrusive. If the applicant should still desire to clean, assurances should be obtained that these old repairs will be removed and correctly coarsed and pointed indents with carefully matched natural stone should be sought.

Figure 2   Glasgow Cathedral: The 'best' effect of the controlled field trials undertaken at the Cathedral in 1987. A prior investigation revealed the use of tinted mortar repairs at various stages during early consolidation campaigns and a heavy build-up of carbon deposits in areas associated with high water run-off. Such an inspection revealed the folly of the argument for the need to undertake cleaning to reveal defects. In general, these can be assessed in a pre-cleaned situation. Following the trials the unsatisfactory nature of the finished job was revealed. High iron staining emanated from stones containing much ferrous content, colloidal silica deposits resulted from excessive dwell times, and heavy carbon deposits were impossible to remove without surface damage to the stonework. Tinted dense cement mortar repairs were strongly adhering to the more porous sandstone and were liable to prove extremely damaging, if not impossible, to remove. An overall assessment of the scale of these difficulties lead to the conclusion that it would be inadvisable to clean the Cathedral, given the unsatisfactory nature of what would result.

Partial cleaning should never be permitted except as part of a paint removal exercise on stonework not originally painted; blasting of any kind, carborundum tools and other abrasive methods should never be used since damage and distortion will invariably result; unobtrusive test panels, for all methods, preferably chemical (hydrofluoric acid based and not alkaline, applied only by a specialist contractor as acid must always be used with care), should always be required and studied for damage or adverse reaction. Chemical cleaners should never be used in the proximity of ceramic detail, polished granite or marble without protection as they will remove the polish. Buildings with a combination of hard and soft stones may require a mixture of techniques. No building should ever be so severely cleaned that the polish or tooling is removed from the ashlar face or that putty or mortar joints are left proud of the stone as this will always result in long term damage.

Applicants should always be advised never to enter into a cleaning contract until test panels have been examined and found satisfactory. Where test panels indicate potential damage cleaning should not proceed.

The summary findings of the Glasgow Cathedral site trials proved to be consistent with the previously issued general guidance, and this conclusion set the trend for what was to follow.

A major factor which also emerged at this time was a growing awareness within the staff of the then Scottish Development Agency (SDA) that their grant aided support for the stonecleaning of buildings, as part of their environmental improvements programme, was leading to a number of difficulties. Some buildings were rapidly requiring recleaning, and others were showing signs of increasing and accelerated maintenance needs as a result of earlier works. (Figure 3). Although Historic Scotland (and HBMD before it) has never grant-aided cleaning, joint funding of conservation schemes with SDA frequently occurred. This approach enabled a considerably improved environmental package to be realised in a manner which was intended to be both architecturally sympathetic and historically correct. However, with the realisation of the concern, that potential permanent damage was being caused by cleaning, (Figure 4, Figure 5) agreement was reached that the problems deserved detailed scientific attention. The foundation for a jointly funded detailed research project was therefore established.

RESEARCH BACKGROUND

In essence, SDA contributed considerable financial backing to a large number of stonecleaning projects throughout urban Scotland. Many of the cleaned buildings were either listed by HBMD as being of outstanding historical or architectural importance or formed part of designated Conservation Areas. An appreciable number of cases had also been the subject of application to HBMD for historic building repair grant to assist with associated conservation work. Although HBMD had reservations on the widespread cleaning of historic buildings, these doubts could not be well articulated because of the lack of detailed knowledge on the long term effects of cleaning, the nature and quality of the products used, and the standard of workmanship involved. At the same time HBMD recognised the positive impact that cleaning of buildings could have on an area, and thereby hung the dilemma.

In developing the operating parameters for a joint research project it was readily agreed that the entire question should be considered in all its aspects, as far as available funding would allow. Associated guidelines emerged from detailed discussions between SDA and HBMD officials and a two year project

Figure 3   Lynedoch Terrace, Glasgow: An exercise in stonecleaning for the sake of it, and not carried out as part of a scheme of comprehensive repairs. Roof, masonry and window works left undone begs the question why undertake such works at all. Faulty gutters, behind the single block upstanding parapet, are evident through the continuous staining of the plain face ashlar below the string course, the exfoliation of surface repairs, and the general concentration of iron staining in the vicinity.

was decided upon. The resulting brief suggested that the research should examine in some depth the:

– general reasons for stonecleaning, setting down the pros and cons of using cleaning as an environmental tool;
– various available cleaning methods, with a view to making an appropriate assessment of each to establish its suitability;

Figure 4   High School, Glasgow - Phase I

– variety of stones used in Scottish buildings, assessing their strength and
weakness to appropriate stonecleaning techniques;
– amplification of a guide to assist those in the decision making process as to
whether or not to clean;
– establishing of quality assurance standards for use in choosing appropriate
supervisory staff and skilled contractors;
– need for guidance to determine appropriate building maintenance treatments,
to ensure the continued well-being of the structures after cleaning.

It was acknowledged that some early research had been carried out both in
Britain and abroad. On the whole this was not summarised in a readily
digestible form, and the British research, in particular, was predominantly on
limestone. Clearly this had little relevance to the main Scottish building
material, sandstone. Consequently there was ready acceptance that a literature
review of stonecleaning procedures and techniques was necessary as a
preliminary step in the research programme.

As the primary stimulus for stonecleaning was generally the expectation of
environmental or visual gain, it was also agreed that the reasons for cleaning
should be assessed against the knowledge of what it actually did to the building
fabric – visual gain might well be offset by disadvantages in long term physical
damage (Figure 6). If this hypothesis were to be proved correct, a not
inconsiderable financial commitment might be required in future to effect

associated remedial works. (Figure 7) As a result there was ready acceptance that this factor should be assessed in detail.

Figure 5   High School, Glasgow - Phase II
A comparison of similar details cleaned under two separate contracts reveal the extent of damage emerging from an unsatisfactory Phase I. Here, much of the moulded work, arrises and architectural features were badly damaged. Phase II works produce a more sympathetic approach although some arris damage occurred. Some unfortunate cement mortar repairs have previously been undertaken on the eroded surfaces.

The main aim of historic building repair grants is to render properties wind and watertight and to put them into a sound state of repair, using appropriate craft skills, and the correct traditional materials and techniques. Against this intention, many grant applications relating to buildings which were due to be cleaned were of particular concern to HBMD where, for example, the specification called for damaged stones to be disguised or patched over with disfiguring repairs using modern 'liquid' or 'plastic' stone materials. (Figure 8) .

Concern was also expressed where other critical defects were left outstanding, and unattended to, as part of an environmentally orientated face-lift scheme. Work undertaken solely from that point of view, was also recognised as being inadvisable if carried out in isolation and without forming part of a properly co-ordinated, omnibus, repair and maintenance approach. To ensure the overall integrity of the finished product HBMD considered it paramount that historically important facades should be treated in a unified manner. Not infrequently, part cleaning, cleaning by different methods, and cleaning at different periods, produced visually unsatisfactory results and negated much of both organisations operational intentions (Figure 9, i-v).

Figure 6   St Enoch's, Glasgow: A considerable opening-up of the natural bedding planes resulted from an excessive high pressure wash-off during this chemical cleaning exercise. The subsequent appearance of salt crystallisation in the vicinity of mortar beds and joints reveals the fact that an unpleasant chemical reaction has taken place. Increased water absorption into the stone will result from the opened up surface, thereby exacerbating the wetting/drying and encourage possible further efflorescence and decay.

All such variations were identified as being potential causes of permanent visual disfigurement to buildings in the urban setting. Whilst not denigrating the apparent improvement which cleaning was lending to run down areas, concern was expressed that short-term benefits should not be achieved at the expense of the building's long-term welfare. The need was to establish a method of identifying and categorising the complex issues involved.

PRACTICAL AWARENESS

On the practical side, stonecleaning problems were summarised at the time as follows:

– the 3 dimensional geometry of buildings inevitably leads to associated complex weathering patterns and surface water run off problems (Figure 10);

Figure 7   St Andrew's Cathedral, Glasgow: A post-cleaning view where flat wall surfaces, pilasters and carved details have been ripped open as a result of the processes used. The pilaster shafts, and bedding planes through the eyes of the terminating hood-moulding corbel, are particularly badly affected. Increased water penetration will inevitably result in increased erosion and possible frost damage.

– cleaning can be very damaging to tooled or polished ashlar and, particularly, carved decorative work;
– cleaning can expose naturally disfiguring bedding faults, or open up weaker beds, exacerbating erosion (Figure 11);
– cleaning reveals poor repairs and non-matching stones;
– in depth staining, as a result of defective rain water goods and flashings, are made more obvious and can never be totally removed (Figure 12);
– surface rust staining is created or exaggerated in stones with a high ferrous content (Figure 13);
– surface algal growth, and 'greening' of water retention features is made more obvious (Figure 14), or exacerbated by cleaning;
– cleaning emphasises inherent building problems, such as rising damp and water retention features such as scarcements, parapets and ledges (Figure 15).

Subsequently these issues were to form the basis of understanding which led to the formation of the research commission brief.

    Following cleaning it was also noted that chemical changes seemed to occur within the stone structure on some buildings. Lime mortar bedding was also observed to be affected, and the risk of accelerated erosion appeared to be enhanced following the formation of salt efflorescence in many buildings which

Figure 8 Woodlands, Glasgow: An unsatisfactory situation where principal elevation chimneys have been omitted from this facelift cleaning. This is doubly unfortunate as both stacks require fundamental repairs to eroded masonry and open joints. The lighter 'ashlar' blocks under the left-hand stack is the unfortunate effect of applying a liquid stone onto the face of a cut-back original block. The damp stain between the lower windows is the effect of a condensation dew-point in an unlined gas fired flue. Resoiling wall face runs have re-established themselves under supporting brackets of the projecting hood mouldings over the central windows.

had been cleaned. In addition, the inter-relationship of newly applied chemical constituents with previous treatments seemed to pose further risks, particularly when the building's history was not fully understood, or recorded, in the first instance.

The recognition of such difficult and unsatisfactory factors were being acknowledged not only in Scotland. Elsewhere, near identical issues were being expressed in print. A recent article in Building Cleaning (2) introduced the subject with a statement:

> There are numbers of buildings in British towns and cities suffering severe surface sickness, a familiar after-effect of inappropriate building cleaning methods in the hands of poor operatives. Although most of the mal-treatment occurred in the first flush of grant-aided 1960s enthusiasm for clean buildings when little was known of the long term effects of bad cleaning methods, there are still too many mistakes and too many inexperienced operators; too many inadequate specifications,

and poor supervision ... But the variety of building materials and the extent and nature of dirt deposits are so varied that no one solution can be applied to all buildings, and in some cases an individual building may need more than one cleaning method.

Figure 9a Rutland Square, Edinburgh

Concern was also expressed abroad. HBMD contact with the Danish Ministry of the Environment, National Agency for Physical Planning, in 1988, led to the opinion being aired that the technical and aesthetic problems cannot be solved in isolation from each other. With regard to the technical issue, the Danish officials were uncertain as to the end result of cleaning because of the unknown long term effect, possibly made worse by short-term cosmetic gain. In addition, the emerging research need was considered to be of direct interest to the Eurocare Eureka Umbrella Project EU140. Here, it was suggested that appropriate research and monitoring policy links could well be forged between Scotland and Sweden, to mutual advantage.

HBMD/SDA STONE CLEANING RESEARCH COMMISSION

Against this background, the two year research commission into cleaning sandstone, jointly funded by HBMD through the Scottish Development Department, and SDA, was let in February 1989.

Figures 9b i-v
This series of five detailed and one general view illustrates the effects of individual owners working to legally defined building responsibility lines in a Square conceived as an architectural entity. Colour variation on the ashlar blocks which actually cross the legal line illustrate complete lack of control in cleaning in a unified manner. Colour changes are not associated with the use of different stone types but are the direct result of the individual specifications used, and a variety of timescales to undertake the work. Hard masking of the legal line creates the most abrupt visual change from the uncleaned property to that of its neighbour. Less well defined masking leads to over-application of chemicals beyond the legal line, revealing, by tonal change, a double application. Spill, and occasional wind drift, leaves further visual disfigurement. The variable degree of the mobilisation of the ferrous content within the stone compounds the effect. Future weathering will result in false differentials, and the visual architectural unity of the Square will remain totally upset forever.

Figure 10   Caley Cinema, Lothian Road, Edinburgh: The inherent staining of this early 1920s structure reveals a pattern which is related to orientation, exposure and water retention. The upper work, exposed on all five surfaces to the atmosphere; the weather courses; projecting facework with uppermost exposed edges, and upper surfaces of the carved work are consistently wetted to a greater extent than the sheltered masonry below the projecting details. Microclimatic effects are at work where the left-hand vertical arrises of the pilasters divide the air flow, whilst the right-hand pilaster steps alternate between fast-moving and eddying air across the flat surfaces. The prevailing weather conditions approach from the right. To a lesser extent a similar pattern emerges on the two ashlar blocking courses above the projecting principal cornice. The clean triangular area lying to the left of the upper part of the central medallion, is the effect of the adjacent building and a stepping out of the cornice to accommodate the change in architectural detail. A further complexity is evident in the light unstained masonry, in the form of a 25mm wide band, around masonry beds and joints of the ashlar. Here, an interaction between the stone and bedding material appears to reject surface staining where the masonry is subjected to less severe wetting. Such complexities are rarely understood in deciding how to undertake a cleaning exercise.

Figure 11   St Vincent Street, Glasgow: An unhappy combination of cleaning on top of already eroding sandstone. The curved corner blocks are suffering from contour scaling, and general erosion from wetting and drying, coupled with wind erosion. A rising damp contour follows the profile of the pavement and access steps. The unsatisfactory physical removal of an adjacent ashlar block reveals the use of cement mortar, and a white cement mortar patch exists on the parapet.

Its main purpose was to investigate the cleaning of Scottish sandstone buildings and to assess the use and limitations of different cleaning methods.

It was awarded to The Robert Gordon Institute of Technology, Aberdeen (RGIT) following a tendering procedure which invited six academic teams to present a detailed submission outlining their proposed methodology for satisfying the requirements of the brief to the client panel (Annex C). In this process, an integrated multi-disciplinary approach was considered paramount and essential to the success of the project.

From the outset, it was recognised the main reason for cleaning was for perceived environmental and aesthetic gain. However, the project team was required to investigate the short and long term technical implications of the cleaning processes, from which informed decisions might be made to balance out the risk of potential damage against these gains.

Within the original study requirements, an element of research into the aesthetic aspects was included. With greater public awareness of the programme, it became increasingly clear that additional research into this hitherto subjective element would be required. This was thought necessary to

Figure 12   Queen Street, Edinburgh: Considerable in-depth staining has resulted from a long standing failed parapet gutter in the vicinity of the rain water head. Such penetration can also lead to the risk of dry rot occurring in timbers attached to the internal wall face. Staining of this nature tends to be exacerbated by the cleaning processes.

supplement the complex detailed technical issues already earmarked for scientific analysis. The continuing pressure to clean buildings, without waiting for the research findings, clearly illustrated the strength and widespread desire to do so. Despite the possibilities of actually causing further physical damage and accelerated erosion, technical decisions were, unfortunately, being taken on an insufficient database. Whilst that has remained the position throughout the duration of the research project, the early reluctance to defer decision making only served to support the need for a more detailed understanding as to why cleaning was being perceived as desirable in the first place.

Figure 13   City Chambers, Glasgow: A post-cleaning view, where the chemical treatment has exacerbated the inherent natural effects of different coloured beds within the original stone. The result is an unfortunate visual disturbance, and an increase in ferrous staining from the iron-rich bedding plants.

Figure 14   City Chambers, Glasgow: In a post-cleaned view all upper water retentive surfaces suffer fron an active colonisation of algal growth. This is particularly severe on the upper edges of weather exposed elements, scarcements, cornices, sculpture and dome details.

Figure 15 City Chambers, Glasgow: Low level colonisation illustrates a link with the 'splash' zone from the weathering surface of the string course. This is particularly evident on the left hand column base and shaft where a segmental profile has emerged.

Funding for this additional research was endorsed by the Scottish Office Research Committee and supplementary work on perceptual assessments and techniques was approved and commissioned in July 1989. Because of the high degree of interest in the cleaning issue, it was intended that this project should run concurrently with the main research package. However, its conclusions were required to be presented, in an integrated manner, with the principal findings at the end of the research period.

INTERIM UNDERSTANDING

Whilst waiting on the outcome of the research some private professional practices found it necessary to devise their own ground rules. In asking the question why clean at all, one practitioner argued that it is done to protect the stone by neutralising and removing dirty chemical deposits on the surface, and under-surfaces. In recognising that deposits could seriously attack the stones' structure, cleaning was argued as necessary to improve the appearance of buildings, and their decoration, to enhance the part they played in town schemes, whilst making a major impact on the general environment. Arguing that the 'human spirit' was undeniably lifted, on seeing a cleaned building, it was questioned, whether or not this was being gained at a cost to the building.

At a meeting of the Sandstone Study Group held in Edinburgh during February 1989, the generally accepted view that clean buildings looked better was questioned. The nature of 'dirt' and 'soot' was put under scrutiny and it was thought that much of this appeared to be decayed or carbonised algal growth. Key buildings often looked bleached, or iron stained, once cleaned and prominent irregular staining was noted to occur beneath problem gutters and other water outlets. The balance of patination with uncleaned adjacent buildings was seen as being rarely recovered, and it was considered that all cleaning caused irreversible damage, however slight, to the surface (Figure 16). In the case of some of the most important Scottish buildings, this damage had been severe and the results were now thought unwarranted.

The debate continued, and in April 1990 the Royal Incorporation of Architects in Scotland (RIAS) organised a Sandstone Cleaning Seminar at Culzean Castle, Ayrshire. Following the presentation of a well balanced programme, delegates at this popular event concluded in discussion that stonecleaning was desirable in certain cases, but each case should be assessed individually. Buildings were emphasised as being works of art and it was considered a tragedy that some of Scotland's finest buildings had been treated as guinea pigs to test out methods of stonecleaning (Figure 17). Significantly, the attending Stone Federation representative intimated the setting up of an advisory service for contractors, and recommended a tightening up of the list of contractors who would be allowed to clean buildings. This suggestion was welcomed as indicating an important change in how the industry viewed the current difficulties.

In summary, there was a general feeling that the architectural profession should await the outcome of the HBMD/SDA research commission before cleaning further buildings, and a thorough individual analysis should be adopted before deciding whether to clean at all, and if so which technique should be specified and used (3).

In an attempt to put forward the industry's point of view, a further seminar entitled 'Putting the Record Straight' was organised by the Stone Federation in October 1990. Held in Edinburgh, this event was instigated as a result of 'several detrimental generalisations' having been made concerning the stone cleaning industry in Scotland. In an attempt to clarify matters, the Federation considered 'that many of the problems are caused by the use of the "cowboy element" of the industry' and stressed the importance of employing Stone Federation members who abide by a Code of Conduct, Health and Safety policies and were experienced in the use and correct application of materials and methods for cleaning natural stone. Aimed at architects, specifiers, local authorities, builders and others interested in the stone cleaning industry, the event actually served to re-emphasise many of the concerns which some professionals had already expressed. Indeed, in a literature pack made available to delegates, one firm of stone consultancy services acknowledged the view that 'for every sample of a successful cleaning project there exists an example of one which has sadly gone wrong'. Unfortunately, where such schemes have gone wrong, it is the building which has tended to suffer.

Figure 16 Royal Botanic Gardens, New Palm House, Edinburgh: The unfortunate after effects of physically cleaning this building, where the full intention, crispness and detail of the moulded work has been totally disrupted. Considerable scour has also taken place on the left hand return face.

PUBLIC CONCERN

Concern also continued to grow over the future price our cities may have to pay in consequence of the desire for clean buildings. Both the lay and professional press have taken up the issue. In one newspaper article, produced in June 1989, the author concluded with the view that 'Many people will continue to hurt the buildings they love' (4). In the technical press, a recent editorial (5) raised important questions:

> It seems astonishing that chemical cleaning has been carried out on such an extensive scale (often without expert supervision) before any scientific study has been carried out on the long term effects of the method used on the molecular structure of sandstone. Now, at long last

Figure 17 Royal Scottish Academy, The Mound, Edinburgh: The unfortunate results of an early physical cleaning exercise showing the total disruption of the original carved surfaces.The shadow profiles and wandering arrises particularly reveal lack of control and the capital echinus has lost its original refinement and sophistication.

such studies are being undertaken, by the Scott Sutherland School of Architecture in Aberdeen and by Brian Bluck and Jane Porter in Glasgow ... No restoration architect or conservation officer in stone-built areas should commission any more stonecleaning before reading this research. For, as we have always known about the human body, face lifts can lead to much faster ageing in the end.

Inevitably, degrees of confusion exist. It is suspected that this will remain the position for some time, given the number of those supporting stonecleaning, and those who are generally concerned by it:

Two centuries of grime must not be removed from a Georgian tenement in Edinburgh, local council planners and Scottish Office civil servants have ruled. An attempt to clean up the face of the building in Gayfield Square has been firmly turned down on the grounds that the architectural unity of the street, just off Leith Walk, would be disrupted. The application, on behalf of eight residents in two main door flats and a six house stair in between would, say the planners, have a seriously adverse effect on the architectural character of a listed building in particular and the New Town Conservation Area in general (6).

A project to improve the appearance of Annan's Town Hall has been delayed by up to two years because of concern over stonecleaning methods. Annandale and Eskdale District Council had hoped to have the scheme under way this month while scaffolding is in place for roof repairs. But planners have been advised to refuse listed building consent to allow the work to go ahead until the completion of a two-year study into the methods and results of stonecleaning (7).

Permission to stoneclean one of Edinburgh's most famous landmarks, the Scott Monument in Princes Street, has been refused by the government agency, Historic Scotland. The agency says cleaning the 150 year old building using the chosen poultice method would give it 'a soiled, variegated brown colour, with heavy iron staining', would lead to further damage and would not last (8).

The preliminary announcement of the RGIT research commission findings in April 1991 inevitably heightened the concern of a number of Scottish conservation architects, and the interim official HS position (which was adopted at the outset of the study) had to be restated. This emphasised that the cosmetic nature of stonecleaning buildings is not eligible for grant assistance from Historic Scotland, and that care should be exercised in deciding how to go about determining how a building should be cleaned. Such caution appears to have been sensibly founded (Figure 18). One recent trade magazine article, which introduced poulticing for external cleaning, acknowledged the concern. The firm reported that in the particular case in question, 'conventional cleaning methods were tested without success. In fact, they actually compounded the problem by severely damaging and discolouring the sandstone' (9). Whilst it is gratifying that the industry is also recognising the fact that a problem exists, it is of concern that it has taken so long to do so. In the interim many structures have suffered through having their outer surfaces opened up to the elements and the inevitable consequence of accelerated decay.

EDUCATION

In the current situation, one consistent theme emerges. That is the need for increased education and awareness in all who have to deal with the issue.

Figure 18   St. Andrew's Parish Church, Glasgow: A rich variety of effects in this post-cleaning view. Cleaning appears to have been undertaken with growth remaining on the surface. Considerable colour variations exist in the vicinity of run-off from the column base, over the six courses of the plinth, where growth is re-establishing itself.

Whilst the promoting of the RGIT, and other, research will do much to give a greater understanding of the chemicals, techniques, skills and qualities required for a stonecleaning project, there is also a fundamental need to understand how a building actually performs in the environment, both before and after it is cleaned.

CASEWORK RECORDS AND VISUAL EVIDENCE

It is an unfortunate fact that there are no centralised record–keeping systems at either District, Regional or National level upon which research based analytical work can be founded. It is therefore impossible to obtain an accurate and detailed understanding of what has happened on each cleaned building. Frequently, it is suspected that on site practice and specification intentions have varied to a considerable degree, but the extent of the gap between intention and practice remains uncharted and unknown. What, of course, does remain is the legacy of the result.

Given that the early schemes were generally carried out to achieve visual gain, it is perhaps not inappropriate to assess their outcome in visual terms. The following schedule records some of the changes which are evident in a good many of Scotland's cleaned buildings. Aspects contributing to the difficulties can be grouped into six categories. These are by no means exhaustively listed, but a representative schedule of concerns might be quoted as follows:

Inherent Material Problems:

- Buildings constructed with stones of different colour and texture from a variety of quarry source;
- Natural variations in the bedding planes, giving strong irregular colour banding;
- Stones with high hydrocarbon and iron content, resulting in mineralogical changes;
- Rising damp effects, leading to delamination and frost damage spalling;
- Salt crystallisation, resulting in efflorescence, surface erosion and decay;
- Contour scaling with the loss of tooled surface detail and an opening up of the stone interior;
- Surface delamination, frequently linked to improper bedding.

Incomplete Specifications:

- Partial cleaning of features, or principal elevations only;
- Cleaning single, 'legally defined', buildings in unified facades of integrated design;
- Missing out architectural elements, such as chimneys and dormers;
- Accepting broken or missing stone pieces, without initially effecting repairs;
- Accepting fractured stone, as a result of iron rusting, structural movement etc.

Abrasive cleaning:

- Plain face scallop indentations, due to mechanical disc action (Figure 19);
- Segmental tracks, reflecting operatives' stance and arm swing movements;
- Wandering arrises, due to uneven control of equipment;
- Modified mouldings, particularly of rounded profiles, where flat plane grinding actions have been involved;
- Blunted and distorted carved detail, with loss of tooling and finish;
- Gun-shading, producing a mottled surface effect (Figure 20).

Chemical Cleaning:

- Over saturation of high pressure wash off, leading to bedding plane scour;
- Concentrated run-off on to the top bed of an impervious plinth, or base course, constructed of granite (Figure 21);

Figure 19 Westbourne Gardens, Glasgow: Highlighted by cross lighting, the effects of uncontrolled cleaning by mechanical disc is evident in the segmental scallop markings on the facade. These dig into the surface to variable depths and cross over stone bed and joint alike. A major loss of surface has occurred.

- Chemical penetration and remaining residue through open joints and broken stones;
- Reaction with lime mortar, along bed and joint zones;
- Salt crystallisation contours, resulting from wetting/drying cycles of remaining chemicals (Figure 22, i and ii).

Growth factors:

- Colonisation of algae, lichens and mosses, on opened surfaces;

Figure 20   Cecil Street, Glasgow: A bad example of abrasive cleaning, resulting in gun shading, general disruption to the worked faces of ashlar blocks, and the removal of projecting carved detail and arrises. Inherent weaker bedding planes within the sandstone blocks have been opened up resulting in a generally unsatisfactory job.

-   Discoloration associated with internal dry rot treatments (Figure 23);
-   Proximity of trees and bushes, resulting in organic surface staining

Associated Factors:

-   Linseed oil and oil painted elevations, resulting from early attempts to waterproof;
-   Applied modern water repellants and other chemicals;
-   Kitchen exhaust ventilator fumes, resulting in surface deposits and contamination;
-   Winter road salt contamination, emanating from surface spray;
-   Faulty rainwater goods, gutters and flashings leading to indepth saturation and wall face discoloration;
-   Concentrated rainwater run-offs due to weathering patterns, orientation and micro-climatic effects;
-   'Plastic' repairs of inappropriate materials, resulting in incompatible weathering and decay;

Figure 21   City Chambers, Glasgow: A build-up of salt efflorescence in the first course of sandstone, positioned on top of a more impervious granite base, indicates a concentration of chemicals lying in the interface mortar bed. This failure frequently occurs where insufficient attention has been paid to washing off heavy concentrations of acid. A similar effect has occurred on the uppermost bed of the first ashlar course and appears also to be related to an ingress of chemicals through the open joint. Naturally inherent bedding planes within the stone reveal a significant surface colour change, possibly due to a high iron content.

- Surface graffiti aerosol paint contamination, and applied decoration;
- Iron and copper staining, caused by run-off from roof and metal fixings;
- Applied anti-bird gels, resulting in localised solvent penetration into the stone.

Any one building can, in complex combinations, incorporate a wide variety of these difficulties. Given these intricacies, and an assessment of the available visual evidence from around the country, it is not unreasonable to claim the view that stonecleaning has caused considerable irreparable damage to Scotland's built heritage. In recognising this, HBMD officials were of the opinion that cleaning should, preferably, not take place at all, although much of what occurred was outwith their control on non-protected buildings. Here,

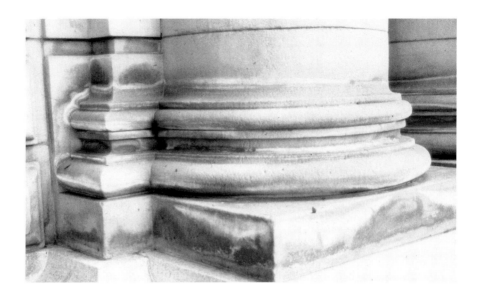

Figure 22 i Usher Hall, Edinburgh (June 1990)
Figure 22ii Usher Hall, Edinburgh (October 1991)
Two post-cleaning views of the same detail, taken 16 months apart, illustrate a developing high concentration of salt contamination in the vicinity of the first course of sandstone on top of the granite base. These contours follow a pre-established mineralogical contour, taking up the moulded details on the plain vertical facework. They also relate to zones in the detail which trap and hold high levels of water and seem to be expanding in dimension with the passage of time.

Figure 23   St. Andrew's By The Green, Glasgow: The dark surface staining extending down from the left-hand jamb of the uppermost window, to the lintel and left-hand jamb of the lower window, may possibly be linked with an outbreak of dry rot which was evident within the building over that area. Three new indent stones are of a slightly more buff colour than the original, which has a high ferrous content, as noted by the surface leaching.

however, the damage is no less severe than that which has occurred on buildings which are listed and covered by statute.

In the desire to reach a possible compromise, approvals were sometimes given to stone wash listed properties, provided such a technique caused no damage. Authorisation centred on the applied use of plain water and the bristle brushing down of all loose surface deposits. Not unfrequently such 'stone washing' approvals were 'converted' into 'stone cleaning' chemical and abrasive techniques on site. This occurred without further reference, or revised application for approval being submitted, or considered. Awareness of this trend heightened concern and served to further endorse the view that a lack of understanding was promoting systems of cleaning which were damaging to the surface of buildings and should be avoided.

FACTORS REQUIRING FURTHER CONSIDERATION

The hitherto accepted approach of inviting contractors to undertake free on-site sample panels of cleaning techniques for visual consideration, and acceptance, can now be seen to be grossly inadequate. As indicated, an attempt was made to break from this established pattern at Glasgow Cathedral in 1987. Following this approach, and a greater awareness of how insufficient limited site tests were coping with the variety of problems encountered, there was a recognised need to ensure that any future trials are more objectively set up and controlled. Inevitably, degrees of subjectivity will enter the assessment but a more appropriate format for determining detailed results has to be devised to cope with this tendency. In compiling this framework a number of questions should be raised and answered:

– Will increases in the recommended dwell times of chemical on the surface cause long-term damage to the stonework? How will this be determined and controlled with regard to the likely variations?
– Will the use of chemicals cause damage to the surroundings, fabric, and drains? How will operatives, the public and adjacent buildings be adequately protected during operations?
– How are large areas of incompatible coloured repairs, different stone type, and in-depth staining to be treated if cleaning is undertaken?
– How will newly 'cleaned' stone weather given the possible mobilisation of ferrous particles, the build up of culloidal silica deposits, and the inability to remove heavy surface deposits of carbon/gypsum etc?
– Where is appropriate matching material to the original going to be obtained, if it is damaged beyond repair through inappropriate cleaning techniques?
– How are the effects of differential weathering on previously cleaned buildings going to be dealt with? How is the unity going to be brought back to a disrupted facade where individual cleaning exercises have been undertaken over a long time span?
– What will the overall true cost of cleaning be, taking account of consequential future maintenance costs of the weakened stonework? How soon will resoiling occur?

Given the considerable sums of monies liable to be committed in the resolution of these matters, what standard measurement can be devised, if any, to prove that a long term gain will result from a cleaning exercise? To assess this, there is a greater need to put the building into a wider context from which an appropriate understanding might flow.

WEATHERING AND SOILING

Geometry, exposure, orientation and detail are all factors that ultimately come to bear on the material used in the original construction of a building. Where that material is sandstone, close inspection will reveal its ready ability to weather, breath, and change its appearance. The complexities increase when the effects of micro-climate, and the wetting/drying, heating/cooling, freezing/thawing cycles, are added to the equation.

Sandstone fresh from the quarry might appear raw and bright, but it visually matures with age. It does so in a pattern which can be summed up with the maxim 'sandstone weathers dirty'. Architectural elements such as spires, finials and parapets are prone to total saturation as virtually all surfaces are exposed to the elements. Other features such as windowsills, weathercourses and scarcements also have to deal with a greater proportion of surface water than adjacent plain face masonry. Consequently, all of these elements can hold a high degree of moisture. In simplistic terms, greater concentrations of water inevitably lead to accelerated wetting and drying cycles. In turn, this leads to concentrated soiling and, ultimately, accelerated decay.

Additional complications can be noted on vertical arrises, pilasters and columns, where the micro-climatic effects on windward and leeward surfaces often reveal common soiling patterns. These result from a situation which depends upon orientation and prevailing weather conditions. Further sophisticated soiling patterns emerge upon close examination of bedding and jointing patterns where, with some sandstones, a chemical action appears to take place with the lime mortar, or whatever may be mixed into it. Add to that, surface variations created as a result of run-off over iron rich stones, where the internal mobilisation of minerals lead to surface soiling from within, and the range of complexities which result is immense. Currently, professional, technical and craft skill training programmes do not address these issues to any great degree and a great misunderstanding of them exists.

FUTURE

As to the future, a greater awareness of these complications is essential if appropriate decisions are to be taken in the stonecleaning debate. Inevitably, each case will have to be treated on its own merits. Gone are the days when a simple one metre square test panel provided all the answers upon which a decision to proceed might be taken (Figure 24).

In should come the need for a more complex series of tests, based on a clear understanding of the issues involved. In, too, should come a greater perception of modern technology, and a comprehension of the implications, and possibilities, of laser energy technology, ice and micro particle cleaning techniques, amongst others. There is also the need to appreciate the interaction of acid rain, the complexities of consolidants, waterproofers and magic 'cure it alls' chemicals, and to effect a greater recognition of associated safety requirements, skills and training needs.

Figure 24 Belfast: Test Panel: A close-up view of a brick, lime mortar and limestone base, where abrasive cleaning has successfully opened up all surfaces, effectively allowing an increase in water absorption which will lead to accelerated decay.

In the past, we have stumbled through the cleaning debate with a limited knowledge, appreciation and awareness (Figure 25). Such an approach is no longer valid. In our care of the heritage, what we do now should not be viewed as an unfortunate legacy. We must aim to progress in an enlightened, sympathetic and appropriate manner if we are serious about our intention to protect the past for the future. We have already created too much permanent damage as matters currently stand.

References

1. 'Memorandum of Guidance on Listed Buildings and Conservation Areas'. 1988.
2. 'Stone Industries', January/February 1989.
3. RIAS 'Sandstone Cleaning in Scotland' Seminar Summary. 1990
4. Observer Scotland, 25 June 1989.
5. Architects Journal, 8 May 1991.
6. Edinburgh Evening News, 3 March 1989.
7. Annandale Observer, 22 February 1991.

8. The Scotsman, 24 September 1991.
9. Pro So Co News, Spring 1990.

Figure 25 Woodside Terrace, Glasgow: The unfortunate effects of an individualistic approach in a unified Terrace elevation. Cleaning has been undertaken to a dissimilar specification within legally defined property limits. The resulting colour differentiation, and time delay between cleaning exercises, will be exacerbated by differential weathering. This will break down the design unity of the Terrace for all time coming. Such common problems stem from a lack of understanding of the need to approach unified designs in a unified manner, and ensure compatibility of specification intentions.

GLASGOW CATHEDRAL: STONE CLEANING TRIALS

GENERAL SPECIFICATION: APRIL 1987

1.00 DESCRIPTION OF WORKS

1.01 The Contractor will be required to provide plant, materials, working platforms and skilled operatives to prepare sample panels of cleaned masonry under the direction of a Supervising Officer from Historic Buildings and Monuments Directorate.

1.02 The methodology for cleaning is set out in Appendix 1. These may, however, be varied on site at the discretion of the Supervising Officer.

1.03 The work will be carried out from 1-5 June 1987 inclusive, with the option of further days as necessary for completion of trials.

2.00 THE SITE

2.01 The trial panels are to be carried out at Glasgow Cathedral. Two bays on the North elevation of the Sacristy have been selected and are illustrated on Drawing no 4/14M/52.

2.02 Access to the site is via double gates at the West boundary then along a made up road to the North of the building. See Drawing no 4/14M/51.

2.03 The permanent electrical installation situated in the treasury block may be used by the Contractor free of charge. The Contractor will be responsible for temporary distribution round the site. See Drawing no 4/14M/51.

2.04 Water for the works will be supplied free of charge and is available from a 12mm supply in the treasury block. The Contractor will be responsible for provision of a branch and isolating valve if a greater supply is required. The Contractor will also be responsible for any temporary arrangements for storage and distribution about the site. See Drawing no 4/14M/51.

2.05 The Contractor must ensure water and compressed air lines are fully prepared for and that adequate drainage is available to the existing gulleys.

3.00 ACCESS

3.01 Scaffolded access with 3 lifts of 2400mm will be required over the area shown on Drawing no 4/14M/53.

3.02 Working platforms will require to be 200mm wide and all tubes must be capped. The scaffold must be fully framed and sheeted for security, with plywood up to 2400 and translucent sheet above and on the roof. A hinged lockable access door will be required at ground level.

4.00 CATHEDRAL FABRIC

4.01 Window glass should be treated with peelable rubber solution, such as Neolith Tak Pro-Peel, brush applied to provide a thick protective film. A small sample area should be tried to ensure no damage will result to glass. Alternatively Visqueen 1000 sheet should be taped over the glass.

4.02 Additionally 12mm exterior grade ply templates, fitted with pipe insulation on the edges, should be pressed into the openings and taped to ensure a tight fit.

4.03 Any loose joints should be raked out and sealed with compressible foam filler, such as compriband foam filler, during the cleaning process.

4.04 Exposed metal should be protected when acid or alkaline cleaning agents are used. Paintwork should be protected if alkaline cleaning agents are used.

4.05 Hopper heads, rainwater gulleys and outlets should be covered and protected from the accumulation of spent abrasive. Spent abrasive should be collected and cleared from site at regular intervals.

4.06 All wet methods of cleaning and surface repair should be suspended if there is a risk of the building fabric becoming frozen whilst saturated with water.

4.07 Trial methods should not be repeated more than twice on any area of stonework.

5.00 PERSONNEL

5.01 Operatives must be fully competent stone cleaners with experience in the use of both chemical and abrasive cleaning techniques. It is envisaged one working foreman, one operative and a labourer will be required.

5.02 All personnel working within the sealed area during chemical processes should wear shields that fully protect the face and throat and full protective clothing, which should be acid and waterproof and include long elasticated gauntlets and rubber boots.

5.03 Abrasive gun operatives must wear a well fitting airline helmet in which a positive air pressure is maintained to prevent ingress of dirt. The air supplied to the helmet must be clean and the use of a high efficiency in line filter is recommended.

5.04 Personnel working within the enclosed area during abrasive operations must be wearing respirators and goggles.

5.05 Trial methods will be supervised and recorded by up to three members of Historic Buildings and Monuments staff, for whom suitable protective clothing must be available on site.

6.00 PLANT AND EQUIPMENT

6.01 Scaffold boards and platforms should be regularly cleared of debris and dust. Debris should be collected from each lift and not swept or thrown onto the ground.

6.02 Scaffold poles and boards should be hosed down regularly to free them from all chemicals.

6.03 Compressors, pipes and airlines, including coupling connectors etc., should be inspected regularly and tested.

6.04 All reasonable precautions must be taken to ensure no damage is caused by oil or petrol spillage from plant.

6.05 Noise levels should be kept to a minimum. Any compressors must have covers closed, and should where necessary be enclosed in an acoustic shelter. For further guidance refer to BS5228. Part 1 1984: Noise Control on Construction and Open sites.

6.06 Blast machines should be from the Hodge Clemco 'craftsman' range or equivalent with both pressure and suction guns and dry and wet blasting options.

6.07 Air lines should be securely fixed to the scaffold to prevent accidental recoil, and guns should be fitted with a 'dead man's handle'.

6.08 All equipment used in handling and applying chemicals should be of plastic.

6.09 All equipment and protective clothing should be cleansed thoroughly after use and stored where it is not subject to contamination.

7.00 MATERIALS

7.01 Hydrofluoric Acid with rust inhibitor such as Neolith 625 ss, or equivalent, will be used for chemical cleaning.

7.02 Caustic Alkali such as Neolith HDL, or equivalent, will be used for pre-washing masonry.

7.03 Abrasive materials should be non siliceous, such as J.Blast Stonegrit extra fine, SC or equivalent.

8.00 GENERAL PROCEDURES

8.01 Chemicals must be handled, stored and applied in accordance with the manufacturer's instructions.

8.02 Washing off of chemicals should be carried out from bottom to top of panels.

8.03 Work should be carried out in accordance with the following standards and recommendations:

BS6270 Part 1 1982 Cleaning and Surface Repair of Buildings,
BS5390 1976 Code of Practice for Stone Masonry.

8.04 Particular attention is drawn to the inherent dangers of working with abrasives and chemicals and the Contractor is reminded of his obligations under the Health and Safety at Work Act 1974.

8.05 The Contractor's attention is drawn to the 'Code of Practice for Users of Inorganic Fluorides and Hydrofluoric Acid' published by Laporte Industries Ltd.

METHOD 1

CHEMICAL CLEANING

Objective: To establish the minimum effective strength and dwell time of hydrofluoric acid cleaner.

Materials: Neolith 625 ss

Protection: In accordance with the manufacturer's instructions, and as set out in the preliminaries section.

Procedure:

1. Pre-wet walls with a water lance using not more than 200 psi until water runs down the walls.
2. Apply Neolith 625 ss at standard strength and observe and record results at the following dwell times:
   a.   2 mins
   b.   5 mins
   c.   10 mins
3. Wash off wall thoroughly with a water lance at 200 psi.
4. If it is felt a weaker solution would provide adequate cleaning then steps 1-3 should be repeated at:
   a.   Half strength
   b.   Quarter strength
5. Record results and determine minimum effective strength and dwell time.

METHOD 2

CHEMICAL CLEANING WITH PRE-WASH

Objective: To establish the effect of pre-washing with a caustic alkali prior to treatment with the minimum effective strength and dwell time of hydrofluoric acid.

Materials: Neolith HDL
Neolith 625 ss

Protection: In accordance with the manufacturer's instructions and as set out in the preliminaries section.

Procedure:

1. Pre-wet walls with a water lance using not more than 200 psi until water runs down the walls.
2. Apply pre-wash Neolith HDL at standard strength for a dwell time of 15 minutes.

3. Wash off wall thoroughly with a water lance at 200 psi.
4. Apply Neolith 624 ss at the minimum effective strength determined during Method 1.
5. After the minimum dwell time again determined during Method 1 wash off wall thoroughly with a water lance at 200 psi.
6. Observe and record results.

METHOD 3

AIR ABRASIVE CLEANING

Objective: To establish the most effective method of cleaning with air/water/abrasive at the lowest pressure, and using the smallest non-siliceous abrasive possible.

Materials
and Plant: Hodge Clemco 'Craftsman' blast machine. Pressure gun nozzle. Venturi gun nozzle. Water atomiser attachment for guns. J .Blast non siliceous abrasive.

Protection: In accordance with the plant manufacturer's instructions and as set out in the preliminaries sections.

Procedure:

1. Use the air abrasive system with the Venturi gun nozzle and the finest abrasive recommended. Start at 15 psi and work up to 40 psi as long as cleaning is effected without pitting or etching of the surface. Observe and record results at:
    A. 15 psi
    B. 20 psi
    C. 30 psi
    D. 40 psi
2. Repeat this operating with a larger abrasive if no effective cleaning is observed.
3. Repeat the operations 1 and 2 with a pressure gun nozzle.
4. Repeat the operations and recording for both guns with the water atomiser attachment.
5. Determine the best combination of nozzle abrasive and pressure for most effective cleaning.

METHOD 4

CHEMICAL/AIR ABRASIVE COMBINED CLEAN

Objective: To establish the effect of combining both methods of cleaning.

Materials
and Plant: As selected in methods 1, 2 and 3.

Protection: In accordance with manufacturer's instructions and as set out in the preliminaries section.

Procedure:

1. Select an area generally successfully cleaned by chemical method, but with an area of heavy soiling left unmoved.
2. Apply the selected air abrasive technique to heavy soiling to determine whether or not this will remove soiling more successfully than by chemicals.
3. Record whether or not 'blending' out of heavy soiling on selected features offers a successful finish.

GLASGOW CATHEDRAL

STONE CLEANING TRIALS REPORT: JULY 1987

INTRODUCTION

A contract for stone cleaning trials was let to Hunter and Clark Ltd. of Glasgow, who set up the scaffold and protective screening on 4 and 5 of June 1987. On Monday 8 June the specified plant and materials were delivered to site and made ready for use on the following day.

The trials commenced on 9 June 1987 under the supervision of Mr J. Ashurst of English Heritage and Mr C. P. Fotheringham and Mr T. Cuthbert of Historic Buildings and Monuments. Mr I. Maxwell (Assistant Director) and Mr N. Hynd (Principal Architect) were also present as observers for the initial setting up procedures.

METHODOLOGY

The appended specification describes the methodology adopted, and is based on the original report prepared by Mr Ashurst. In general the least aggressive techniques were applied first, and gradually increased in strength until visible results could be recorded. It was noted that the soiling of the Cathedral is unusually heavy.

CHEMICAL CLEANING

It was recommended that for hydrofluoric acid cleaning we should begin with normal strength solution with minimal dwell times. The manufacturer recommends a 20 minute dwell time followed by washing down and re-application for a similar period. This may be repeated until sufficient cleaning is achieved. It is however, generally accepted that three applications should give the required cleaning and that further applications may gradually be absorbed by the stone giving subsequent problems of salt migration and crystallisation. The wall was washed down and chemical was applied as follows:-

Chemical	Dwell Time	Applications	Results
Neolith 625ss	2 mins	1	No effect
Neolith 625ss	8 mins	1	Slight lightening of surface
” ”	15 mins	1	Surface lightening with heavy soiling remaining

Neolith 625ss	2 mins	2	Slight lightening of surface
" "	2 mins	3	Further lightening of surface

The results achieved were not sufficient to remove soiling and it was therefore decided to attempt to break down the carbonaceous surface layer with an aggressive alkaline cleaner, followed by application of the hydrofluoric Acid. A new area of wall was selected and washed down before application of the following chemicals, again at full strength:

Chemical	Dwell Time	Applications	Results
Neolith HDL	15 mins	1	Break down of surface layer
Neolith 625ss	8 mins	1	Good cleaning but slight soiling remains
Neolith 625ss	8 mins	1	Further improvement but soiling remains
Neolith HDL	10 mins	1	Little improvement
Neolith 625ss	8 mins	1	No improvement, soiling remains

The results were an improvement on the application of acid alone, but still did not achieve an adequate finish. The next step was to try a combination of stronger chemicals produced by the same manufacturer. Neolith 425, a strong alkaline degreaser, and Neolith 625HD, formulated for heavily soiled sandstone were then applied to further sections of wall as follows:

Chemical	Dwell Time	Applications	Results
Neolith HDL	30 mins	1	Break down of surface layer
Neolith 625ss	5 mins	1	Good cleaning slight soiling remains
Neolith 625ss	10 mins	1	Further improvement light soiling remains

Chemical	Dwell Time	Applications	Results
Neolith 425	30 mins	1	Break down of surface layer
Neolith 625ss	5 mins	1	Good cleaning slight soiling remains
Neolith 625ss	10 mins	1	Further improvement light soiling remains

Chemical	Dwell Time	Applications	Results
Neolith HDL	30 mins	1	Break down of surface layer
Neolith HD	5 mins	1	Good cleaning slight soiling remains
Neolith 625ss	10 mins	1	Further improvement light soiling remains

Chemical	Dwell Time	Applications	Results
Neolith 425	30 mins	1	Break down of surface layer
Neolith HD	5 mins	1	Good cleaning slight soiling remains
Neolith HD	10 mins	1	Further improvement light soiling remains

From the consistency of results it was observed that given a longer dwell time the Neolith HDL was providing as good a break down of the carbonaceous layer as the Neolith 425. The subsequent application of Neolith 625ss also had a similar effect as a second coat to the two base coats. The only significant difference between the series of tests was the combination of Neolith 425 and HD which left the cleaned surface slightly browner than after application of the 625ss. A subsequent clean with 625ss brought the stone back to the same colour. This is explained by the slight bleaching effect acid has on stone.

ABRASIVE CLEANING

Abrasive cleaning was also attempted, again beginning with the finest possible abrasive at very low pressures. J. Blast Stonegrit extra fine was first applied at 15 psi using a venturi gun and water injection system. It was found that this had little effect on the outer carbonaceous layer, and the pressure was therefore increased to 30 psi and finally 50 psi. This removed much of the outer layer, but even after prolonged blasting did not remove all soiling.

A further panel of blasting was attempted using a larger abrasive, J. Blast Stonegrit Fine, at lower pressure. Once again this technique proved ineffective at 30 psi and had to be increased to 50 psi. At this level of pressure the larger abrasive was having a marked effect on the stone surface, removing up to 5mm of the face. This meant that pointing, which is generally harder than the stone, was left proud and exposed. The force of blasting was causing additional damage by knocking off all loose and friable stone. Because of the extent of damage being caused it was decided to abandon further samples of blast cleaning.

CONCLUSIONS

From the results it is obvious that soiling is considerably worse than generally encountered. The initial trial dwell times of 2, 8 and 15 minutes for chemicals, although normally acceptable, were inadequate if it is hoped to provide an even clean surface.

It was in fact necessary to move up to the following procedure to achieve an acceptable finish:

Chemical	Dwell Time	Applications
Neolith HDL	45 mins	1
Neolith 625ss	15 mins	1
Neolith 625ss	5 mins	Spotting up only

This is providing an acceptable degree of finish on all but the most heavily soiled areas, where the following procedure was adopted.

Chemical	Dwell Time	Applications
Neolith HDL	45 mins	1
Neolith 625ss	15 mins	1
Neolith HDL	30 mins	1
Neolith 625ss	10 mins	1
Neolith 625ss	5 mins	Spotting up only

It would therefore appear from the results obtained that abrasive techniques are generally too aggressive for the work, and while chemicals are providing a satisfactory finish a number of further questions must now be answered:

1.   Will the use of the longer dwell times cause any long term damage to the stonework?
2.   Will the use of chemicals cause damage to the surrounding fabric, or can all areas be protected during operations?

3.   Large areas of coloured plastic repair have been exposed by cleaning and a decision will have to be made on how they should be treated if further cleaning is proposed.

4.   How will the newly cleaned stone weather?

5.   What would be the overall cost of cleaning and restoration?

In addition to the outstanding technical points it must now be assessed whether or not the results are acceptable visually and from that, whether monies should be committed to what is a cosmetic exercise.

HISTORIC BUILDINGS AND MONUMENTS/SCOTTISH DEVELOPMENT AGENCY

FINAL BRIEF FOR RESEARCH COMMISSION
FEBRUARY 1989   PAPER A2

STONECLEANING IN SCOTLAND

Programme

The research project shall last for two years from the date of commission.

The research project shall be led by a named member of staff of a University, who will be the project director.

All of the work described in the project brief shall be completed, and all reports submitted within the two year period. Future monitoring as described in item 11 should be set up at the end of that period.

The reports described in items 1, 2 and 3 should be submitted within six months of the start of the programme. Interim reports on the other items should be issued to the steering committee.

The research director shall report to a steering committee, through the project officer. Any changes or additional expenditure shall be cleared in advance.

The steering committee shall comprise officials from Scottish Development Agency and from Historic Buildings and Monuments Directorate, who are joint sponsors of the project.

Brief

1. (i) Investigate available information from Scottish, British, European or other   sources on, or relevant to, the cleaning of sandstone buildings, and the weathering or other changes in cleaned buildings; arrange translation as necessary.
    (ii) Compile checklist of the information that is available.
    (iii)Analyse the information and summarise the main points. The summary should be presented in a form suitable for widespread dissemination.
2. In general terms, study, analyse and report on the reasons for stonecleaning and the benefits of stonecleaning as an environmental instrument, by reference to certain specific schemes, standards achieved and techniques used.
3. (i) Prepare checklist of all currently available cleaning methods and materials.
    (ii) For all commercially available chemical products used in cleaning, obtain detailed chemical analysis.
    (iii) Submit detailed report, and summarise in a form suitable for widespread dissemination and publication.
4. Carry out laboratory testing to establish short-term, medium or long-term effects of cleaning and recording all physical and chemical changes in the materials, across the following range:
    using:

(a) all commercially available chemical treatments (concentrating on this aspect);
(b) wet grit at a range of pressures and abrasives;
(c) dry grit at a range of pressures and abrasives;
(d) water washing;

on:

(i) mortar of various types;
(ii) a number of identifiable sandstones;
(iii) sandstones previously treated with chemicals or pollutants (e.g. silicones, lamp black, linseed oil, herbicides, atmospheric pollution);
(iv) sandstones previously stained by various causes (eg. dry rot, prolonged water penetration);
(v) if resources allow, a range of brick, granite, concrete and other structures.

5. Field tests over the range described above, with emphasis on the interaction between mortar and sandstone during and after cleaning.
6. For the samples of both field tests and laboratory testing analyse the theoretical and actual susceptibility of the cleaned stone to various physical and chemical stimuli (e.g. organic growth, atmospheric pollution, increased   weathering). Also record the visible, aesthetic change. Assess and analyse the efficacy, use of short and long-term effects of treatments proposed to rectify or limit the weathering of cleaned stone.
7. Provide detailed report of all the tests 4-6.
8. Prepare summary defining the limits of use of each cleaning method, and the likely effects of each treatment on stonework etc. across the range, to include comparative cost indicators.
9. From the tests, recommend testing procedures to check efficacy of stonecleaning and likely results and damage on any individual building on which cleaning is proposed.
10. Identify areas in need of further research.
11. From the field trials or otherwise identify buildings for future monitoring and set up framework for this monitoring. Compile and set up a register of stonecleaning projects, to record technical and contractual information.

Session I
THE BROAD ISSUES

2 A brief history of grime: accumulation and removal of soot deposits on buildings since the 17th century

PETER BRIMBLECOMBE
School of Environmental Sciences, University of East Anglia

INTRODUCTION

Buildings have been exposed to polluted air for very long periods of time. This means that it is often important to understand the historical changes in air pollution to fully appreciate the causes of long-term deterioration. An early realisation of the damaging effects of smoke led to sporadic attempts at solving the problems it caused. At times the cure was worse than the disease, which means that it is also useful to examine how treatments may have changed with time.

EARLY AIR POLLUTION

Cities have probably been polluted for as long as they have existed. The problem was serious enough for smoke to be recognised as a nuisance in Roman law (1) and the following case is of particular relevance:

> Aristo ... did not think smoke could legitimately be allowed to penetrate from a cheese-factory into buildings higher up the road ... no more can you

throw water or anything else from a building higher up on those lower down ... smoke is just the same as water.

Damage to materials is recorded from the dwellings of pre-classical Europe in Books 16 and 19 of Homer's *Odyssey* which describes the tarnishing of the weapons of Odysseus by the fires. Additionally, poets in ancient Rome complained about smoke damage to the temples.

The shift from wood to coal as a fuel introduced dramatic changes in urban air pollution. In south-east England this transition began in the 13th century after the depletion of wood supplies around some major towns.

When a fuel is changed, there is often a shift in the perceptibility quality of emissions and sulphur dioxide associated with coal can be especially corrosive. This seems to have been realised by the year 1512, at least for indoor furnishings. It was not until the late 16th century, with the widespread construction of household chimneys in England and London particularly, that the coal began to be used domestically (2).

The transition to coal was virtually complete in London by the early 17th century. However this is not typical of European cities. In Paris for instance, coal remained unpopular (3). When English coal was introduced in the 18th century there was a general outcry claiming it: 'vitiated the air, soiled linen set to dry, caused chest infections and impaired the delicacy of the female complexion.' In some Mediterranean countries coal was not important even at the beginning of the 20th century (4).

The success of coal as a fuel led to a rapid increase in the density of its use in urban areas. The industrial revolution brought with it the ability to use coal in even larger quantities. Railways also enabled it to be transported cheaply to localities that had not been served by water. By the mid–18th century London was using more than one million tons of coal a year, in a city that had barely grown beyond its medieval boundaries. Little wonder that smoke concentrations rose dramatically.

It is possible to model the dramatic increases in air pollutant concentration over time (5). As expected, cities where coal was adopted early show a rapid increase in concentrations of the traditional pollutants, smoke and sulphur dioxide. Interestingly the few reliable measurements, usually of deposited solids and solutes in industrial towns of England, still lead us to believe that the concentrations of soot and sulphur dioxide were probably higher in about 1900 than at the present time (2). Air pollution seems to be a characteristic of cities that adopted coal as a fuel quite early on in their development.

In London the reason for an early peak in the concentrations of sulphur dioxide and smoke (Figure 1) may be due to an increase in emission of these pollutants followed by their dilution as the city expanded with the development of an urban transport system. A somewhat similar picture is available for New York, although it was well into the 20th century before these primary pollutants seem to have reached a maximum (6). A decline in suspended particulate material, i.e. smoke concentrations, is characteristic of many cities around the world where industrialisation came early, but there are still a number where the concentrations are increasing.

The decreases in particulate load in cities may need to be treated with some caution. In Hamburg it has been observed that, despite substantial reductions in the emission of particulate material, the improvement has been confined to the larger size fractions (7,8). The increasing amounts of diesel smoke in cities have also provoked much comment and this now represents an important contribution to the soiling of the urban fabric (9).

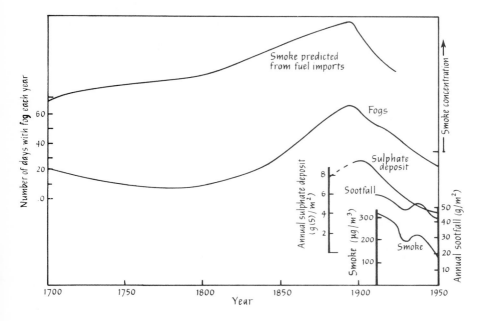

Figure 1 Air pollution in London since the 17th century comparing predicted changes with fog frequency and more recent measurements.

EARLY OBSERVATIONS OF DAMAGE

The blackening of buildings by smoke is such a ready observation that it is hardly surprising it was noted in ancient Rome. Making such an observation presumably required an appreciation of architecture as art, which may explain the early description of smoke damage by visitors, topographers and architects. On the academic side the besooting quality of coal smoke in London was described by Platt in 1603 (10), but received more detailed attention by the mid 17th century. Sir Kenelme Digby and Margaret Cavendish believed in atomic theories of coal combustion. Apart from the smoke penetrating everywhere it was argued that coal smoke contained a very volatile salt, whose sharp atoms filled the London air (2).

John Evelyn, the 17th century diarist had a lively interest in architecture (e.g. *A Parallel of Architecture* (1664)) and he claims that his book on air pollution

Fumifugium (1661) was written because he was unable to view the palace of Charles II at Whitehall, surrounded and infested, as it was, by smoke from chimneys near Scotland Yard. The effects of smoke, as described in *Fumifugium* were numerous: churches and palaces looked old, clothes and furnishings were fouled, paintings were yellowed, the rains, dews and waters were corrupted, plants and bees were killed, and human health and well–being were ruined. His parallel interest in architecture reminds us of the aesthetic nature of arguments about smoke and buildings.

Descriptions of damage to buildings from the late 17th century are really quite sophisticated, because they are not simply arguments about soiling. They recognise the corroding effects of the coal smoke, as indicated in a description of Westminster Abbey by Keepe in 1683 (11):

> On the north side you rather behold the skeleton of a church than any great comeliness in her appearance, being so shrivelled and parcht by ... the continual smoaks of the sea-coal which are of a corroding and fretting quality, which have added more furrows to her declining years.

EARLY ACTION

At the beginning of the 17th century there seem few remedies to smoke damage. King James I gave money for repairs to St Pauls Cathedral because it was so badly damaged by coal smoke. Financing assumed a more thoughtful character under Archbishop Laud who fined the brewers of Westminster for burning coal, perhaps attempting to link the polluters to damage. King Charles I gave a thousand pounds towards repair of the fabric of York Minster in 1632 and forbade both the erection of further buildings around the Minster, for aesthetic reasons, but there were also hints of smoke and dirt from them. Clearances were not uncommon in the centuries that followed. The demolition of nearby dwellings reduced the problems, but there is a strange irony in that the money obtained from renting these properties frequently was an important contribution to the fabric fund.

It was not only large public buildings that suffered. External soiling by coal smoke caused economic loss to ordinary householders. In the London of the 18th century, the rate of darkening to the paintwork of some houses was so rapid that repainting needed to be frequent (12). During the early decades of the 19th century it became evident that the stucco facades of classical or Italianate (e.g. John Nash style) houses hitherto fashionable in London were no match for the air pollution in London. The Italianate style continued to be popular, but stucco was covered with oil paint in attempts to preserve it.

Architectural attempts to counter the air pollution damage to buildings resulted in much use of 'durable' and more importantly washable materials such as glazed tiles, bricks, marble and glass throughout the century. The use of red brick and terracotta for the building of public institutions (i.e. Victoria and Albert Museum or 'New Scotland Yard' by Norman Shaw) was both a reaction against the Italianate style and a response to the problems posed by atmospheric pollution in London. However, even these techniques were vulnerable:

Red brick and terracotta discolour; coloured stones and marbles grow dim and perish in shocking haste; and it would seem as if no building material but what had got practically a glass face to it would be able to contend against the corrosion of the air of a manufacturing town .(13)

APPROACH AT YORK MINSTER

Relatively little is known of the early techniques employed in dealing with smoked covered buildings. However cleaning at York Minster, initiated under Dean Gale in the early 18th century, involved the removal of smoke and 'scurff' (an archaic word for a saline or sulphurous encrustation) from the stonework (14). This was undertaken by a man sitting in a bosun's chair which he fixed on any part that was to be cleaned. The work was completed under the guidance of Gale's successor, Dean Finch, and a tourist visiting the city in 1725 commented that the Minster was 'preserved both of the inside and outside in the best order of any Cathedral church I have yet seen' (14). Drake hinted at the sources of corrosion in the stonework when describing the repair work recently undertaken: 'might yet bid Defiance to Time and Weather for many succeeding Generations.'

John Britton in 1819 (15) noted that corrosion to the exterior of York Minster had proceeded rapidly in the 18th century and emphasised the need to mitigate the sulphurous smoke '..owing to the slow but continual decomposition of its surface, has never acquired the fine russet that clothes the exterior of Lincoln and Peterborough Cathedrals or the neighbouring fabric of Beverley Minster.'

Dean Purey Cust also expressed concern about air pollution damage to the fabric in a series of occasional papers written between 1899 and 1908. In 1901 he argued that the new stone put up in place of 'crumbling fragments' would be 'rapidly remedied by the dense smoke which seems to be more and more enshrouding the good city of York. It has already done extensive mischief to the fabric of the Minster and will continue to do so.' This he said would continue to be the case since, 'the march of intellect, when it clashes with vested interests, is sure to be slow' (16). In a paper of 1907 he warned of the wider implications for York's citizens of the smoke nuisance saying: 'The prevalence therefore of smoke not only affects the Minster, (but also) the health of the City ...' (17). The damage also received general comment in the York City Council Minutes and authorities were interested in the role of hydrochloric, sulphuric acid and microbial action of the limestones.

The interwar years show occasional comment rather than commitment. After the Second World War interest was maintained by incidents such as the London Smog of 1952 and smoke abatement conferences. Scaffolding, evidence of necessary renovation, remained on the west front of the Minster for 17 years until the major restoration by Feilden began in 1967 (18). As part of this, 'Operation Eyesore' (19) was undertaken to clean the stonework and to remove the scaffolding. This involved an understanding that washing was more than a matter of aesthetics, it was very important for conservation in the long term. The stonework was washed to remove 150 years of coal-smoke. However, even when York became a clean air zone it was realised that the struggle was not over because pollution from petrol-engine exhausts close to the Minster were seen to be an increasingly significant problem.

Indurations

Recently, Bowler and Brimblecombe (1991) have compared activities at Westminster Abbey, the Houses of Parliament and Hampton Court Palace over the last two centuries. A detailed study reveals a pattern of activity that appears somewhat more variable that at York. In particular the development of treatments for stone are much clearer for these buildings. The history of techniques and treatments is illustrated in Figure 2.

At the beginning of the 19th century Westminster Abbey and Westminster Hall both underwent renovation with the replacement of exterior stone. The potential for damage to the exterior fabric of the Houses of Parliament was apparent to the designers in the 1830s, so resistant stone was demanded. This was particularly necessary for a new building with so much fine Gothic detail. Indeed William Morris' preference (20) for buildings of the previous century was because their '... artistic value chiefly lay in the fact, that owing to the action of wind and weather, the surface was not unpleasant.'

Despite the effort in choice of stone for the Houses of Parliament, the building stone began to suffer almost immediately. The first symptoms of decay were manifested by a blackish discolouration of the stone, which appeared to be caused by absorption of 'the moisture and filth of the atmosphere ... (which) yielded a disagreeable odour, similar to that of a chimney flue.'

Subsequent stages of decay were the eruption of a coating of discoloured material under which the natural colour appeared, but in powder form. The damage was so great that it created something of a scandal during construction.

There were numerous proposals for treating the stonework and trials of Daines' Stone Preservation Solution in 1854, but the technique was discredited by 1856. At an early stage, Charles Barry, the architect, favoured the indurating formula of Mr Szerelmey 'as a specific against all decay; and in a great degree against all discolouration arising from absorption of the filth and impurities of

Figure 2 History of treatment of various buildings and parliamentary acts with smoke abatement clauses. 1821 S.A.Smoke Abatement Act. 1845 R.C.C.A.Railway Clauses Consolidation Act. 1847 T.I.C.A. Towns Improvement Clauses Act. 1848 N.R.D.P.A.Nuisances Removal and Diseases Prevention Act. 1848 P.H.A .Public Health Act. 1851 L.S.A .City of London Sewers Act. 1853 and 1856 S.N.A.M.A. Smoke Nuisance Abatement (Metropolis) Act. 1853 H.T.A. Health of Towns Act.1858 L.G.A. Local Government Act. 1866 T.S.A. The Sanitary Act. 1891 P.H.L.A. Public Health (London) Act. 1907 P.H.A.A. Public Health (Amendment) Act. 1910 L.C.C.G.P.A. London County Council (General Powers) Act. 1926 P.H.S.A.A. Public Health (Smoke Abatement) Act. 1936 P.H.A. Public Health Act. 1956 C.A.A. The Clean Air Act.

SMOKE ABATEMENT ACTS

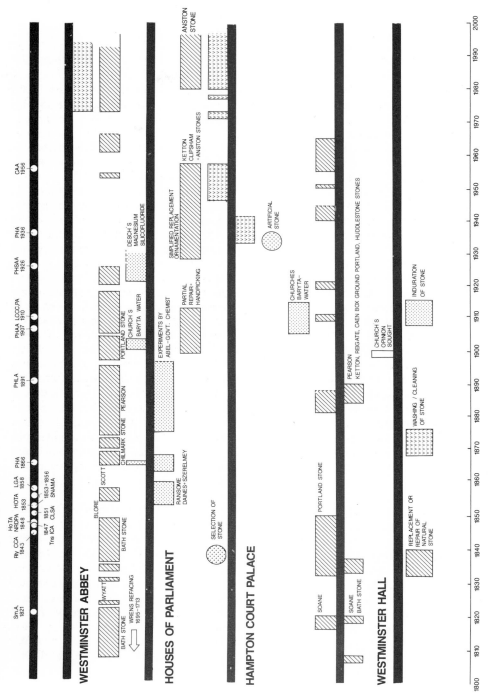

WESTMINSTER ABBEY

HOUSES OF PARLIAMENT

HAMPTON COURT PALACE

WESTMINSTER HALL

the atmosphere'. E.M. Barry rightly queried the general effectiveness of the stone treatment employed at the Houses of Parliament. The techniques of preservative experts included application of: linseed oil, beeswax, paraffin, gums, resins, silicate solutions of varying types, none of which were effective in halting subsequent stone decay. The detrimental effects that some of these methods had on the stone they were trying to preserve was startling. The application of oils (linseed, paraffin or beeswax) resulted in dark oily discolouration with small light coloured spalls on the limestone. Past applications of silicates had produced grey patchy discolouration pitted with small spalls. The stone indurators often wreaked more havoc than centuries of decay and weathering (21).

Despite the attempts to treat the stone deterioration at the Houses of Parliament by indurations, during the 19th century, the problem remained acute. Professor Church and later Desch tried to adopt preservatives to the needs of other buildings, but induration became of less interest to London architects by the end of the century. At this time there was increased discussion of smoke abatement as a method of improving urban air quality and the durability of stone along with it. It was realised that whatever the architectural effect of an edifice it was of little consequence 'for a grim spectre spreads its sooty mantle on all alike.'

The relative merits of brick, stone and artificial stones were discussed, but each succumbed to air pollution. Damaged brickwork presented perhaps the most depressing aspect. Even recent works of red brick would not last, 'the grimy zephyrs ... year by year adding one more fold of the dreaded shroud, will finally wrap them in obscurity.' The action of atmospheric impurities in buildings of limestone used in conjunction with brick was disastrous in setting off a chemical or electrical action. Portland stone weathered black, as did many 'coloured' stones. The weathering 'idiosyncrasies' of Portland were described by near contemporary authors as being typically a whitening of the stone on the south west but darkening on the far sides chiefly at the east and north east sides 'which creates a world of shadows and highlights all of its own' (22). Granites would prove impervious, but 'this is a dream of a Utopian age, when the coin of the realm shall no longer hold sway in human concerns'. Terracotta appeared to hold great promise as a building material and seemed to remain clean for some considerable time after being placed *in situ* although soot deposits had still to be regularly cleaned from its surface.

Ironically, the other side of the coin in this theory of new colour for towns was that the role of Time and Nature's work were also required to play a part in 'softening' the buildings. Into this scheme of things the acceptance of smoke in the air had somehow to be slotted. Thus, while some argued that all that was required to bring colour back to London was to wash buildings regularly with water, others argued that: 'If nature was charged with smoke they must accept it as such' and in designing their architecture they ought to do so that in time it would become 'beautifully coloured by Nature charged with smoke'. Portland stone was believed to weather the best under the effects of smoke. Unfortunately, corrosive elements in the air did more than simply coat the exterior with an aged look: 'In clear atmosphere Time works on the architect's behalf, flinging a broidery of texture and colour over his work, but in manufacturing towns Time's hand is against the architect, and, with Time's permission, the corrosive gases of the atmosphere gnaw into and devour his building.'

Following the failure of induration as a method of solving the problems of damage to stone we see a return to replacement in the renovation of deteriorating areas (Figure 2). There was also some interest in artificial stone at specific localities to strengthen the fragile portions, but because of aesthetic considerations the argument went: 'it is not desired to proceed until assurance can be given that no harm will result.'

The most significant change one observes in the current century is the widespread adoption of washing and cleaning as a technique in treatment and preservation.

CONCLUSION

The long history of air pollution and our attempts to lessen its effect on building materials is more than interesting reading. It reminds us that cause and effect are never as obvious as they might seem and that past remedies are sometimes today's disasters.

References

1.   Brimblecombe, P. (1987a) 'The antiquity of smokeless zones'. *Atmospheric Environment*. 21:2485.
2.   Brimblecombe, P. (1987b) *The Big Smoke*. (Methuen: London).
3.   Simonin, L. (1867) *La Vie souterraine, ou les mines et les mineurs* (Paris).
4.   HMSO (1905) *Reports on the laws in force in certain foreign countries in regard to the emissions of smoke from chimneys,* Cd.2347. Miscellaneous No.1.(London).
5.   Brimblecombe, P. (1977) 'London air pollution, 1500-1900.'*Atmospheric Environment*.11:1157-1162.
6.   Graedel, T.E (1987) 'Copper patinas formed in the atmosphere III'. *Corrosion Science*. 27:741-69.
7.   Winkler, P. and Kaminski, U. (1988) 'Increasing submicron particle mass concentration at Hamburg I Observations'. *Atmospheric Environment*. 22:2871-8.
8.   Kaminski, U. and Winkler, P.(1988) 'Increasing submicron particle mass concentration at Hamburg II Source Discussion.' *Atmospheric Environment*.22:2879-83.
9.   Hamilton, R.S. and Mansfield, T.A. (1991) 'Airborne particulate elemental carbon: its sources transport and contribution to dark smoke and soiling.'*Atmospheric Environment*. 24A:715-23.
10. Platt, Sir H. (1603) *A new, cheape and delicate Fire of Coleballes ...* (London).
11. Keepe, H.(1900) *Monumenta Westmonasteriensia* (London).

12. Malcolm, J.P. (1770) *Anecdotes of the Manners and Customs of London during the Eighteenth Century* (London).

13. Ricardo, H. (1896) *Art and Life and the Building and Decoration of Cities*. A series of lectures by members of the Arts and Crafts Exhibition Society, delivered at the 5th exhibition of the society in 1896 (Rivington Percival & Co.: London).

13. Ricardo, H. (1896) *Art and Life and the Building and Decoration of Cities*. A series of lectures by members of the Arts and Crafts Exhibition Society, delivered at the 5th exhibition of the society in 1896 (Rivington Percival & Co.: London).

13. Ricardo, H. (1896) *Art and Life and the Building and Decoration of Cities*. A series of lectures by members of the Arts and Crafts Exhibition Society, delivered at the 5th exhibition of the society in 1896 (Rivington Percival & Co.: London).

14. Drake, F.(1736) *Eboracum, or the History and Antiquities of the City of York, from its origins to the present time. Together with a history of the Cathedral Church and the Lives of the Archbishops* (London).

15. Britton, J. (1826) *The Original Picture of London.* (Longman & Co.: London).

16. Cust, P.(1901) *The Restoration of York Minster Third Report* (Belgrave Press: Leeds).

17. Cust, P.(1907) *The Restoration of York Minster Tenth Report* (Belgrave Press: Leeds).

18. Feilden, B.(1976) *The Wonder of York Minster (*Cerialis Press: York).

19. YML, (1973) *York Minster Newsletter,* June 1973 (York Minster Library).

20. Morris, W. (1900) *Architecture and History, and Westminster Abbey* (Longmans: London).

21. Ashurst, J. (1985) 'Options to bodging'. *Architectural Journal,* Special conservation issue, 21st and 28th August, 40-43.

22. Bone, J. (1925) *The London Perambulator* (Jonathan Cape Ltd: London).

3   Towards an aesthetic theory of building soiling

CHRIS ANDREW
The Robert Gordon Institute of Technology

ABSTRACT

Two studies were conducted to investigate the relationship between building soiling, stonecleaning, and aesthetic evaluations of architectural facades. In study 1 subjects were asked to make evaluations of photographs of architecturally identical facades which varied in terms of level of soiling. Significant differences ($P<0.01$, $P<0.05$) were found in semantic differential evaluations between cleaned and soiled facades. In study 2 subjects were asked to evaluate photographs of buildings according to soiling level, aesthetic value and the degree to which buildings would be aesthetically improved or deteriorate following cleaning. Results showed that in some situations soiling can add to the aesthetic value of buildings. Following from these studies a model is proposed which relates soiling to visual complexity and architectural aesthetics.

INTRODUCTION

Buildings are stonecleaned for a variety of different reasons, but underlying all motives to clean is the assumption that buildings are visually improved as a result of cleaning. The way in which perceptions change following the cleaning of building facades has not been widely researched. In one of the few studies reported in this field Steffan (1) used semantic differentials to study perceptions of the south west and north east facades of the department of architecture at Delft University. Architecturally, this is a modern multi-storey building of concrete and glass construction. The south west facade shows relatively little soiling, whereas the north east facade has moderately heavy soiling clearly visible on parts of the facade. Significant differences were found between the perceptions of the two facades of this modern building, as measured by the selected semantic differentials. The way in which soiling and cleaning might effect the perception of more historic buildings constructed in different materials is not fully understood.

A knowledge of the nature of soiling patterns on the facades of different buildings, and the way in which these interact with architectural aesthetics should be the starting point for any stonecleaning decision making process. Yet decisions on the suitability of cleaning different building types, which vary in the nature and extent of their soiling, etc., are made in the absence of research based guidelines.

The objectives of the present study were firstly to investigate more fully the nature of the change in perception which results from the cleaning of a range of different soiled buildings, and secondly to study the effects of soiling patterns and levels on facade complexity and architectural aesthetics. The aim being to develop a model of the way in which the cycle of building soiling affects the perception of architectural aesthetics.

Method

Study 1

In order to investigate the change in perception which occurs as a result of cleaning a series of buildings were selected and photographed for study. Each set consisted of architecturally similar buildings which, as far as possible, varied only in terms of their level of soiling and which, in effect, were examples of particular types of buildings before and after cleaning. Each example of the sets of buildings occurred in the same street, in most cases occupying positions adjacent to each other. Only buildings which were considered to have the least additional variance besides soiling were used. The selected buildings were photographed using a 35mm camera and, where possible, an architectural shift lens was employed.

In order to compare evaluations of the photographs of the before and after cleaning buildings, a series of carefully selected semantic differentials were used. In addition subjects were asked to estimate the age of each building. A related design experimental procedure was used in which each subject was shown, and asked to rate on the semantic differentials, a selection of the photographs of the before and after cleaned buildings. These were ordered in such a way that subjects were unaware that they were evaluating pairs of similar buildings.

Results

The semantic differential ratings for each set of buildings was subjected to Wilcoxon statistical analysis.
Results for each set of buildings are presented in Figures 1-6.

Discussion

In general, the results from the semantic differential evaluations of the pairs of buildings, revealed quite large changes in the perceptual evaluation of buildings before and after cleaning. In every case the cleaned building tended to be rated more positively than their soiled counterparts.The large and significant differences found may in part be due to the examples selected, in that in general, very soiled buildings were being compared to relatively recently cleaned ones. The differences in evaluation between the various sets of soiled and cleaned buildings showed some interesting variations. The least differences in evaluation was found between the ratings for Nos. 3 & 4 Magdala Crescent, Edinburgh. Indeed No.3 Magdala Crescent, the soiled building was rated slightly higher on the dimensions of orderly, has character, dignified and high status than the cleaned No.4 Magdala Crescent, although the differences were not significant. It seems likely that the results of the cleaning to 4 Magdala Crescent have contributed to the smaller shift in evaluation than is apparent with the other buildings used in this study. Cleaning has resulted in a pale bleached facade and there is considerable staining on large parts of the facade. Staining is apparent on 3 Magdala Crescent in similar places to 4 Magdala Crescent but is mainly obscured by the soiling. 4 Magdala Crescent seems to suffer from a combination of poor cleaning coupled with the revealing of existing soiling leaving a largely unattractive facade.

While it is difficult to make direct comparisons between the various cleaned buildings used in this study, some comparisons are possible. Figure 7 represents the evaluation of six different cleaned buildings which can be seen as representing a range of stone finishes produced by cleaning. The evaluation for the semantic differential of pleasing colour-displeasing colour varies for each building. The most pleasing colour being for the evenly coloured yellow/brown facade of 5 Park Circus Place followed by the slightly darker brown coloured facade of the East Claremont Street tenement. The uniformly coloured but rather bland pale facades of 6 Palmerstone Place and 23 Rutland Street were preferred next with the heavily stained facades of 4 Magdala Crescent and 58 Palmerstone Place liked least. It is interesting to note that the dimensions of warm-cold and well looked after–shabby follow a very similar pattern. What seems to emerge from these results is that stonecleaning produces a positive change in evaluations, but the extent of the change in evaluation is very much dependent on the quality of the finished produced by the actual cleaning process.

The change in evaluation on the various semantic differentials was not uniform. Figure 8 gives the mean percentage change in each semantic differential across all pairs of buildings studied. From this it can be seen that cleaning influences some dimensions more than others. Not surprisingly, the dimensions of clean and light are the most markedly changed. Also, quite large

Figure 1 Comparison of soiled and cleaned buildings: 93-97 & 99-103 East Claremont Street, Edinburgh

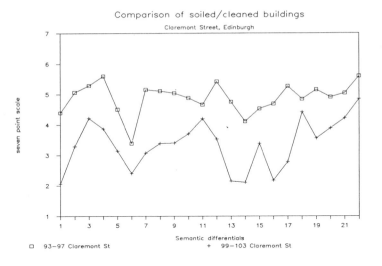

Comparison of soiled/cleaned buildings
Claremont Street, Edinburgh

□ 93-97 Claremont St   + 99-103 Claremont St

	P . VALUE
1.WELL LOOKED AFTER.............SHABBY	0.000**
2.IMPRESSIVE............................UNIMPRESSIVE	0.000**
3.DELICATE................................WEIGHTY	0.000**
4.DISTINCTIVE ....ORDINARY	0.000**
5.INVITING ....REPELLING	0.000**
6.ORDERLY................................IRREGULAR	0.001**
7.CHEERFUL ....GLOOMY	0.000**
8.WARM......................................COLD	0.000**
9.ATTRACTIVE...........................UNATTRACTIVE	0.000**
10.DELIGHTFUL..........................DREADFUL	0.000**
11.HAS CHARACTER.................HAS NO CHARACTER	0.108
12.SOFT......................................HARD	0.000**
13.CLEAN...................................DIRTY	0.000**
14.TIDY ....UNTIDY	0.000**
15.FRIENDLY..............................UNFRIENDLY	0.000**
16.LIGHT ....DARK	0.000**
17.PLEASING COLOUR ....DISPLEASING COLOUR	0.000**
18.ELEGANT...............................CLUMSY	0.000**
19.UPLIFTING ....DEPRESSING	0.000**
20.DIGNIFIED.............................UNDIGNIFIED	0.001**
21.HIGH STATUS ....LOW STATUS	0.002**
22.UNIQUE..................................COMMON	0.007**

* *Significant at P<0.01

Figure 2   Comparison of soiled and cleaned buildings 23,25 Rutland Street, Edinburgh

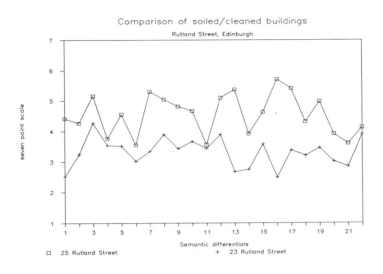

		P . VALUE
1.WELL LOOKED AFTER.............SHABBY		0.000**
2.IMPRESSIVE............................UNIMPRESSIVE		0.000**
3.DELICATE................................WEIGHTY		0.000**
4.DISTINCTIVE ....ORDINARY		0.406
5.INVITING ....REPELLING		0.000**
6.ORDERLY................................IRREGULAR		0.007**
7.CHEERFUL ....GLOOMY		0.000**
8.WARM......................................COLD		0.000**
9.ATTRACTIVE...........................UNATTRACTIVE		0.000**
10.DELIGHTFUL..........................DREADFUL		0.001**
11.HAS CHARACTER ....HAS NO CHARACTER		0.476
12.SOFT......................................HARD		0.000**
13.CLEAN....................................DIRTY		0.000**
14.TIDY ....UNTIDY		0.000**
15.FRIENDLY..............................UNFRIENDLY		0.000**
16.LIGHT ....DARK		0.000**
17.PLEASING COLOUR ....DISPLEASING COLOUR		0.000**
18.ELEGANT................................CLUMSY		0.000**
19.UPLIFTING.............................DEPRESSING		0.000**
20.DIGNIFIED.............................UNDIGNIFIED		0.000**
21.HIGH STATUS ....LOW STATUS		0.000**
22.UNIQUE..................................COMMON		0.296

* *Significant at P<0.01

Figure 3 Comparison of soiled and cleaned buildings 6,8 Palmerstone Place, Edinburgh

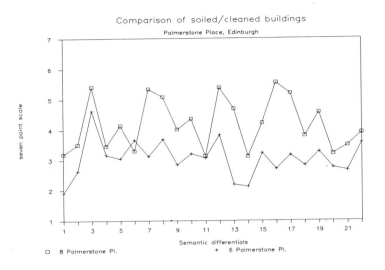

	P . VALUE
1.WELL LOOKED AFTER.............SHABBY	0.000**
2.IMPRESSIVE............................UNIMPRESSIVE	0.006**
3.DELICATE...............................WEIGHTY	0.001**
4.DISTINCTIVE ....ORDINARY	0.247
5.INVITING ....REPELLING	0.001**
6.ORDERLY...............................IRREGULAR	0.151
7.CHEERFUL ....GLOOMY	0.000**
8.WARM....................................COLD	0.000**
9.ATTRACTIVE...........................UNATTRACTIVE	0.002**
10.DELIGHTFUL.........................DREADFUL	0.004**
11.HAS CHARACTER..................HAS NO CHARACTER	0.864
12.SOFT....................................HARD	0.000**
13.CLEAN..................................DIRTY	0.000**
14.TIDY ....UNTIDY	0.001**
15.FRIENDLY.............................UNFRIENDLY	0.001**
16.LIGHT ....DARK	0.000**
17.PLEASING COLOUR ....DISPLEASING COLOUR	0.000**
18.ELEGANT..............................CLUMSY	0.001**
19.UPLIFTING ....DEPRESSING	0.000**
20.DIGNIFIED............................UNDIGNIFIED	0.1
21.HIGH STATUS ....LOW STATUS	0.002**
22.UNIQUE................................COMMON	0.236

* *Significant at P<0.01

Figure 4 Comparison of soiled and cleaned buildings 58,60 Palmerstone Place, Edinburgh

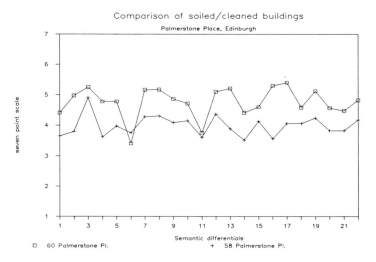

Comparison of soiled/cleaned buildings
Palmerstone Place, Edinburgh

□ 60 Palmerstone Pl.   + 58 Palmerstone Pl.

		P . VALUE
1.WELL LOOKED AFTER	SHABBY	0.005**
2.IMPRESSIVE	UNIMPRESSIVE	0.000**
3.DELICATE	WEIGHTY	0.068
4.DISTINCTIVE	ORDINARY	0.000**
5.INVITING	REPELLING	0.000**
6.ORDERLY	IRREGULAR	0.111
7.CHEERFUL	GLOOMY	0.000**
8.WARM	COLD	0.000**
9.ATTRACTIVE	UNATTRACTIVE	0.001**
10.DELIGHTFUL	DREADFUL	0.001**
11.HAS CHARACTER	HAS NO CHARACTER	0.446
12.SOFT	HARD	0.001**
13.CLEAN	DIRTY	0.000**
14.TIDY	UNTIDY	0.000**
15.FRIENDLY	UNFRIENDLY	0.021*
16.LIGHT	DARK	0.000**
17.PLEASING COLOUR	DISPLEASING COLOUR	0.000**
18.ELEGANT	CLUMSY	0.020*
19.UPLIFTING	DEPRESSING	0.000**
20.DIGNIFIED	UNDIGNIFIED	0.001**
21.HIGH STATUS	LOW STATUS	0.010**
22.UNIQUE	COMMON	0.002**

* Significant at P<0.01
**Significant at P<0.05

Figure 5 Comparison of soiled and cleaned buildings 3,4 Magdala Crescent, Edinburgh

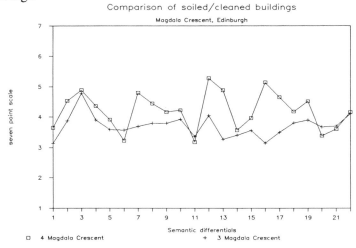

		P . VALUE
1.WELL LOOKED AFTER	SHABBY	0.024*
2.IMPRESSIVE	UNIMPRESSIVE	0.000**
3.DELICATE	WEIGHTY	0.659
4.DISTINCTIVE	ORDINARY	0.026*
5.INVITING	REPELLING	0.200
6.ORDERLY	IRREGULAR	0.099
7.CHEERFUL	GLOOMY	0.000**
8.WARM	COLD	0.004**
9.ATTRACTIVE	UNATTRACTIVE	0.113**
10.DELIGHTFUL	DREADFUL	0.764**
11.HAS CHARACTER	HAS NO CHARACTER	0.266
12.SOFT	HARD	0.000**
13.CLEAN	DIRTY	0.000**
14.TIDY	UNTIDY	0.515
15.FRIENDLY	UNFRIENDLY	0.068
16.LIGHT	DARK	0.000**
17.PLEASING COLOUR	DISPLEASING COLOUR	0.000**
18.ELEGANT	CLUMSY	0.132
19.UPLIFTING	DEPRESSING	0.004**
20.DIGNIFIED	UNDIGNIFIED	0.070
21.HIGH STATUS	LOW STATUS	0.462
22.UNIQUE	COMMON	0.739

* Significant at P<0.01
**Significant at P<0.05

Figure 6 Comparison of soiled and cleaned buildings 5,7,9 Park Circus Place, Glasgow

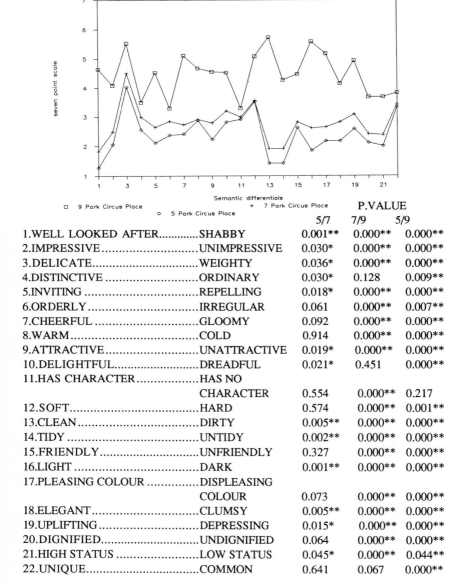

Comparison of soiled/cleaned buildings
Park Circus Place, Glasgow

□ 9 Park Circus Place   + 7 Park Circus Place   ○ 5 Park Circus Place

		P.VALUE	
	5/7	7/9	5/9
1.WELL LOOKED AFTER.............SHABBY	0.001**	0.000**	0.000**
2.IMPRESSIVE...........................UNIMPRESSIVE	0.030*	0.000**	0.000**
3.DELICATE...............................WEIGHTY	0.036*	0.000**	0.000**
4.DISTINCTIVE ....ORDINARY	0.030*	0.128	0.009**
5.INVITING ....REPELLING	0.018*	0.000**	0.000**
6.ORDERLY...............................IRREGULAR	0.061	0.000**	0.007**
7.CHEERFUL ....GLOOMY	0.092	0.000**	0.000**
8.WARM....................................COLD	0.914	0.000**	0.000**
9.ATTRACTIVE..........................UNATTRACTIVE	0.019*	0.000**	0.000**
10.DELIGHTFUL..........................DREADFUL	0.021*	0.451	0.000**
11.HAS CHARACTER...................HAS NO			
CHARACTER	0.554	0.000**	0.217
12.SOFT.....................................HARD	0.574	0.000**	0.001**
13.CLEAN...................................DIRTY	0.005**	0.000**	0.000**
14.TIDY ....UNTIDY	0.002**	0.000**	0.000**
15.FRIENDLY.............................UNFRIENDLY	0.327	0.000**	0.000**
16.LIGHT ....DARK	0.001**	0.000**	0.000**
17.PLEASING COLOUR ....DISPLEASING			
COLOUR	0.073	0.000**	0.000**
18.ELEGANT..............................CLUMSY	0.005**	0.000**	0.000**
19.UPLIFTING............................DEPRESSING	0.015*	0.000**	0.000**
20.DIGNIFIED.............................UNDIGNIFIED	0.064	0.000**	0.000**
21.HIGH STATUS ....LOW STATUS	0.045*	0.000**	0.044**
22.UNIQUE.................................COMMON	0.641	0.067	0.000**

* Significant at P<0.01
**Significant at P<0.05

Figure 7 Comparison of semantic differential ratings of a number of cleaned buildings

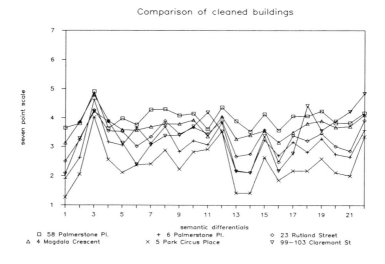

Comparison of cleaned buildings

1.WELL LOOKED AFTER..............SHABBY
2.IMPRESSIVE ............................UNIMPRESSIVE
3.DELICATE.................................WEIGHTY
4.DISTINCTIVE ....ORDINARY
5.INVITING ....REPELLING
6.ORDERLY ....IRREGULAR
7.CHEERFUL ....GLOOMY
8.WARM.....................................COLD
9.ATTRACTIVE...........................UNATTRACTIVE
10.DELIGHTFUL..........................DREADFUL
11.HAS CHARACTER..................HAS NO CHARACTER
12.SOFT.....................................HARD
13.CLEAN...................................DIRTY
14.TIDY ....UNTIDY
15.FRIENDLY..............................UNFRIENDLY
16.LIGHT ....DARK
17.PLEASING COLOUR ....DISPLEASING COLOUR
18.ELEGANT...............................CLUMSY
19.UPLIFTING.............................DEPRESSING
20.DIGNIFIED..............................UNDIGNIFIED
21.HIGH STATUS ....LOW STATUS
22.UNIQUE..................................COMMON

Figure 8 Mean percentage change in semantic differential rating following cleaning

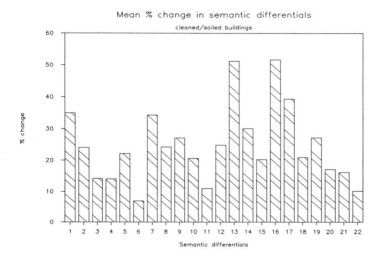

Mean % change in semantic differentials
cleaned/soiled buildings

1.WELL LOOKED AFTER.............SHABBY
2.IMPRESSIVE............................UNIMPRESSIVE
3.DELICATE...............................WEIGHTY
4.DISTINCTIVE ....ORDINARY
5.INVITING ....REPELLING
6.ORDERLY................................IRREGULAR
7.CHEERFUL ....GLOOMY
8.WARM.....................................COLD
9.ATTRACTIVE...........................UNATTRACTIVE
10.DELIGHTFUL.........................DREADFUL
11.HAS CHARACTER ....HAS NO CHARACTER
12.SOFT.....................................HARD
13.CLEAN ....DIRTY
14.TIDY ....UNTIDY
15FRIENDLY..............................UNFRIENDLY
16.LIGHT ....DARK
17.PLEASING COLOUR ....DISPLEASING COLOUR
18.ELEGANT..............................CLUMSY
19.UPLIFTING............................DEPRESSING
20.DIGNIFIED............................UNDIGNIFIED
21.HIGH STATUS ....LOW STATUS
22.UNIQUE.................................COMMON

percentage changes occur along the dimensions of pleasing colour, cheerful, tidy and well looked after. To a slightly lesser extent the dimensions of tidy, attractive, impressive, warm, soft, friendly, elegant and uplifting are also improved following cleaning. Least affected by cleaning are the dimensions of orderly, character, unique, impressive and weighty. It would seem that these characteristics are probably more influenced by the architecture of the building rather than the level of soiling.

Subjects in this study were also asked to make estimations of the age of the buildings. There was a general tendency to estimate the age of the cleaned building as being slightly younger than their soiled counterparts (no soiled building was estimated as being younger than its cleaned counterpart). In most cases the differences were not large. It seems that the architectural style of the building was the main influence in judging the approximate period of the building, but stonecleaning had the effect of shifting estimations to the later part of the period. Evidence from the study showed a general tendency, with both the soiled and cleaned buildings, to underestimate the age of buildings. With this general tendency to underestimate combined with the effect of stonecleaning on estimations large scale stonecleaning might reduce the sense of age of urban areas.

Study 2

Introduction

The previous study of the appraisal of buildings before and after cleaning revealed significant shifts in semantic differential evaluations following the cleaning of heavily soiled buildings. However, evidence reported by The Masonry Conservation Research Group (2) from surveys of architects and non professionals has revealed that soiling can aesthetically enhance and add to the character of some buildings. The question then arises as to when and how buildings are aesthetically improved by cleaning. The aim of this second study was to investigate more fully the relationship between type of building, materials used in construction, aesthetic value and whether the building would be aesthetically enhanced or deteriorate following cleaning.

Method

In order to investigate the relationship between the nature of soiling and building aesthetics a series of buildings were selected and photographed. The basis of selection was to achieve, as far as possible, a reasonable cross section of buildings which varied in terms of soiling, materials used in construction, age and style. Subjects were presented with photographs of each building and asked to rate them on three scales. The scales measured:

1. Degree of soiling;
2. Aesthetic appeal of building;
3. The degree to which subjects believed the aesthetic appeal would be improved or deteriorate following cleaning.

Results

Results from these ratings were then drawn up on three dimensional graphs a selection of which are shown in Figures 9-12.

Discussion

This study illustrates the complex interaction between soiling, architecture and aesthetics. While study 1 revealed significant shifts in semantic differential evaluation following the cleaning of heavily soiled buildings, study 2 shows that soiling would appear to enhance the aesthetic appeal of buildings in some circumstances. Results from this study would seem to confirm the potential aesthetic improvement brought about by the cleaning of heavily soiled buildings. Where soiling is perceived to be heavy, most subjects were agreed that cleaning would improve the aesthetic appeal of the building, e.g. Argyle Arcade, Glasgow and Royal High School, Edinburgh. These buildings are interesting in that subjects varied considerably in their judgement of the aesthetics of the building. This may be due to some subjects paying relatively little attention to the soiled surface layer and responding at a 'deeper' level to the underlying architectural features of the building, and thus rating them as aesthetically pleasing. Others may have responded at a 'surface level', and, on seeing the buildings heavily soiled, rated the buildings as aesthetically displeasing, without tending to look closer at the underlying architecture. Although it may simply be that the architectural style of these buildings are aesthetically more pleasing to some individuals. Results from those buildings which display light and moderate levels of soiling also produced interesting results, particularly where subjects were of the opinion that cleaning would be detrimental to the look of the building. Buildings which appeared in this category included 244 Royal Mile and Lady Stair's House. Although there are clearly individual differences in judgement these appear situations where soiling seems to enhance their aesthetic appeal.

Aesthetic theory

Results from the two previous studies indicate that soiling and weathering on the surface of buildings changes the visual character of their facades. Building soiling can be seen to progress through a cycle with facade cleaning interrupting this progression and returning the building to an earlier stage in the cycle.

Initially, light soiling on surfaces which have an uneven texture (e.g. tooled stone) lodges mainly in crevices and on horizontal surfaces which rainwater has difficulty in dislodging. Similarly, light soiling around architectural detail adds to the visual complexity of the building by increasing contrast and shadowing effects. Verhoef (3) argues that in northerly cities of Europe soiling can emphasise architectural designs which for much of the year would be lacking due to the absence of sharp, well defined shadows. Moderate soiling of building facades results in a change in the visual appearance of the building which has an interactional effect with the underlying architectural features or

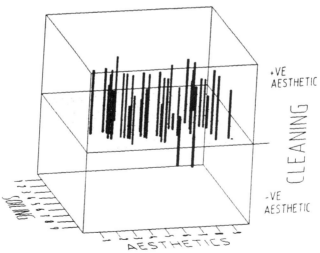

Figure 9 Argyle Arcade, Glasgow

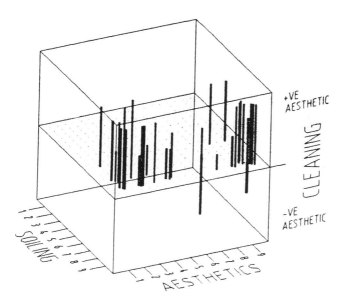

Figure 10 Royal High School, Edinburgh

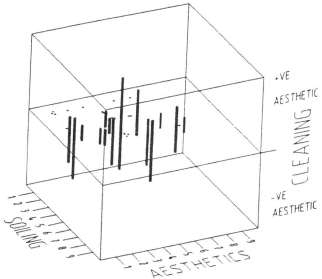

Figure 11 244 Royal Mile, Edinburgh

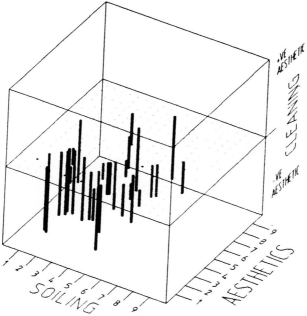

Figure 12 Lady Stairs House, Edinburgh

stone surface. Moderate soiling changes the visual complexity of the building (by obscuring some detail, colour and texture, etc.)while at the same time adding a pattern of soiling which was originally absent. This interactional effect may well change with different stone surfaces. While initially this soiling may be related to the underlying architectural surface, with continued build up patterns of soiling eventually arise which are unrelated to the underlying detail. Heavy soiling eventually leads to a uniform blackening of the surface of the building which reduces the visual information of architectural details and completely obscures the colour, texture and any shadowing effects. In effect the visual complexity of the facade is reduced by the even and complete blackening of the building facade. Entire buildings may progress through this pattern of soiling in a relatively consistent way or parts of facades may soil at different rates.

The concept of complexity is related to the concept of information rate, derived from information theory. Moles (4) applied the original theory to human perception, partitioning communication into redundancy and message. This was taken further by Krampen (5) who used the concept of the type-token ratio as a measure of the variability of facade designs. Studies in experimental aesthetics (6) have shown that ratings of pleasingness of relatively complex patterns varies from those of relatively simple patterns.

The cycle of building weathering suggests that soiling affects building complexity and thus aesthetic value in a relationship shown by Figure 13. The precise shape of this graph may vary considerably due to factors such as type and age of building, material used in construction, etc. Figure 13 may hypothetically be seen to represent the weathering pattern of many rock faced and tooled ashlar stone buildings.

Initially after construction, the building has a positive aesthetic value. After a number of years of weathering, where accumulations of dirt are consistent with the architectural features and the stone texture, complexity is increased and aesthetic value rises to a peak. Thereafter it begins to decline as soiling increases, becoming unrelated to underlying architectural features. As soiling becomes increasingly heavy complexity is reduced and aesthetic value decreases to a point where the whole facade is blackened and complexity is at a minimum. In Figure 13 cleaning a building at the point of maximum soiling has the effect of returning it to a point nearer the beginning of the graph, and the soiling cycle is again reintroduced. The point at which it returns and the subsequent weathering effects may well depend on the method chosen for cleaning and the success of the cleaning process. The model of building weathering and architectural aesthetics proposed at least in part supports Berlyne's model. The model would predict that heavily soiled buildings are aesthetically less pleasing than when cleaned, clear evidence for this is seen in study 1. The model also suggests that old buildings with light soiling are aesthetically more pleasing than the same buildings without soiling, study 2 gives indications of this being the case.

In addition to interacting with the visual complexity of the facade, soiling also adds a further historical dimension to building facades. Evidence from The Masonry Conservation Research Group (2) shows that removal of all soiling from buildings, removes a sense of the history of buildings. Perhaps the best

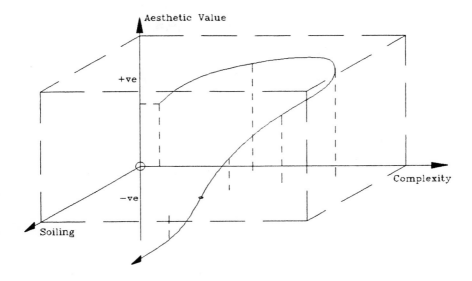

Figure 13 Relationship between aesthetic value, soiling and complexity

example of this historical association is seen in the general opposition to the cleaning of Edinburgh Castle were soiling in addition to giving increased complexity to the building also adds a historic significance which would be lost on cleaning.

References

1. Steffan (1988) in Verhoef, L, G, W (1988) ref.3.
2. The Masonry Conservation Research Group (1991) Stone cleaning in Scotland, report to Scottish Enterprise and Historic Scotland.
3. Verhoef, L.G.W. (ed), 1988 Rilem Report, Soiling and cleaning of building facades, Chapman Hall.
4. Moles, A. 1966 Information theory and aesthetic perception, Univ. of Illinois Press.
5. Krampen, M. 1979 Meaning in the urban environment, Pion.
6. Berlyne, D.E. 1974 Studies in the new experimental aesthetics, Wiley.

4 Stone cleaning – a professional view

JAMES SIMPSON
B Arch FRIAS RIBA FSA Scot

(ABSTRACT)

This paper gives a professional viewpoint of architect, historian and conservator; the place of stone in Scottish architecture and townscape and the concept of architectural geography; the comparative behaviour and appearance of Scottish stone; and the character of the Scottish city and burgh.

The origins of the desire to clean stone are covered; as well as the mid 20th century 'modern' view of finite building life; neglect followed by rediscovery of need to retain, repair and improve; travel, comparison with other cities and developments in, e.g. London and Paris; political discovery of public relations and marketing; cleaning stone a cheap, fast and popular way of making an impact, boosting economic confidence and social morale; parallel thinking in public and private sectors; shift of commercial and housing architects and builders with little experience of old buildings into 'refurbishment' and 'rehabilitation'; public perception of stone cleaning as a necessary and integral component of 'environmental improvement'.

Serious professional opinion initially interested but increasingly concerned and cautious about the consequences of cleaning, e.g. attitudes of ENTCC, AHSS, HS, RIAS etc.; sandblasting, discing etc. rejected, but only after serious damage to important architecture; chemical methods accepted for a time by some, but increasing awareness of insidious damage, increased water retention, algae growth, unnaturally bleached and generally unsatisfactory appearance etc., the arguably, irresponsible attitude of SDA and confusion in public minds, including those of planning committee members.

Professional awareness of lack of knowledge and understanding of the nature and behaviour of sandstone in building; work of SSG, SPAB, Professor Bluck, Professor Webster and the RGIT team; chemical and physical composition, mechanisms of discolouration, weathering and decay and the effects of chemical cleaning all considerably clarified; professional opposition to cleaning, particularly chemical cleaning, considerably strengthened; current opinion a general presumption against cleaning stone, but where, very exceptionally justified, small scale dry air abrasive preferred; likely to be very slow and expensive by present standards.

Twenty year affair with stone cleaning a minor disaster for Scottish architecture and townscape; c.f. the effect on interiors of the remedial treatment industry's largely discredited, destructive, chemically based approach to dry rot eradication; 'modern' technological approach to the 'improvement' of the traditional building stock second only, in seriousness and financial consequences, to the period of comprehensive redevelopment; serious professional opinion now moving firmly towards a less interventionist, more traditional, craft based, genuinely environmental approach.

Judgement of today's actions by tomorrow's historians; stone cleaning acquiring 'down market' associations; uncleaned areas, e.g. the New Town, the Colonies etc. clearly preferred; this perception growing; long term effects of cleaning likely to be negative, possibly seriously so; enormous task still ahead to get the traditional building stock into good order; much good real work done, though perhaps inevitably some bad too, through repair grant programme; real effort needed to 'educate' owners and building manager about systematic maintenance, quinquennial routines etc.; against this background, the promotion of cleaning a serious mistake; need for acknowledgement of this, and for efforts to be concentrated on real repair and improvement work; a professional view.

5 Sources of building soiling and a review of the stone cleaning industry 1991

TRUDIE MANSFIELD
Air Quality Division, Department of the Environment, London
and Ron Hamilton, Middlesex Polytechnic, London

INTRODUCTION

'Where there's muck there's brass' was traditionally used to describe the polluting industrial landscapes of centuries past; nowadays it could be equally transposed to the stone cleaning industry ... 'Where there's muck there's money to be made from removing it!

Improvements in the level of sulphur dioxide and smoke experienced in our cities over the past 30 years have provided an impetus for stone cleaning. Buildings were not cleaned in earlier times when smoke levels were greater than they are now, because property owners felt re-soiling would occur too quickly and that they would be wasting their money. For example, Parker (1) quotes that buildings in Pall Mall were painted cream in colour and that even before the paint was dry the surfaces had collected numerous black specks and that within two years such buildings had lost their 'exterior freshness' and were distinctly soiled. However, there is every reason to believe that as time progresses, the trend towards cleaner buildings will continue. The research I have undertaken since 1987, indicates that stone cleaning may have more benefits to the owners apart from purely an aesthetic one and that the public will continue to remain intolerant of soiled buildings. The sources of today's soiling material and the stone cleaning industry are described in the following sections.

SOURCES OF SOILING PARTICULATE MATTER

To identify the sources of a pollutant, an emission inventory needs to be carried out. An emission inventory is a list of the amount of pollutants from all sources entering the air in a given time period. Table 1 shows an emission inventory for UK black smoke emissions from 1979 to 1989 (2). Emissions fell continuously from 655,000 tonnes in 1979 to 482,000 tonnes in 1984 during the miners' strike. After a rise to 585,000 tonnes in 1986, emissions fell again to 512,000 in 1989. The contribution from domestic sources fell from 58% in 1979 to 37% in 1989; whilst that from road transport rose from 18% to 39% over the same period. These changes are reflected in the analysis of fuel type which shows between 1979 and 1989 a substantial reduction in emissions from coal combustion and an almost doubling of emissions from diesel contribution.

Table 1 Black smoke: estimated emissions by emission source and by type of fuel[1]

ited Kingdom — Thousand tonnes

	1979	1980	1981	1982	1983	1984	1985	1986	1987	1988	1989	Percentage of total in 1989
By emission source												
mestic	382	316	297	292	271	212	285	300	247	223	191	37
mmercial/public service[2]	7	6	6	6	6	6	6	5	5	4	4	1
wer stations	33	29	27	26	24	33	28	26	26	26r	25	5
fineries	4	4	3	3	3	3	2	2	2	2	2	-
riculture	1	1	1	1	1	1	1	1	1	1	1	-
her industry[3]	102	93	90	91	89	89	89	91	87r	89r	88	17
ilways	2	2	2	2	1	1	1	1	1	1	-	-
ad transport	121	118	112	116	124	135	141	155	167	184	198	39
vil aircraft	1	1	1	1	1	1	1	1	1	1	1	-
ipping	3r	3r	2r	3r	3r	3r	3r	2	2r	2	3	1
tal	655r	572r	541r	539r	521r	482r	555	585r	538r	533	512	100
By type of fuel												
al	413	341	322	315	294	228	306	326	274	251	218	43
lid smokeless uel	21	21	19	19	19	15	20	17	17	16	14	3
troleum: Motor spirit	12	12	12	12	13	13	13	14	14	15	15	3
Derv	109	105	100	103	111	122	128	142	152	169	182	36
ias	11	10	9	9	8	9r	8	8	7	7	7	1
uel oil	32r	24r	20r	20r	16r	31r	19r	15	12	14r	14	3
ther petroleum	1	1	1	1	1	1	1	1	1	1	1	-
her emissions	56	58	58	60	59	64	60	62	60r	60r	60	12
tal	655r	572r	541r	539r	521r	482r	555	585r	538r	533	512	100
Emissions (tonnes)/GDP (£ million)[4]												
	2.0	1.8	1.7	1.7	1.6	1.4	1.6	1.6	1.4	1.3	1.2	

ncludes miscellaneous emission sources.
xcludes power stations, refineries and agriculture.
ower stations, refineries and a proportion (57%) of other industry.
iDP measured at 1985 market prices.

85

So although many stone buildings have been cleaned in the past 30 years, they are being re-soiled; the contribution from coal burning to this soiling is in decline, whilst emissions from diesel vehicles are deemed to be the major source of soiling matter in urban areas. Figure 1 illustrates diesel's increasing contribution to the UK's black smoke emissions.

Diesel exhaust is a rich source of very fine carbon particles known as Particulate Elemental Carbon (PEC). It is now recognised that PEC emissions from diesel vehicles are the main source of soiling in European towns (3). Table 2 shows a PEC emission inventory for London (1980) and Figure 2 illustrates diesel and total PEC emissions for the UK from 1971-1989.

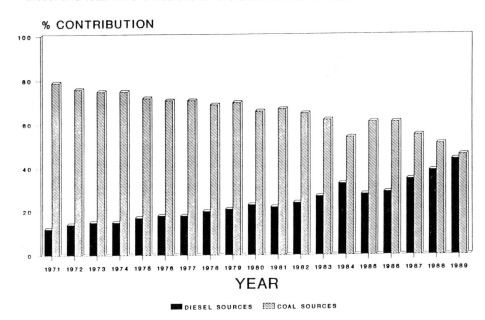

Figure 1 The percentage contribution of UK dark smoke mass from coal and diesel combustion from 1971-1989

Thus, such results from emission inventories for dark smoke and PEC indicate that diesel emissions are responsible for much of the airborne particulate matter responsible for the surface soiling of buildings observed in urban areas. Although PEC is chemically inert, the particles produced by diesel engines are very small, being about 0.02μm in size and they are very sticky in nature because of their hydrocarbon content. Thus, a diesel particle landing on a surface is more likely to become strongly adhered to it. It is additionally much less water soluble than a suspended soil particle which may be readily removed by rain washing. PEC's surface tension properties have implications for potentially damaging reactions which may occur within the patina of a building's facade. Acidic gases such as sulphur and nitrogen oxides can in turn

Table 2 Mass of PEC emissions (in tonnes) according to fuel use for London (1980).

Fuel type	Amount of fuel consumed (10^3 tonnes)	PEC emission factor (86) (% by mass)	Amount of PEC emitted (tonnes)	% of PEC Total by fuel type
Coal: domestic	50	0.0001	0.05	0.004%
Coal: industrial	250	0.0001	0.25	0.02%
Solid smokeless fuel	350	0.0001	0.35	0.03%
Gas oil	1000	0.01	0.1	0.009%
Fuel oil	600	0.002	12	1%
Petrol	2200	0.002	44	4%
Diesel	520	0.2	1040	94.8%

TOTAL : 1096.75

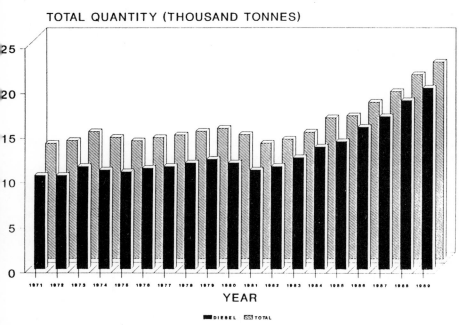

Figure 2 Diesel and total PEC emissions (in thousand tonnes for the UK from 1971-1989

become easily absorbed on to the surface of such particles and once deposited on a soiled stone surface may act synergistically with it. Also, PEC due to its electronic structure and π-electron system may aid in the catalytic conversion of such acidic gases to the sulphate and nitrate forms respectively.

Once sulphuric and nitric acids are present on the building fabric surface, they may then react for example with limestone and convert it into gypsum or calcium nitrate respectively. These latter compounds are more soluble and leachable with rainfall than limestone and thus elevated erosion rates may occur. Calcium nitrate is more leachable than gypsum and considering the emissions of nitrogen oxides are increasing within the ambient atmosphere (over 40% of the national emissions of nitrogen oxides are vehicularly derived) this may be a factor in explaining the fact that rates of building erosion are similar to when ambient levels of pollution of smoke and sulphur dioxide were much greater than they are now.

For example, research carried out on the erosion rates of balustrades on St. Paul's Cathedral, London, indicate that limestone was being eroded at a rate of 8mm every 100 years during the 18th century and the rates today are very similar despite a dramatic decrease in the levels of sulphur dioxide and smoke. Perhaps this is due to the 'memory effect' of stone and/or the increasing contribution to erosion rates by the emission of NO_x and subsequent formation and effect of nitric acid on the stone surface (4). As will later be illustrated, one of the benefits of stone cleaning as stated by stone cleaning companies is that cleaning prolongs the life of the building fabric. Although the impact of such carbon-catalysed reactions has not been well studied, it may well be that soiling may not only be a nuisance in terms of an aesthetic blight but also in terms of enhancing the rate of fabric erosion.

MEASUREMENT OF SOILING RATES WITHIN THE URBAN ENVIRONMENT

A study was set up to determine soiling rates for a variety of materials at nine sites within central and metropolitan London. Measurements of the percentage of the material's original reflectance were obtained used an Eel reflectometer and carried out for a total of 18 months. An example of the soiling rates achieved at one of the sites, on the Euston Road, where the smoke level of $20\mu g/m^3$ (typical for an urban area) is given in Figure 3.

These results are typical of those experienced at the other sites; soiling appears to be very rapid at first following initial exposure (a decrease of 32% of the original reflectance within seven days). Perhaps, Quentin Crisp's theory applies: 'There was no need to do any housework at all. After the first four years the dirt doesn't get any worse' (5). Circumstantial evidence from stone cleaning companies tends to support my measurements of soiling; after cleaning, re-soiling does appear to happen fairly quickly; I was told that this was known as 'toning down' within the trade. Figure 3 illustrates that the reflectance measurements oscillated, indicating a cleansing and re-soiling process.

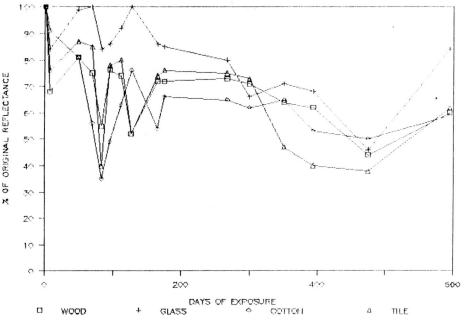

Figure 3 Changes in reflectance for materials exposed on Euston Road, London

As mentioned in the previous section, resuspended road dust and soil derived particles may be deposited on materials but are more likely to be removed by rainfall than a deposited diesel particle.

A SURVEY OF THE STONE CLEANING INDUSTRY

A repeat of the survey I carried out on the stone cleaning industry in 1987 was sent to 415 stone cleaning companies in the UK (6). The questionnaire sought to explore:

(i)   The principal customers of the industry and the motivation for building cleaning;
(ii)   The cost of cleaning by various methods, the recommended cleaning frequency for a variety of locations, and the factors responsible for any noted difference in frequency;
(iii)   The major areas of the country where cleaning occurs, their turnover for 1990/91, with estimates of the value of the annual stone cleaning market.

The companies were identified from the Stone Federation handbook and Yellow Pages.

THE INDUSTRY'S CLIENTELE

Nearly 60% of the work came from the private sector, a common ratio of 80:20, private to public, was quoted. The categories and proportion of customers served within the private and public sectors respectively are given in Table 3. More than 60% stated that the public sector's motives for cleaning were the same as the private sector's. The reasons for cleaning were as follows:

42% Appearance
27% Restoration/identification of faults
10% Part of lease/refurbishment package
 6% To blend in with surrounds
 5% To decrease long term maintenance costs
 4% To increase value of the property
 4% Upgrade housing stock
 2% An alternative to painting

Very few respondents attempted to assess the annual value of the UK cleaning market, those that did put it between £10 million and £200 million. In 1987, the range was £5m to £100m. Not all companies were prepared to give their turnover and others were not able to estimate it for stone cleaning activities alone where these were only a small part – less than 15% – of their turnover. Once the buildings had been cleaned, major faults are identified, which cost more to rectify than the original cost of stone cleaning. The market for stone cleaning is not spread evenly throughout the country but appears to be most active in London, Manchester, Leeds, Sheffield, Glasgow and Edinburgh.

However, it was possible to calculate an average turnover of £190,000 for each of the 415 companies, giving a total market value of £79m. This compares reasonably well to the figure I calculated for the industry in 1987, which when adjusted for inflation would be worth around £110m in today's terms. The decline in the value of the stone cleaning industry may well be attributable to the recession rather than improvements in air quality. Over 30% of replies stated that the recession was detrimentally affecting business. Meanwhile, more than 50% thought business would improve; especially given:

(i)   The current decrease in the number of new properties built;
(ii)   Stone cleaning was proving to be a viable alternative to painting;
(iii) New non-destructive cleaning techniques were being developed and
       easier access was permissible with the latest developments in scaffolding.

Some also noted that many of the larger stone cleaning companies were mainly administrative centres, sub-contracting the vast majority of their work to 'cowboys'. However, 48% of the companies thought their prices would not increase by more than the rate of inflation, 16% thought it would be less and 35% thought it would increase by more. Table 4 illustrates the range in price for different stone cleaning techniques for 1990/91.

Table 3 The categories and proportion of customers served within the private and public sectors for 1990/91 and 1986/7

Percentage of customers in the private sector	1991	1987
Banks	28	23
Domestic housing	16	12
Building societies	14	7
Property development agencies	13	10
Offices	9	14
Shops	7	18
Insurance companies	5	9
Gas and Electricity boards	4	-
Hotels	2	7
Farms	2	-
Percentage of customers in the public sector	**1991**	**1987**
Local authorities	52	39
Property Service Agency	18	24
Churches	16	14
Museums/galleries	4	-
Schools/universities	4	7
British Rail	2	9
Health authorities	2	7
Sport facilities	2	-

Table 4 The ranges in price for different stone cleaning techniques

Method	Range of prices/m^2	Typical cost/m^2
Water clean	£1 - 15	£3
Degrease and water clean	£1 - 12	£4
Dry abrasive	£1 - 22	£5
Wet abrasive	£1 - 16	£7
Use of sealant	£1 - 8	£3

In answer to a question on the recommended frequency for stone cleaning in a major city, a figure of every eight years was calculated; for a town, the frequency was 11 years and for rural areas every 21 years. The survey contained a question which sought to explore the source/variation in frequency between city and rural areas; over 40% attributed diesel exhaust directly, 32% quoted general pollution, 16% industrial pollution, 8% mentioned carbon deposits and 4% sited aircraft emissions as the main factor responsible for these frequencies.

FUTURE TRENDS IN DIESEL EMISSIONS

In March 1991, the European Community reached a common position on an amending directive prescribing stricter limits on emissions of carbon monoxide, hydrocarbons and oxides of nitrogen from new diesel-engined trucks and buses over 3.5 tonnes. Limits on emissions of particulates are also set for the first time. There will be two stages, the first of which will take effect in 1992-93 and the second in 1995-96.

Also, the Royal Commission on Environmental Pollution recently undertook a study of emissions from heavy goods vehicles (HGVs)(7); and whilst endorsing the above directive, recommended that the problem of emissions from existing HGVs should also be addressed. For example, buses such as the Route Master have a very long service life (20-30 years); replacement of such a fleet will take many years. So, the Government have been asked by the Commission to consider strongly the possibility of retrofitting the existing fleet with particulate control technology; or to consider using alternative fuels to diesel.

The Government is looking into ways of introducing an instrumented smoke check in the annual HGV and Public Service (PSV) tests, and in roadside checks. The in-service regulations about smoke emissions are being made stricter. The public can also contact local Traffic Area Offices (TAO) to report excessively smoky HGVs. Assuming all the relevant details have been provided by the complainant, a letter is sent to the vehicle owner asking them to get it checked and to send a written report back to the TAO within 10 days.

Such initiatives should help to decrease the mass emission of soiling matter from diesel engines in the future; though diesel's contribution to UK dark smoke and PEC emissions will probably dominate such inventories for the foreseeable future.

CONCLUSIONS

Emission inventories of dark smoke and PEC indicate that diesel vehicles appear to be the main sources of soiling matter in urban areas.

Measurements of soiling for a variety of materials (percentage of original reflectance lost with time) may oscillate due to the removal of larger particles such as resuspended dust/road/soil particles with rainfall; diesel particulate is less easily removed from such surfaces. Rates of soiling on to a surface follow an exponential decrease – Quentin Crisp theory.

A survey of the UK stone cleaning industry in 1990/91 was undertaken – it was estimated to have a value of £79m; this compares to a value of £110m for 1987. The current recession was mentioned as a factor for this decrease in value.

References

1. Parker, A. (1955) 'The destructive effects of air pollution on materials'. Colliery Guardian, vol.191, pp.447-450.
2. Department of the Environment (1990) 'Digest of environmental protection and water statistics, no.13' HMSO, London.
3. Ball, D.J. and Hume, R. (1977) 'The relative importance of vehicular and domestic emissions of dark smoke in greater London in the mid-1970s, the significance of smoke shade measurements, and an explanation of the relationship of smoke shade to gravimetric measurements of particulate.' Atmospheric Environment. vol.11, no.11, pp.1065-1073.
4. Pearce, F. (1985) 'Acid eats into Britain's stone heritage'. New Scientist, 28/9/85. pp.26-27.
5. Crisp, Q. (1968) 'The naked civil servant'. Fontana paperbacks, London.
6. Newby, P.T., Mansfield T.A., Hamilton, R.S. (1991) 'The economic implications of building soiling in urban areas'. Science of the Total Environment. vol.100, pp.347-365.
7. Royal commission on Environmental Pollution (1991) 'Fifteenth report: Emissions from heavy duty diesels vehicles'. HMSO. London.

Acknowledgements

The authors are grateful to T.Tarazawa and F.Segawa for updating the emission inventories and for production of the graphics.

Session II

CASE STUDIES AND EXPERIMENTAL INVESTIGATION

6 To clean or not to clean buildings within Edinburgh

ALASTAIR MILLIGAN
DA DIP TP (Edin)
City of Edinburgh Planning Department

INTRODUCTION

Judgement has to be made on whether alterations, including cleaning, would damage the fabric, or adversely affect the character or appearance of the many important listed buildings within the City of Edinburgh. Many of these buildings form a part of the Old and New Towns within the central residential and commercial heart of Edinburgh. These are areas of architectural and historic importance which make a major contribution to the image and traditional character of Edinburgh. Most but not all are centred around the High Street and to the north of Princes Street. There are significant areas of high environmental quality beyond the centre of the City. These include high quality residential areas, the green belt villages and the villages and historic centres along the northern shores of Edinburgh from South Queensferry to Portobello.

It is the stated aim of the City Development Plan to preserve as far as possible the unique and distinctive environmental character of our designated Conservation Areas. Within these any development must be of an appropriate scale and character and must not dominate the important view of the Castle, the Castle ridge, the Calton hill and Arthurs Seat or the important interaction of quality and scale of the streets and townscape of the Capital. The quality of the New Town 'should be preserved intact'.

THE OLD AND NEW TOWNS

Before looking in some detail at the repair and cleaning of historic buildings we need to know more about the beginnings of Edinburgh and consider whether planning was at work in those early days. A visitor to the City wrote the following description of the Old Town in 1598:

> And so I came to Edenbaro. The city is high seated in a fruitful soyle and wholesome aire, and is adorned with many Nobleman's Towers lying about it, and aboundeth with many springs of sweet waters. At the end towards the east, is the Kings Palace, loyning to the Monastery of the Holy Cross, which King David the First built; over which, in a Parke of Hares, Conies and Deare, on high mountain hangs called the Chaire of Arthur. From the Kings Palace at the east, the city still riseth higher towards the west, and consists especially of one broad and very faire street (which is the greatest part and sole ornament thereof). The rest of the sid streetes, and allies being of poore building, and inhabited with very poore people; and the length from the east to the west is about a mile, whereas the breadth of the City from north to south is narrow and cannot be half a mile. At the further end, towards the west, is a very strong Castle and from the Castle, towards the west, is a most steepe Rocke pointed on the highest top, out of which the Castle is cut; but on the north and south sides, without the walls lie plaine and fruitful fields of corne. The houses are built of unpolished stone, and in the faire street a good part of them is of free stone, which in that broad streete would make a faire show, but that the outsides of them are faced with wooden galleries built upon the second storey of the house.

The early plan of the Old Town was tightly contained within the City Walls and it was built like this for many good reasons with the huddling together of its Old Town of Edinburgh giving a sense of security. Those who lived there came to accept an urban way of life. The Lands – high flats piled one upon the other with the long central street; a promenade. The promenade where business deals were agreed or for walking about, all well within the security of the city. Even in the 18th century the Old Town maintained greater similarities to the ancient walled cities of Europe and it was Scotland's turbulent history which did not encourage its Capital to spread.

This acceptance of a particular way of living was to have a profound effect on the design of the New Town and on public attitudes to its making. James Craig was 23 when his New Town Plan was accepted and it was some time before prosperity gradually grew before the stage was set for the awakening of the new Town. Provost Drummond several times Lord Provost of Edinburgh and a man of resolve and integrity, for years worked to extend the city. A policy statement was prepared which was in fact the planning brief for the New Town. Once an act of Parliament was passed to allow for the extension of Edinburgh to the north, plans were set to build Craigs New Town.

Planning rules (guidelines today) were published in 1767 by the City Fathers, e.g. pavements were to be 10ft wide and laid at the householder's expense, there was to be a uniform building line, signs were not to project from walls. For their part the Corporation built sewers, roads and provided the water supply. Although plans were carefully laid there was some difficulty in keeping to the brief. This was when the ground was feud on the south side of Princes Street to allow the building of the North British Hotel (now the Balmoral). Only when agreement was reached not to allow any more building on the south side of Princes Street was the seal set on the building of the New Town.

Within six years in 1782 the appeal of the New Town had been established which was soon to become, 'a distinct social impetus' to abandon the Old for the New. With the completion of Charlotte Square the first phase of building, extending over a period of 25 years was complete. This included buildings designed by Robert Adam, Sir William Chambers, David May and James Craig.

The planning guidelines were followed by a fue charter to speed implementation of the proposals. This charter, enforced by the Acts of 1782 and 1785 in effect entrusted a committee, very like our own Planning Committee, to grant a fue only after approving plans and elevations, signed by the applicant. They decided that in the principal streets no house was to be above three storeys excluding 'garret and sunk storeys' with the overall height not exceeding 48ft. The mews lanes were only to contain stables an coach houses. Anyone who infringed those guidelines were fined with this cost being added to the site costs and also liable to further penalty if their proposals were not altered. Those who had bought the ground had only one year to start building otherwise they would loose their site and be fined.

Strict rules they were indeed, and probably more so than those included in present day planning legislation and policies. The present planning committee are very conscious of this heritage and the need to preserve the character and quality of the City environment. Policies have been agreed and implemented aimed at the careful conservation of these two areas of early town planning. Restoration work within the Old and new Town is ongoing with grant aid being administered by the Edinburgh New Town Committee for Conservation and the Edinburgh Old Town Committee for Conservation and Renewal. Applications for alterations including the repair and cleaning of listed buildings are processed by the Planning Department and the City Planning Committee. All applications to clean listed buildings require listed building consent.

STONE CLEANING AND REPAIR

In Edinburgh the cleaning of buildings for aesthetic reasons is not encouraged although dirt often obscures the colour and character of differing stones altering them to an unattractive, some say attractive uniformity. This can cause to the eye some loss of detail which could be seen in many of the buildings on or near rail lines to and from Waverley Station. Many of these buildings of national importance have been cleaned, some many years ago, e.g. the Scottish and National Galleries on the Mound, The Caledonian Hotel and Rutland Square. Dirt is not only an aesthetic problem but often hides structural faults within the stonework, levels the quality of detail and often hides open joints and as a result can be a major cause of decay. Atmospheric pollution and dirt react with sandstones forming a thin hard dirt collecting film which can rarely be removed with water alone, as the silica component within the stone binds the dirt. The only way to loosen this surface skin in the past has been by the use of chemicals and abrasive or mechanical methods of cleaning, the latter of which is not being encouraged in Edinburgh.

The National Gallery

The sandstones of Edinburgh were originally quarried locally. Some of these quarries were temporary, e.g. the Old Town Quarries of Greyfriars Port (Society or Bristo Port) dating from the 14th century and at Windmill Lane – at the connection of Chapel Street and George Square. Other quarries were to be found in the Meadows and at Bruntsfield at Burgh Muir where there was quarrying for more than 200 years. Princes Street Gardens, where Bearfords Quarries stretched from near the west end of Princes Street as far as the Balmoral Hotel. One of the quarries (12m deep) was rediscovered when the foundations of the Scott Monument were being laid. Other quarries were to be found to the east of the Calton Hill where I understand there are still traces within Royal Terrace Gardens. At the Queens Park where some of these can still be seen especially along the Salisbury Crags sill. Other early 14th century quarrying was to be found at Craigmillar, Broughton, Joppa and Niddrie where quarrying was carried on for almost three hundred years.

One of the largest quarries was at Granton where many stones were moved by sea to Leith and in 1835 Granton Sea Quarry was opened by the Duke of Buccleuch to provide stone for the east and west breakwaters of Granton Harbour. By that time the quarry extended for eight acres and was 24m deep.

It was only second to the great quarry of Craigleith. Craigleith was and still is the best known and largest quarry in Edinburgh and it was from here that most of the building stone for the New Town of Edinburgh was quarried. However, stone was first taken from here in the early years of the 15th century and towards the end of its life there was difficulty in keeping the quarry dry. The last major project in which Craigleith stone was used was in the building of Leith Docks, begun in 1895. The quarry was worked up until 1942 and afterwards was gradually filled in until today, when little rock lies exposed. It might be of interest that in Victorian times doctors were drawing attention to the health hazards from the fine stone powder – so much so that the quarrymen were advised to grow beards and moustaches to act as respirators!

Other quarries in this same rock formation were Maidencraig (Blackhall) from which stone was used to build parts of Edinburgh Castle and for North Bridge in 1773, Barnton Quarry in the middle of Bruntsfield Golf Course as well as Redhall and Hailes Quarries. Because of the huge demand for stone in the 17th and 18th centuries the builders of Edinburgh looked to West Lothian to the quarries of Binnie and Humble, both located near the Union Canal. However, with the new railways the quarries of Fife and northern England began to send stone to Edinburgh.

Since the early 1970s there has been a renewed interest in quarrying stone for restoration work and to date 11 Scottish quarries are now working, with other stones being sent from northern England from the quarries of Dunhouse, Springwell, Stainton, Wellfield and Woodkirk. These stones are used for quality restoration work and many stones from these quarries are being used today for indenting repairs to many of Edinburgh's listed buildings. In fact a new replica building at Glenfinlas Street to the north of Charlotte Square used stone from the Dunhouse Quarry.

CLEANING POLICY

Matching stone for specialist repair work is perhaps less difficult and certainly less controversial than deciding whether a building should be cleaned and if so, which method should be used for that cleaning. Because of this, the Planning Committee over the last 18 years or so, have carefully considered and implemented policies for stone cleaning within the city. These policies have been amended over the years and all were aimed at ensuring that minimum damage was done to the stone. Especially the detailing to the fronts of many of our buildings which have been listed by the Secretary of State.

The main concerns were limiting damage to the fabric of the building and the effect cleaning would have on a building's character. Also whether changing the appearance of a building within an area of high townscape value e.g. within the Old or, possibly more so, in the New Towns of Edinburgh. This is of equal importance because of the need to maintain the strong unity of design and the striking combination of architecture and landscape within these areas. They decided therefore that properties forming part of continuous elevations should not be individually cleaned although the cleaning of whole crescents and terraces could be acceptable. Individual buildings e.g. galleries, churches, hotels could and have been cleaned.

It is important to remember that rarely do the Committee approve cleaning for cosmetic reasons only. Rather they expect cleaning to be the first stage of comprehensive restoration work which must include stone repair.

At all costs what is referred to as 'piecemeal' cleaning of ashlar stone must be avoided or any form of cleaning which would disrupt the unity of elevations – a feature of central Edinburgh and some of the surrounding residential areas.

Melville Street

Atholl Crescent

However, buildings of rubble stone will be considered on their own merits and may be cleaned individually. Evidence of this is to be found in the Old Town and the South Side.

These policies over the years have had the support of the Scottish office and local amenity bodies.

Within the last five years grants have been available from the City Housing Department for comprehensive repairs mainly to tenement flats. Through these stone cleaning was grant-aided.

CHEMICAL CLEANING

Preliminary studies suggest that chemical cleaning, the favoured method and often, if administered properly, a method achieving good results, may cause long-term damage. This is caused by chemicals which have not been completely removed from the stone at the time of treatment.

A paper listing the conclusions of a Technical Forum at English Heritage discussed cleaning sandstone. It was considered that because of the unpredictable element of some methods the cleaning of sandstones should be avoided. Following this, a research project has been sponsored by Historic Scotland and Scottish Enterprise from The Robert Gordon Institute of Technology, Aberdeen. This was because there was an 'awareness' that the cosmetic improvement given to buildings by stone cleaning may be achieved at too high a price and that cleaning could result in accelerated erosion. Also it was thought that there was a lack of sound, informed advice on some aspects of stone cleaning. In the interim District Councils were advised by Historic Scotland to clean buildings with caution and only after a detailed site assessment and survey. This should consider current defects, future weathering, fully monitored and recorded site trails, backed up by laboratory tests and analysis of stone samples and the effects of a variety of methods on cleaning particular stones. After a period, it was advised that site trials be retested for any noticeable or chemical change. Only at this stage a detailed report should be prepared with satisfactory conclusions detailing technical specifications including the cleaning method or methods to be used. Historic Scotland considers that if doubt persists cleaning should not be undertaken. If however, cleaning is agreed experienced contractors under good supervision should carry out the contract based on the individual study of that particular building.

A section of the brief for the study suggests that areas should be identified for further research. In my view an area which requires to be covered is the chemical deposition on stone which forms a part of the natural weathering process.

Acid rain often contains elements including sulphur dioxide and nitrogen oxides. These oxides are generated by the vehicles using our cities and roads in ever increasing numbers. Pollutants can be deposited either almost directly on buildings or absorbed into rain clouds. Fogs and mist are another means of deposition and these often contain higher levels of acidity than raindrops. Some work on pollution levels has been done in Lincoln on the Cathedral and although pollution levels on average were found to be much lower than was seen in the smogs of the 1950s, there are still peak levels, 16 times higher than the average, these levels often lasting for several hours at a time.

Perhaps the question could be asked: by not cleaning pollutants from stone surfaces are they breaking down or weathering stone more quickly than if these surfaces were cleaned from time to time?

It is significant to say that there is no scientific evidence at present to show that long term damage is being done to stonework by cleaning with chemically based cleaners. I would have considered that if the proper testing of samples within the laboratory and on site is carried out in accordance with the Scottish office guidelines it may be difficult to resist cleaning. All buildings are different because of their detailing, type of stone, location and exposure to pollutants, wind and rain. As a result general advice on cleaning for specific locations may not be entirely relevant.

CONCLUSIONS

People like to see clean buildings and in some areas Government Authorities have expected, by funding cosmetic cleaning, to improve confidence. In Leith this has had the desired effect. There has been an upsurge in enthusiasm backed by financial investment which has lead to regeneration. The District Council except in these special situations do not encourage cleaning buildings unless it forms a part of a contract for including significant stone repair. In certain areas where there are terraces of 'A' and 'A' group listed buildings cleaning is discouraged not always because of any damage which may result from the cleaning process, but because cleaning individual buildings within this group would adversely affect the character of the area. Control in these areas is just as important now as it was over two hundred years ago when Edinburgh first expanded beyond the confines of the Old Town.

References

1.   City and Royal Burgh of Edinburgh, Development Plan 1965 Review, Written Statement.
2.   Memorandum of guidance on listed buildings and conservation areas – Historic Scotland.
3.   Two Hundred Summers in a City, Edinburgh 1767-1967.
4.   The Making of Classical Edinburgh, A.J. Youngson.
5.   Architects Journal Information Library – Technical Study 3.
6.   Building Research Establishment Digest 280.
7.   Building Stones of Edinburgh, Bunyan, Fairhurst Mackie & A.A.McMillan.
8.   HBMD Papers 1 and 4 – the cleaning of sandstones – 1988.
9.   HBMD/SDA Final brief for research Commission Paper A2 – 1989.
10. Acid deposition and stone – Dr R.N.Butlin.

7   Scott Monument – a brief study report

HURD ROLLAND PARTNERSHIP and JOHN DIXON
Department of Geology and Geophysics, Edinburgh University

INTRODUCTION

Without doubt the Scott Monument belongs to that elite group of landmarks recognised worldwide and is as much associated with Edinburgh as the Eiffel Tower is with Paris and the Brooklyn Bridge with New York. It is a national monument of significant importance.

Edinburgh District Council commissioned the Design Team in June 1989 to study the need and the practicalities of stone restoration, and to research cleaning of the stonework.

It was generally felt that the Scott Monument would be an ideal test for research of this nature and it could well be the guide for future stonework restoration projects of national importance.

Full scaffolding would be required for the study with the thought that this would remain in place during the three stages of the project, namely 'study period', 'limited consideration period' and 'implementation'.

HISTORICAL RESEARCH

The Sir Walter Scott Monument, erected between 1840 and 1844, was designed by George Meikle Kemp as a soaring tiered spire, rich in ornate Gothic detail.

Scott's association with the Capital made it the most obvious place for his memorial and immediately after his death a committee was appointed. £7,000 was soon raised for the monument, and various sites were mooted: the West End, Calton Hill, Charlotte Square, Moray Place and Randolph Crescent.

In 1836 more than fifty design competition entries were received and eventually three were selected as prizewinners but differences existed within the committee over the designs and the competition re-opened. Kemp worked to improve and elaborate his earlier proposal, and on the 28th March 1838 the committee recommended the acceptance of his revised design. At the same meeting John Steell's design for the statue of Sir Walter Scott was accepted. As Parliament had decreed against all building in Princes Street Gardens a special Act of Consent for the erection of the Monument had to be sought.

The supervision of the construction of the Monument was entrusted to Kemp; the building contract was assigned to Mr David Lind, and sandstone from Binny Quarry, Uphall was selected. Kemp persuaded the committee to consent to full excavations down to rock – a shaft of 52 feet deep was required.

BINNY SANDSTONE

The quarry which produced the stone was located on the East Binny Estate, near Uphall and it is recorded that stone was being taken as early as the 1790s. In addition to the Scott Monument, Binny was also used in the Tolbooth St. John's Church, the New College and Assembly Hall and Donaldson's School. The National Gallery was built of Binny stone in the 1850s and the Bank of Scotland headquarters on the Mound was enlarged with Binny Stone in the 1860s. Terraces in Rutland Square and Randolph Crescent were primarily constructed of Binny Stone.

In 1925 the quarries were 'now deserted and full of water', 'the cost of working the quarries led to their abandonment'. After World War Two, the pits were gradually filled in and this area is now completely grown over. The site near East Binny House was more recently worked and here the remains of operations are most noticeable.

> The Binny sandstone is well known to be a very durable building material. It might be contended that the small amount of oil in it contributes to this durability by excluding water; but the oil probably has another effect. The Scott Monument and Art Galleries, which are largely built of Binny Sandstone, are disfigured by black patches on the surface of the stone. These patches are generally said to be caused by the smoke of the city, and by the smoke of the locomotives of the railway close at hand. But a close inspection of the distribution and shape of the sooty patches and bands, coupled with the knowledge that the rock does contain oil, suggests the conclusion that the darker markings are oily patches to which cling a specially thick coating of soot. (1, 2)

TESTING FORMAT

Laboratory analysis was required to allow the chemical manufacturers to tailor their agents to the nature of the stone and soiling problems. Dr John E.Dixon, Senior Lecturer at the Department of Geology, University of Edinburgh, carried out the analysis; cores were taken from soiled and the sample cleaned areas for the following laboratory tests:

1. Thin Sections: Study of the character of grains and matrix of the surface layer and sub-surfaces;
2. Scanning Electron Microscopy: Revealing the nature of clay minerals in matrix; determination of organic/inorganic presence on grains revealing physical surface changes by weathering or previous sample cleaning;
3. X-Ray Diffraction: Supports findings of Sections and SEM;
4. Gas-chromatography mass-spectrometry: Identification and abundance of natural hydrocarbons; the nature of original bituminous impregnation and the degradation of it by atmospheric contact;
5. Water Absorption and Porosity: Determination of rate and Saturation Coefficient – giving insight into pore structure;
6. Initial Surface Absorption: Indication of ability of stone to absorb atmospheric pollutants. With the Saturation Coefficient test contributes to understanding the stone's vulnerability to water-borne deterioration.

Neolith Chemicals Ltd and ProSoCo Inc. conducted trials using variations of their alkaline/acid treatments. Visually these trials showed that the soiling could be removed without undue discolouration of the stone.

The data gained from the laboratory tests was issued to the chemical specialists to enable them to consider cleaning components and methods most suited to the stone and surface soiling with an invitation to provide further samples of cleaning.

Secondary cleaning trials were undertaken in November 1990 by Neolith, ProSoCo and Structural Chemicals Ltd. The firms arranged their own core sampling and petrological and chemical analyses for review by Dr Dixon.

Initial inspection of the secondary trials show that while some areas of the Monument may be cleaned with relative ease, more ingrained soiling would require careful supervision of cleaning operatives (2).

STONE SURVEY FORMAT

A collection of original contract drawings was located in the National Buildings Record, but as they did not provide a complete cover they were of limited use to the study. It appeared that no drawings exist of the Monument as built.

To provide the necessary accurate drawings, a photogrammetric survey of the Monument was instructed and to affect this, Mr R.Dallas of the Institute of Advanced Architectural Studies in York was commissioned to prepare a specification.

The shooting of the scaled stereo photographs was carried out in the Spring of 1990 from a Simon Hoist. 1:20 scale drawings have been plotted from the photographs and recorded on computer discs. The photographic exercise of each elevation was done prior to the erection of scaffolding entailing the use of a Simon Hoist.

Due to the complex nature of the Monument, certain areas were inaccessible to the camera, and to complete the survey these areas were measured and drawn by hand for later insertion. The survey data on the computer is recorded in such a way as to permit full flexibility of the drawings to give desired degrees of scale and detail, including that of major architectural features or carved work; the most important facility being the provision of accurate drawings in 2–D or 3-D.

In order to facilitate the immense task of recording repair data, the Monument was sectioned according to the 29 levels of scaffolding of 'lifts' and sectioned further according to the four public landings. The stone courses were numbered on the drawings in ascending order.

In addition to the ashlar, the Monument's architectural features were identified and inspected according to location. These elements included: pinnacles, finials, brackets, buttresses, flying buttresses, parapet, quatrefoils, gargoyles, statuettes, canopies, arches, ribs, sills and cornices. To determine the condition of individual stones a systematic inspection of the stonework was carried out, painstakingly recording stone deficiencies and the degree of repair or replacement. Stones requiring repairs (replacement, indenting, dressing back, etc.) were marked in situ with coloured chalk, colours being used to differentiate the repairs links to a coding system on the drawings. These were recorded on to A3 reductions by the architects' field staff and later transferred on to 1:20 scale detailed information drawings. The repair information may be programmed into the CAD system if required. The compilation of repair recommendations was used by the quantity surveyor in the preparation of estimated costs.

FABRIC REPORT

The inspection of the Scott Monument's stonework was carried out between August and October 1990. In general the stonework was determined to be in fair condition, for although the majority of the stones are sound there are many localised areas of severe decay. The cumulative number of stones requiring repair is high, but relative to the overall size of the Monument the percentage is quite low.

Deterioration is most common among ornamental carved features. This decay is the result of extreme weathering conditions pushing the stone to the limits of its natural capabilities. Most often these finials, brackets, mouldings and cornices have decayed where the stone is finely carved or thin in section. During the inspection many finials, for example, were found to be sitting loose on their dowels or the thin gravity alone. Certain elements in a perilous state have been taken down and these have been noted in the structural engineer's Report.

It would appear that the Monument has no strict pattern of stone decay.

Owing to the complex shape of the Monument with its many recesses, niches, returns, arches and pinnacles there are innumerable 'microclimates' affecting the weathering of small, individual areas. Swirling winds, driving rain and atmospheric pollutants around and through the multi-faceted structure causing a myriad of soiling and erosion conditions. A further contributing factor to the inconsistent resistance to decay of the Monument's stonework would be the variations in the natural characteristics of the Binny Stone as it was extracted from different sections in the quarry. Certain inherent weaknesses (e.g. soft beds, shakes, etc.) are apparent at various points in the building, probably corresponding with the quality of blocks from various depths in the quarry pit.

Throughout the structure the most pervasive condition is the shallow surface flaking or scaling; this surface breakdown can entrap moisture and promote further deterioration. There are also many areas of black cement which had been applied during previous repair works in order to retard erosion. This cement is deleterious to the stone, is highly unsightly and must be removed.

Whilst some cornices and ashlar blocks require full indents, there are few entire stones requiring full replacement other than a number of finials which are badly decayed or have been removed during previous repair works. There are, however, large numbers of part indents required, particularly to the varied ornamental elements. Finials, crockets, tracery, mouldings, cusps and canopies are the most delicate carved features and many of these have not weathered well or many suffered from the excesses of previous repair attempts. In addition, many of the statues and statuettes have deteriorated and require part indents; it is recommended that a sculptor or statue conservator is employed to carry out this work.

During earlier repair works certain finials and crocketed pinnacles in the upper reaches of the Monument were replaced with coarsely carved blocks only barely resembling the outline of the originals. In order to renew the consistency of the Monument's appearance it is recommended that these elements are carved properly.

Minor repairs to the stonework include the filling of cracks with a clear epoxy resin whereas small holes would be filled with lime mortar; most of the holes to be filled are redundant doors and other old fittings. Most epoxy repairs occur on finials and pinnacles where black cement is to be removed as the features are re-fixed. These epoxy and mortar repairs are small in number and will not affect the overall appearance of the structure. It is thought that 75% of the pointing might be defective although this is difficult to establish until repair work proceeds.

The extent of the stone deterioration is more graphically described on the Study drawings (2).

The Carrera marble statue of Sir Walter Scott is in fair condition having suffered small areas of etched graffiti. It is recommended that specialist advice is obtained regarding treatment.

The drainage of rainwater is a problem at all four public landings. At present water collects on the stone platts and is directed to narrow (20mm) holes in the parapet walls of the top three landings and is channelled over projecting cornices. At the first landing the water is carried to the eight gargoyles above the corner buttresses. All of these passageways require enlarging and the area behind the gargoyles should be screened to prevent the collection of debris and pigeon residue.

The ornamental balustrade and steps in the gardens to the south of the Monument were built in Binny Stone in the 1850s. These areas require some minor stone repairs, and repointing, and it is recommended that they are stone cleaned.

STRUCTURAL ENGINEER'S REPORT

Following completion of the scaffolding the structural engineer undertook a comprehensive inspection of the Monument. It was quickly concluded that with the exception of the pinnacle on the North West buttress there were no major structural problems. The top ten stones or the northwest pinnacle were rocking on a bed joint and thus is a dangerous state. The pinnacle is now temporarily restrained by the scaffolding until permanent repairs are carried out.

The structural engineer has identified that it is necessary to take off, repair and replace all the finials. Pinnacles that are not gravity stable should be stitch drilled to the lower stones so that the back weight of the lower stones can be utilised for the stability of the upper parts of the pinnacles. The large statues require to have all the fixings removed from the shoulder of the statues and properly embedded using modern fixing materials. The small statues should be removed to ensure that the mild steel fixings in the back of the statues and the monument are removed. The statues would then be replaced and refixed using new fixings in more appropriate positions. The traceries will require to be removed and refixed (2).

CONCLUSIONS

For nearly 150 years the Scott Monument has been a prominent landmark in the Edinburgh skyline with its ornate Gothic profile dominating the valley of East Princes Street Gardens and acting as a counterpoint to the bulk of the Balmoral Hotel. It is Category 'A' in the Statutory List of Building of Special Architectural and/or Historical Interest and thus the Monument's importance requires that work to its fabric must be of the highest standard and faithful to the original materials.

At present the Monument's stonework is in fair condition although areas of severe decay are evident in the many carved elements, some of which have become dislodged or have been removed. Over the years the Monument has been subjected to many necessary and emergency repairs which have contributed to the present shabby appearance. Some poor quality repairs from the 1970s have proved detrimental in the long term and certain deficiencies not addressed in previous years (e.g. rainwater drainage) must be rectified and ancillary items such as stair and floodlighting should be improved.

The issue of whether to clean historic buildings has become increasingly complex and problematic in recent years. Poor results and uncertainty regarding the long term effects of chemical cleaning have prompted a call for a moratorium to allow for further research.

The decision to clean an important building such as the Scott Monument must consider all aspects of the discussion and therefore a programme of laboratory analysis was commissioned to ensure that any decision would be based on clear and judicious information. This analysis shows that the soiling does not appear to adversely affect the weathering capabilities of the stone and that once the soiling is successfully removed the stone would continue to weather normally. Heavy soiling, however, does obscure the decaying of the stone, structural faults and open joints, and therefore can allow deterioration to progress unchecked.

It must, however, be undertaken without damaging the physical integrity of the stone. It must also be made clear that there is no known chemical product which can clean the Monument's stonework to its original pristine appearance: weathering over many decades (particularly the migration of iron) – has permanently altered the appearance of the stone and also, the varying degrees of soiling around the structure will result in different levels of 'cleanliness' after even the most careful cleaning. Thus the Monument might appear somewhat mottled though still with much of the Binny stone's natural brownish grey colour dominating.

In conclusion, the Design Team's recommendations are as follows:

1. The fabric study indicates that extensive stone repairs are necessary;
2. Improvements to 'ancillary items' should be undertaken;
3. The decision to clean must consider the following:
   a. Removal of soiling will enhance appreciation of the Monument by transforming the dark silhouette and liberating the delicate Gothic ornamentation from decades of accumulated soot.
   b. Cleaned stone shows defects for present and future maintenance.
   c. Although cleaning will show much of the stone's natural colour, the overall appearance will be characterised by differential weathering of individual stones.
   d. Laboratory analysis has shown that, of the methods tested, the ProSoCo poultice is acceptable, but in order to clean the stonework properly it requires strict adherence to a complex specification. Thus it is very labour intensive, making it at least three times more expensive than traditional acid cleaning. According to D.Dixon, the ProSoCo poultice appears to be gentler than Neolith or Structural Chemical products.
   e. Analysis shows that soluble salts are deposits in the stone during both the poultice and standard acid treatments. ProSoCo have adjusted their proposed specification to neutralise these salts with an interim rinse with acetic acid and Neolith states that an additional water rinse would be required to remove the salts. Although these proposals to minimise salt deposits are vital, it is still unclear what the long term effects would be.

References

1. Tait, D. 'The Occurrence of Petroliferous Sandstones in the

Carboniferous Rock of Scotland and the relation to certain Black Sandstones'. Transactions of the Edinburgh Geological Society. Vol.12, 1932.
2. Bunch, H.M., Dixon.Dr., Edinburgh District Council. 'Scott Monument Restoration Study 1990'.

8   The cleaning of the Palace of Westminster

CHRIS TUCKER
BSc ARICS

INTRODUCTION

This paper provides a summary of 10 years of experience of the cleaning of the Palace of Westminster more commonly known as the Houses of Parliament. It must be emphasised at this point, that the cleaning only formed part of the repair, restoration and conservation of the external stonework.The main purpose of the cleaning was to reveal the full extent of defects evident in the stonework and to enable repairs to be scheduled. However, the dramatic change in appearance following cleaning does raise an interesting question often debated in conservation groups over whether or not historic buildings should be cleaned with the associated loss of the 'patina of age'. There is no easy answer to this question, although this must be considered before embarking on any cleaning works. For this project English Heritage were consulted and made fully aware of the extent of works being undertaken.

Although much of the information provided is peculiar to this building, I hope that some of the points raised will be both educational and promote debate. One of the major lessons I have learnt from this project is that the text book solutions cannot always be applied and a flexible approach is required to achieve the most suitable solution.

BRIEF HISTORY

The old Royal Palace of Westminster and its parliament buildings were destroyed by fire on 16 October 1834, with the exception of Westminster Hall,

Cloister of St Stephen and Chapel of St Stephen. In March 1835, a select committee of the House of Commons was appointed to 'consider and report upon such a plan as may be most fitting and convenient for the permanent accommodation of the Houses of Parliament'. The committee decided that the style of the new building should be either Gothic or Elizabethan, the design to be chosen by open competition. Ninety-seven designs were submitted and the first prize was awarded to Charles Barry (later Sir), who produced a design based on Gothic style of the Tudor period. Barry's original drawings no longer remain, although it is thought that many amendments and alterations were made both to suit the whims of Parliament and the practicalities of the immense project. It is acknowledged that Barry was responsible for the major concepts of the design however much of the detailing was designed by Augustus Welby Pugin.

The foundation stone was laid by Mrs Barry in 1839/40 and a greater part of the works was completed in 10 to 12 years; the House of Lords was occupied in 1847 with the majority of the building completed and Royal Entrance used by Queen Victoria in 1852. The Clock Tower was completed in 1858 and Victoria Tower was completed two years later in 1860. This represents a comparatively rapid rate of building when compared to St Paul's which took 35 years to build.

The stone originally selected was a magnesian limestone from Bolsover Moor. However, within a very short period it was found impossible to obtain blocks of sufficient size and the same difficulty was experienced with the alternative magnesian limestone, Mansfield Woodhouse. After a delay of approximately six months a decision was taken to use Anston, another magnesian limestone from Yorkshire.

The first evidence of decay in the structure was discovered even before the building was completed, the Chief Clerk of Works of the building stated at committee that he first observed symptoms of decay in 1849. A number of early trials to arrest this decay were instigated by Sir Charles Barry although these were not pursued after his death in 1860.

The Committee investigating the decay in 1861 reported that one of the major contributing factors in the decay of the stonework was the polluted atmosphere in London. A later memorandum on the Defective Condition of the Stonework at the Houses of Parliament dated 1926, 'estimated that the annual consumption of coal in the London area to be 17 – 20 million tons, the annual output of soot being approximately half a million tons'. This burning of raw coal lead to an appreciable amount of sulphur passing into the atmosphere in the form of sulphur dioxide which on oxidation becomes sulphuric acid. On contact with the stonework via rain or snow this acid attacks the calcium carbonate matrix of the stone resulting in rapid decay. This memorandum also reported that prior to 1926 at least 70 tons of loose fragments were repaired or refixed and since that date a further 103 tons were removed by hand and another 25 tons were ready for removal.

In 1926 the main causes of decay were found to be due to atmospheric impurities; face bedding; faults in the stone and corroding ferrous fixings. Following the investigations and recommendation made by the Committee investigating the decay of the stonework a major repair, restoration and conservation programmes were carried out during 1920s and 1950s. It is not clear if this restoration included the cleaning of the stonework. The type of stone used for the restoration works was Clipsham, an Oolitic limestone from the old country of Rutland. The majority of the stonework above parapet level and large parts of the elevations were replaced. The Anston can be differentiated from the Clipsham by its much finer texture and mellow gold colour compared to the more shelly texture and grey colour of weathered Clipsham. This colour variation is particularly noticeable following cleaning.

REPAIR, RESTORATION AND CONSERVATION PROGRAMME

The current repair, restoration and conservation programme commenced in May 1981 and to date there have been eight Phases on a rolling programme. The latest Phase, VIII, is due for completion in 1994 and at that time the whole of the external elevations will have been cleaned and conserved. However, there are many inner court yards which in area approximately equates to the complete area of the external elevations. Works on these court yards are yet to commence.

The works carried out as part of the repair, restoration and conservation programme include cleaning of the stonework; stone repairs including pointing, plastic repairs and replacement of stone; window repairs; anti-corrosion treatment to cast ironwork; regilding and redecoration works; leadworks; glass repairs and other associated works. The stone cleaning formed a significant part of these works.

The works were project managed by the Parliamentary Works Office and Weatherall Green & Smith were appointed as supervising officers. A full time Clerk of Works was employed to monitor the works and ensure compliance with the contract documentation. Stone cleaning works formed part of a tendered package generally using bills of approximate quantities prepared by chartered quantity surveyors. A preferred list of stone cleaning sub contractors was attached to the contract documentation. The main contract used was the GCE Works 1; Edition 2.

In the following sections I have concentrated on the alternative cleaning methods used; the problems encountered and solutions adopted.

STONE CLEANING (introduction)

1973 Feasibility Report

In 1971/72 a feasibility study was carried out by the Department of the Environment (English Heritage) to determine the most suitable method of cleaning the stonework. This study considered all of the alternative methods of cleaning available including wet and dry abrasive cleaning; chemical cleaning; water washing and poultice cleaning. Cleaning trials were carried out and the findings of the trials and investigations were detailed in 1973 'Report on the feasibility of stone cleaning to the facades of the Palace of Westminster'.

Although many advantages and disadvantages were identified with each method, the report concluded that the most appropriate form of cleaning would be by water washing including an element of air abrasive blasting to remove stubborn deposits thus avoiding the risk of overwashing.

Repair, Restoration and Conservation Programme

The majority of the stonework has been cleaned using the wash and blast method recommended in the 1973 Feasibility Report with certain refinements. However, two Phases, the River Terrace and Victoria Tower, had to be cleaned by an alternative method of semi-dry abrasive cleaning. An alternative method of cleaning had to be used because a guarantee could not be given that some water penetration would not occur which on these Phases could have caused irretrievable damage to special finishes and unique documents/books.

In the next section of this paper, I have reviewed the two principal methods used, the problems encountered and solutions adopted.

Wash and Blast Cleaning

As stated previously this has been the principal method of cleaning adopted on the majority of Phases. The method of cleaning involves the spraying of water onto the face of the stonework to soften the surface deposits but avoiding the saturation of the stonework with the associated problems of damp penetration internally, frost damage and the forcing of contaminants deeper into the stone. Stubborn deposits were removed by localised air abrasive cleaning following water washing operations. The risk of overwashing, saturation or water penetration was reduced by the following methods:

1. Nebulae nozzles were used to ensure that water was applied as a fine mist which limited the quantity of water being applied.
2. Limitations were imposed on the size of nozzles used to 15 gallons per hour to one spray head.
3. The spacing of nozzles was restricted.
4. The period of washing was restricted to one hour on, two hours off.
5. Hand held bristle or phosphor bronze brushes were used to dislodge stubborn deposits.
6. Polythene protection was applied over the windows including temporary mastic seal.
7. Overnight washing was not permitted.
8. Slurry gutters were erected to collect water running down the elevation. The gutters restricted the area being cleaned, prevented the saturation of the ground and provided an effective means of collecting and disposing of the water. Samples of the water were taken to determine the level of contamination before disposing of the water into the drainage.
9. Water meters were provided which were checked on a daily basis to ensure that the quantity of water used did not exceed the specified limits.
   On Phase IV, The Clock Tower, a sophisticated monitoring system was developed to record quantity of water delivered to each nozzle, location of

nozzle and period of cleaning. However, the success and effectiveness of the system was limited due to the number of occasions it was inoperative. A certain amount of reluctance was encountered from the sub-contractor in using this method of control.

10. Problems were encountered on all Phases as a result of water penetration through defective mortar joints. The degree of surface contamination prevented a realistic assessment of the amount of repointing required prior to cleaning. To reduce this problem on later Phases all joints were cleaned using a suction gun and defective joints repointed prior to cleaning operations. Although this approach reduced the number of incidents of water penetration, some water penetration still occurred.

11. Even though extensive protection measures and preliminary works were carried out, water penetration still occurred. To avoid the potential risk of damage to finishes, fixtures and fittings, an operative with a two way radio was located internally at all times to monitor for signs of water penetration. As soon as any water penetration was identified washing ceased until the point of entry could be ascertained and appropriate additional temporary sealing carried out. In some instances the point of entry could not be ascertained and in such circumstances no further water washing was carried out.

12. To reduce the risk of over washing, stubborn deposits were removed by air abrasive cleaning. This was only used in isolated areas and the principal method of cleaning was water washing.

During Phases II, the West Front and Westminster Hall and Phase IV, the Clock Tower, moisture readings were taken at various depths in the wall before, during and after cleaning operations. These tests revealed that even with strict controls over the quantity of water used, the stone became saturated after a relatively short period of washing. Furthermore, the stone took a number of months to dry out fully.

From these tests it was readily apparent that the risk of water penetration and saturation of stonework in part depended on the period required to clean the stonework. This point was confirmed on Phase VII, South Elevation, when only a few incidents of water penetration were encountered as a result of this elevation being cleaned more rapidly than other Phases. The reason for the faster rate of cleaning was attributable to the elevation having been cleaned more recently in the early 1970s. This point raises a number of interesting questions on planned maintenance and frequency of cleaning, which is outside the scope of this paper.

As discussed above, one of the major problems encountered on all Phases was the lengthy period required to remove the surface contamination. This was probably attributable to the fact that the contamination had built up over many decades forming a hard impervious layout. Due to the extended period of cleaning required, the sub-contractors were constantly requesting relaxation of the specification to speed up the programme. This point emphasised that stone cleaning is an inexact science and the tendering process involves a number of risks and problems. The alternative solution would have been for some form of negotiated contract however this has its own problems. There is no definite answer to the best form of contracting procedure, but the essential requirements is to ensure that the specification is fully researched and comprehensive.

Another risk identified was frost damage during cold periods. To minimise this risk water washing was not permitted when the temperature fell below 5°C. Furthermore water washing was not permitted during the Winter months, 30 November to 31 March. This restriction did not have significant programme implications because stone cleaning progressed more quickly than following operations such as stone repairs.

Air Abrasive Cleaning

As discussed previously, Phase V, River Terrace and Phase VIII, Victoria Tower were cleaned by semi-dry air abrasive techniques. The cleaning method again followed the principals set out in the 1973 Feasibility Report subject to certain refinements to take into account latest technology and results of further trials. From our initial investigations it become apparent that a grading system of cleaning had to be used which would minimise the risk of damage but also achieve a reasonable rate of progress. I have detailed below the grading system developed:

a)   Original carving details which were in a friable and a vulnerable condition were cleaned using a pencil gun. The use of this type of gun ensured strict control over the zone of cleaning (spread of abrasive) and reduced the risk of damage. This type of gun is impracticable on large areas and was therefore only used on particularly vulnerable details.

b)   All remaining carving details were cleaned using Hodge Clemco SCW/028 with a nozzle size not exceeding 6.3mm. Again with this type of gun, the zone of cleaning is small which is essential when cleaning ornate carvings.

c)   Ashlar and tracery were cleaned using Hodge Clemco, NC, SCW and SCWB equipment with a nozzle size not exceeding 12.5mm.

d)   On particularly valuable or unique details, poultice cleaning was carried out where there was risk of damage even when using the pencil gun.

Trials were carried out prior to completing the specification to test various equipment and cleaning procedures. These trials also identified an optimum pressure and cleaning distance from the stone which would remove the surface contaminants but not damage the stonework. Risk of damage was increased when the pressure was too low or too high.

A number of potential problems with air abrasive cleaning of stonework were identified and these were minimised by imposing extensive requirements and restrictions in the specification. The following summarise the main requirements imposed in the specification:

a)   The type of abrasive was selected by trial. The abrasive specified was 'J Blast Finesse'. This abrasive contained no free silica.

b)   The control of dust was important both from environmental and health and safety points of view. On the environmental side the scaffolding was enclosed with lapped flexible sheeting or rigid profiled sheeting. One of the main purposes of this sheeting was to contain dust generated by the cleaning process. As a further precaution, a small quantity of water was entrained at the nozzle to damp down the dust.

On the health and safety side, all operatives were required to wear protective helmets which also provided fresh air. Filters were specified to clean the air supplied to helmets which also removed any residue moisture which could freeze in cold weather.

c) One of the major problems with the air abrasive cleaning process is the noise generated by plant and the use of associated equipment. To reduce this problem maximum noise levels were specified for the main compressors and on one Phase, the compressor was located within an acoustic enclosure. In addition all other equipment was to be new and provided with silencers.

Due to the sensitivity of the occupants the periods of working were also restricted.

d) Gauges were provided to monitor pressure levels at various locations to check that specified levels were being complied with. A significant pressure drop does occur at the gun and therefore a hypodermic pressure gauge was also used to check pressures at the work face.

e) Radio communication was required between the 'gun' operative and the 'pot' operative. In addition an operative was located internally to monitor for signs of dust penetration.

f) Protection in the form of polythene sheeting, sealant, zinc sheet and plywood was provided to windows. Protection was also provided to carvings during abrasive cleaning of adjoining tracery and ashlar work.

g) Grit and dust arising from the cleaning operations was collected in a slurry gutter, similar to that provided for water washing. Grit was collected in polythene bags and disposed of at an approved site.

Two major disadvantages/risks of air abrasive cleaning are damage to the stonework and gun shading. The risk of damage was monitored by inspecting certain details before and after cleaning to check that fine tooling marks had not been removed. This monitoring proved that no significant visual damage (loss of detail) was caused by the cleaning process. However, with Clipsham stone, soft beds were susceptible to damage. This emphasised the need for the operatives to be fully trained and made aware that cleaning should cease immediately if any damage became apparent. It was found that due to the ornate feature work, it was not possible to remove all surface contamination without a significant risk of damage. A decision was therefore taken not to require a 100% clean, but rather to ensure that the majority of the contamination was removed.

On the problem of gun shading, this was minimised by ensuring the operatives were full trained and sample areas prepared which set the standard of finish required. However, some gun shading had to be accepted rather than requiring a further clean to be carried out with the greater risk of damage. A recent inspection of The River Terrace, Phase V completed in 1985 has revealed that gun shading becomes more apparent as the building weathers.

As part of the pre-contact investigations the Supervising Officer and Clerk of Works attended a course on air abrasive cleaning. This ensured that the most suitable equipment was specified. It also acquainted the professional team with the limitations of the equipment, and enabled problems encountered on site to be resolved without undue delay or argument.

Unlike water washing, air abrasive cleaning was permitted during the winter months due to the small quantity of water being used. However, no cleaning was permitted when the temperature fell below 5°C.

SITE CONTROL

Most of the restrictions imposed in the specification varied 'standard practice' adopted by the stone cleaning subcontractors. Problems were encountered with subcontractors in convincing them of the need to change 'standard practice' and ensuring compliance with the specification. This situation may have been exacerbated by the need to obtain competitive tenders. However, it would also be fair to say that site operatives often showed a responsible attitude to the works. The risk of non-compliance with the specification and/or abuse was reduced by the client employing a full time Clerk of Works who was fully experienced in the type of works involved.

CONCLUSION

Two main methods of cleaning, water washing and air abrasive cleaning have been used on the cleaning of the facades of the Palace of Westminster. Various refinements have been made to these methods to minimise the risks and disadvantages with varying degrees of success. It is apparent that the most effective cleaning and best appearance particularly after a period of weathering is achieved by water washing with limited air abrasive cleaning. However, occasions will arise when the most effective solution will not be practicable and therefore it is essential that a flexible approach is adopted when considering the alternative methods available. Before a final decision is reached on the most suitable cleaning method trials must be carried out. This will provide invaluable guidance and information when preparing the specification. The end objective must be to protect the fabric of the building and avoid any damage.

9   A conservator's approach to architectural stonework

JANE PORTER
Stone and Metalwork Conservator,
The Burrell Collection, Glasgow

(ABSTRACT)

GENERAL CONSERVATION PARAMETERS

The treatment of stone in the museum and archaeological world over the last 40 years has developed from a simple restoration to a fully scientific conservation approach.

Structured guidelines of professional conservation practice have been developed in which pre-treatment analysis and research is considered essential for the most successful choice of treatment. Such research must be specific to the artefact under treatment and its problems, but the following general considerations should be included:

a)   A thorough understanding of the stone: its geology and technology, and its causes of soiling and decay (including its history and use and earlier treatments);

b)   A thorough understanding of the nature of the materials and methods being considered for treatment and their likely effects on the stone over both a short and a long-term period (with direct reference to the weathering process and environmental conditions of the stone to be treated);

c) A thorough evaluation of the risks of materials/methods in relation to the problems of the stone and to the environmental conditions in which it will eventually be sited post-treatment.

To evaluate his/her decision on treatment correctly, a conservator must therefore proceed through a carefully structured process of pre-treatment research strictly relevant to a choice of treatment. He should be sufficiently trained in basic materials/applied science to enable him to formulate general answers to these questions, who to approach for more refined scientific testing and how to evaluate the results of research in relation to his conservation requirements. Ideally he should be able to refer to a sound body of general conservation research already carried out on the long-term effects of specific methods and materials used on the particular type of stone he is treating.

Ultimately the choice of treatment will be the conservator's responsibility and its success will depend on the thorough understanding of what he is trying to do and the effect he is wishing to achieve, together with the degree of skill and control he has in applying it.

In deciding on method, some principle considerations should be:

a) The treatment chosen should aim to prolong the life of a stone artefact and where it risks accelerating decay or where there is insufficient knowledge of its long-term effect, treatment should not proceed.

b) The chosen method and material should be sufficiently tested over the long-term and within the relevant conditions for its risks to be known and evaluated; testing should have been carried out by accredited research institutions to conservation specifications. On no account should experimental techniques, unresearched to these specifications, be considered.

c) The method, however well tested elsewhere, should always be tested and monitored in situ on the particular stone to be treated and preferably over varied areas of deterioration and/or soiling.

d) No method should ever be used uniformly over a stone surface which has varied areas of decay as these could react differently to treatment.

e) All methods should have a sufficient degree of control to stop or vary treatment instantly and enable the conservator to visibly monitor reaction to treatment at every stage.

f) Anything put into a porous stone structure, particularly a resin, will be either impossible or damaging to remove in the future and could risk accelerating the stone's natural process of weathering/decay; this could be accelerated if the material is forced in under pressure or heat, and it is itself susceptible to decay.

Passive/preventive conservation, ie. removing any external sources of harm and improving conditions, may often be a more effective way of prolonging the life of a deteriorated object than attempting to interfere with a structure using risky or inadequate methods.

ARCHITECTURAL STONEWORK: SPECIFIC CONSERVATION PARAMETERS

Choice of treatment for deteriorated stone in a controlled museum environment, however, may prove an easier option than that for stone in exposed and weathered conditions, susceptible to the most severe climatic conditions. In such conditions, architectural sculpture and decorative stonework may prove just as vulnerable as deteriorated Egyptian limestone reliefs stored in museum basements, and often the more difficult to diagnose for treatment due to the dynamic nature of their decay. In their case, then, it would appear even more critical that strict conservation codes of practice and scientific testing apply both in pre-treatment research and in post-treatment monitoring.

Together with the general parameters given above, a conservator will require to consider additional factors in order to assess the decay and weathering process of architectural stonework and its subsequent treatment. Principle considerations will be:

Environmental weathering conditions:

a)   The degree of water permeation/retention through the stone structure affecting surface breathing, patination build-up, internal composition, structural breakdown and decay.
b)   The degree of exposure to fluctuations in temperature, wetting and drying, freeze-thaw conditions, sunlight and wind.
c)   The degree of pollution and formation of impermeable surface skins from lichen, salts and industrial pollutants.

Design and technology of an architectural monument/sculpture:

The design of a stone structure and/or its position in a larger architectural structure will fundamentally affect its weathering pattern and mechanism of decay. Surface tolling, carving refinements, methods of dowelling, mortars, and differences in composition of adjacent materials will directly affect such considerations, and also diagnosis for treatment.

Historically-applied treatments:

Residues of materials resulting from earlier methods of cleaning, consolidation, restoration and surface protection, and their degree of deterioration from weathering, will often prove the cause of decay and will fundamentally affect or impede treatment.

THREE CASE STUDIES IN GLASGOW

In relation to the above conservation parameters, the author has chosen to review the problems associated with the cleaning and restoration of three principle city monuments in Glasgow, all of which comprise important sculpture and decorative detail. Two of these monuments were cleaned and restored in the late 1980s:

Kelvingrove: the city's principle museum and art gallery, built of Locharbriggs new red sandstone in 1900 and incorporating eight over life-size figure sculptures and much decorative relief carving.

Stewart Memorial: the city's principle fountain sculpture, built in 1872 to commemorate the bringing of fresh water to Glasgow and representing in multiple carving the flora and fauna of Scott's poem 'The Lady of the Lake'; constructed principally of carboniferous blonde sandstone, it also comprises polished Portsoy (limestone) marble columns, inset metal coloured enamels and a granite basin.

Both buildings were cleaned using chemical cleaning systems and problems with cleaning were complicated by the existence in the stone of residual preservative/water-repellent mediums applied at the time of building. The author will review the approach to cleaning taken, the effects of treatment three years on, and the conservation implications of the methods and materials used.

The third case study will review a building urgently in need of restoration and cleaning, the St Vincent Street Church designed by Alexander 'Greek' Thomson, Glasgow's most important 19th century architect. Built of carboniferous blonde sandstone and restored over the century with methods including cement fondu and lamp black, this building is in a grave state of deterioration with imminent loss of the surface containing much of Greek Thomson's famous characteristic relief carving and incised decoration. The author will review the decay processes and nature of deterioration over the building and will discuss the conservation considerations required to draw up a correct procedure for pre-treatment analysis and diagnosis for treatment.

10 The composition and weathering of sandstone with relation to cleaning

BRIAN BLUCK
University of Glasgow

(ABSTRACT)

The Carboniferous sandstones of which Glasgow is largely built are arenites comprising quartz, feldspar and clay with a carbonate cement. They weather to rocks which, when mature, comprise five zones illustrated in Figure 1 and commonly found in other sandstones. The outer zone 1 of soiling which is formed mainly by materials external to the stone, is followed inward by a zone 2 where mineral cements dissolved from within the stone are reprecipitated to accumulate as a layer of reduced permeability. Zone 3 is gradational to 2 and is characterised by a colour change. Zone 4 is depleted of mineral cement which has been supplied to zones 2 and 3 and zone 5 is the original rock.

These zones, produced by repeated moisture ingress and egress within the sandstone, are supplemented by the addition of moisture transmitted by other means. Degradation of the surface in Glasgow's buildings commonly takes place by exfoliation and expansion and detachment of exfoliated layers is often at the depleted zone (4). The % of zone 4 is used as a quantitative estimate of the degree of degradation of a stone building surface and preliminary analyses of sandstone buildings built in Glasgow between 1880 and 1910 show a relationship between the estimated degradation and the volume of clay present within the stone (Figure 2).

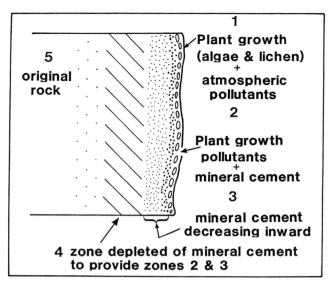

Figure 1 Distribution of zones of weathering in a typical mature Glasgow 'blonde' sandstone.

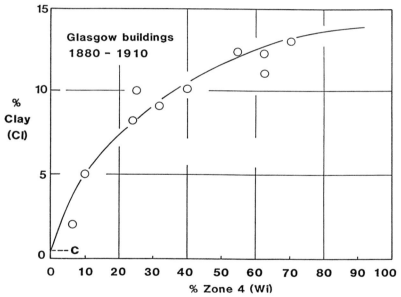

Figure 2 The relationship between clay content and degradation of sandstones of Glasgow buildings. The data are preliminary.

Petrographic and SEM examination of these degraded rocks show them to have a clay enrichment within the zones 2,3 and 4 and a corresponding reduction in feldspars when compared with the feldspars-clay ratios of the sound rock of zone 5. This suggests that sandstones which originally had an acceptable level of clay have acquired more clay by the breakdown of feldspar and the transportation of those elements to the outer zones of the stone where they reassemble as clay minerals.

All clays expand on contact with water, although the extent of the expansion is a function of the clay mineral involved. When sandstones are maturely weathered, water, and particularly water transmitted from elsewhere in the building, becomes trapped in the stone behind the relatively impermeable zones 1 and 2 in the weakly cemented zones 3 and 4. This increase in moisture retention time allows the clays to expand and aids other factors such as frost action to break up the stone.

It is clear that over times spans of hundreds of years, there is a potential for sandstone, which at the time of building was sound, to change to a clay-rich rock which would undergo rapid weathering (Figure 3).

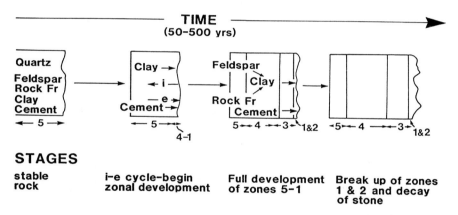

Figure 3 A hypothetical cycle in the degrading of sandstone; i=moisture ingress, e=moisture egress, 1-5 refer to the zones of Figure 1.

There is also great potential for some methods of cleaning to greatly accelerate this weathering process.

11 Abrasive cleaning of sandstone buildings and monuments: an experimental investigation

MAUREEN YOUNG and DENNIS URQUHART
The Robert Gordon Institute of Technology, Aberdeen

INTRODUCTION

The work outlined in this paper forms part of a research commission, sponsored by Historic Scotland and Scottish Enterprise, investigating the effects of cleaning on sandstone buildings and monuments in Scotland. Within this broad area the effects of abrasive cleaning methods on sandstones, particularly the two predominant techniques of wet and dry grit blasting, have received little objective analysis.

There is considerable visual evidence that abrasive cleaning methods have resulted in unacceptable damage to sandstones, in particular, alterations to the surface texture of the stone and erosion of architectural detail. The aim of this part of the research was to establish the mechanisms inherent in these cleaning techniques and to identify the critical factors responsible for damage.

METHOD

To determine the effects of selected wet and dry grit blasting abrasive cleaning methods on sandstone, a testing regime to standardize procedures was devised. This required the construction of a range of test panels (1.5m high by 1.2m wide) at the Faculty of Design, The Robert Gordon Institute of Technology, Aberdeen. Each panel contained 15 different, freshly cut sandstone types as removable prisms (each with a 5cm by 5cm exposed face) for accurate measurement of the effects of cleaning. One panel was left uncleaned to act as a control.

Test cleaning was carried out by trained and highly experienced operators, working under strict supervision, using industry standard equipment.

Ten different grit blasting methods were tested. Details of pressures and grits used are shown in Table 1.

The prisms and grits were subjected to a number of different tests to accurately determine key features before and after they were inserted into the panels.

Table 1   **Grit blasting methods tested**

Pressure(psi)	Grit type	Wet/dry	Ave.grit size (μm)
20	silica sand	dry	550
40	silica sand	dry	550
80	silica sand	dry	550
20	silica sand	wet (2.5gall/min)	550
40	silica sand	wet (2.5gall/min)	550
80	silica sand	wet (2.5gall/min)	550
40	non-silica grit	dry	200
40	non-silica grit	dry	350
40	non-silica grit	dry	900
40	non-silica grit	dry	1600

Weighing

Each prism was oven dried at 103°C and weighed to an accuracy of +/- 0.01g before and after cleaning. The prisms were wrapped in plastic film before being mortared into the test panels to eliminate mortar adhesion problems and the loss of grains during insertion and removal. The prisms were carefully handled between the two sets of weighings so as to minimise any weight loss due to damage other than that caused by cleaning. Weight losses from the test prisms were measured relative to the control prism to exclude any weight losses which were due to factors other than cleaning.

Surface roughness

Surface roughness was measured using Form Talysurf. This works by tracking a fine, diamond tipped needle over the surface of the sample. The vertical displacement of the needle is measured and the result is plotted as a profile on a graph showing deviation from the mean height. A number of statistical data related to roughness are produced. The data used in this study were those of average surface roughness (Ra). This is the arithmetic mean of the departures of the profile from the mean line.

$$R_a = 1/L \int_0^L |y(x)| dx$$

where   L is the sample length
            y is the height relative to the mean
            x is the horizontal distance

It is not possible to scan precisely the same track across the sandstone samples before and after cleaning and this introduces some variability into the results. Measurements were made in two directions at right angles across the sandstones since some sandstones had an observable fabric which could make a difference to the stone's roughness in different directions.

Scanning electron microscopy (SEM)

SEM examinations were made of the surfaces of selected sandstones before and after cleaning. Since the technique can only be used on small samples of sandstone which must be gold coated prior to examination, it was not possible to look at the same area of sandstone before and after cleaning. Control prisms from the test panels were therefore used as examples of uncleaned surfaces.

Grit sizes

The range in size of the grits used were measured by sieving samples of the grits. The results are shown in Table 2.

Table 2   **Sieve sizes of grits used in tests**

Sieve size(μm)	%	passing			
	NS1	NS2	NS3	NS4	Silica sand
2360	100.00	100.00	100.00	96.64	100.00
1180	100.00	99.99	80.06	23.41	99.80
600	99.77	91.47	21.89	5.19	61.14
300	67.66	39.44	5.95	2.00	6.77
150	30.81	13.18	0.92	0.82	0.59
75	10.24	4.05	0.04	0.17	0.07

[NS1-4 are non-silica grits]

RESULTS

Weight loss

The test prisms showed a wide variation in weight losses over the range of cleaning methods used. The large range in weight losses results from the wide range of sandstone types used in the study. Weight losses as large as 2200gm^{-2} were recorded. In a few cases small weight gains were measured after cleaning. This is assumed to be due to mortar or dust adhesion to the prism and weight losses in these cases have been assumed to be zero. These data have been excluded from calculations of regression lines in Figures 3 (a-e). A degree of variability is also introduced due to the random effects of operator control.

The results from cleaning of 15 different freshly cut sandstones were combined to give average results. These sandstones are shown in Table 3.

Table 3   **Data on sandstones**

Sandstone	Type	Calcar-eous	Colour	Ave.grain size (μm)
Blaxter	quartz arenite	no	buff	medium
Cat Castle	sub-arkose	no	buff	coarse
Clashach	sub-arkose	yes	pale-buff	fine-med
Corsehill	sub-arkose	yes	red	fine
Doddington	quartz arenite	no	pink	medium
Dunhouse	sub-arkose	no	buff	fine-med
Gatelawbridge	sub-arkose	no	red	fine-med
Greenbrae	quartz arenite	no	buff	medium
Locharbriggs	quartz arenite	no	red	medium
Newbigging	quartz arenite	no	white	medium
Red Wilderness	lithic arkose	no	red/green	fine
St Bees	sub-arkose	no	red	fine
Springwell	quartz arenite	no	buff	medium
Spynie	sub-arkose	yes	white	fine
Stainton	quartz arenite	no	buff	medium

The averaged weight loss data are shown in Figure 1 along with standard deviations for each data point. Weight losses for each prism have been converted from absolute values to gm^{-2} relative to the control prism.

The effect of pressure water washing at 400psi is also shown since wet grit blasted test panels were washed at 400psi following grit blasting. This wash off must always be done after wet grit blasting as it is necessary to wash off the slurry left on the surface by the blasting process.

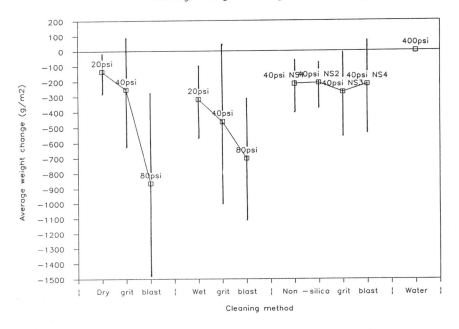

Figure 1 Average weight changes to test prisms due to grit blasting of fresh sandstone. Standard deviations are shown.

Several conclusions can be drawn from this data:

(i) It is clear that the higher the grit blasting pressure, the more weight is lost from the sandstone. For dry grit blasting, doubling the grit blasting pressure approximately doubles the weight loss.

In wet grit blasting, the lower pressures (20 and 40psi) caused greater weight losses than the equivalent dry grit blast. Wet grit blasting is, however, often said to be less abrasive than equivilant dry grit blasting due to the 'cushioning' effect of the water [1,2]. The additional weight loss suffered by prisms after wet grit blasting in these tests may be due to the water introduced into the grit blast jet (2.5 gall/min) and/or to the fact that the stone was washed off using a pressure water jet at 400psi after grit blasting. However, the effects of pressure washing on freshly cut sandstone at 400psi were found to be negligible.

(ii) Changing the size of the grit blasting particles had no observable effect on the average weight losses from the sandstones, despite the fact that the heaviest particles (NS4) were approximately 500 times heavier than the lightest particles (NS1). A comparison of average grit sizes and average lightest particles (NS1). A comparison of average grit sizes and average weight losses are given in Table 4.

Table 4   **Average grit size, relative weight and the weight loss for freshly cut sandstones**

Grit type (dry grit at 40psi)	av. size (μm)	Relative weight	av. weight loss (gm^{-2})
NS 1	200	1	216
NS 2	350	5	210
Silica sand	550	21	254
NS 3	900	91	270
NS 4	1600	512	219

(iii) Differences in the hardness of grit particles had no observable effect on the weight loss. The silica grit has a Mohs' hardness of 7 and the non-silica grit had a Mohs' hardness of 5-6, however, there was no observable difference in weight loss during 40psi dry grit blasting tests (see Table 4).

Surface roughness

Pitting

Sandstone types which contained calcite ($CaCO_3$) cemented patches were affected by pitting of the surface following cleaning (Plate 1). The pits vary in size depending on the size of the calcite patches. In the cases observed they varied in size from about 1 to 4mm diameter and were 1 or 2mm deep. Pitting affected Clashach, Corsehill and Spynie Sandstones. Plate 2 shows a typical calcite cemented patch from Clashach Sandstone.

This pitting develops because the calcite cements in these sandstones are irregularly distributed and concentrated in patches a few millimetres across. Within these patches, the detrital grains (mainly quartz) are relatively uncompacted and cemented together virtually by calcite alone. Outwith these areas, the detrital grains are more compacted and the structure is strengthened by pressure solution and silica cementation. The result is that the sandstone inside the calcite patches is much more vulnerable to erosion (calcite has a Mohs' hardness of 3) than that outside the calcite patches (quartz has a Mohs' hardness of 7). The calcite patches are thus weaker areas of the sandstone and are more rapidly eroded by abrasive cleaning since removal of the calcite cement leads to the additional loss of the uncompacted detrital grains.

Talysurf surface roughness data

Five different sandstones were examined before and after cleaning by Talysurf. These were Blaxter, Cat Castle, Clashach, Locharbriggs and Red Wilderness.

Increases in the average surface roughness (R_a) of the sandstones can have a number of causes. These include: plucking of grains from the surface, preferential erosion of cements or less resistant grains or shattering of grains. Figures 2 (a-e) shows the increase in R_a for each prism after cleaning.

It is not clear from this data whether there are any consistent patterns of roughening with grit blast pressure or grit size. However, the data for weight loss and roughening have been combined in Figures 3 (a-e) to show increased roughness vs. weight loss for each of the five sandstones for which detailed surface roughness data is available.

It is clear from these graphs (except for Clashach Sandstone) that weight loss and increased surface roughness are closely interdependent. In the case of Clashach Sandstone, the spread of data in Figure 3c is probably due to loss of calcite cemented areas. This would tend to increase the average surface roughness more than would be 'expected' from the measured weight loss. The amount of roughening would be dependent on the distribution and amount of calcite in the particular sample.

Higher grit blasting pressures cause both greater erosion (as measured by weight loss) and greater surface roughening.

SEM examination

The surfaces of selected sandstones were examined by SEM before and after cleaning. Plates 3 and 4 show typical examples of Cat Castle Sandstone before and after cleaning at 80psi using dry, silica grit. Before cleaning the surface is relatively free of debris with grains and cements well defined. There are a few damaged grains (caused by sample preparation). After cleaning there is a good deal of surface debris and kaolinite cements are pulverised where they have been exposed to impact. However, there is no evidence of shattering or damage to individual sandstone grains. This suggests that erosion caused by grit blasting occurs by loss of individual, whole grains rather than by shattering of the surface. Similar result have been observed on Clashach and Locharbriggs Sandstones.

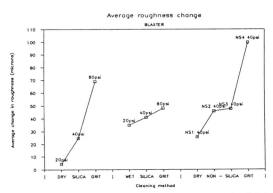

Figure 2a The change in average surface roughness (R_a) of Blaxter sandstone due to grit blasting.

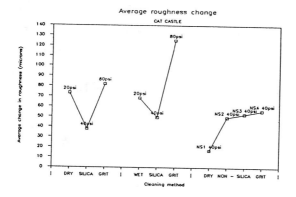

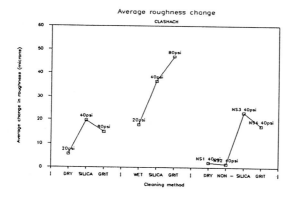

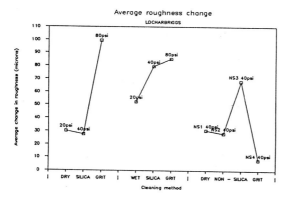

Figures 2 b-d The change in average surface roughness (R_a) of different sandstones due to grit blasting.

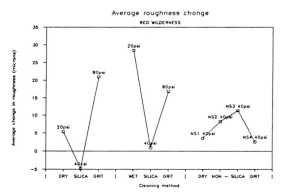

Figure 2e The change in average surface roughness (R_a) of Red Wilderness sandstone due to grit blasting.

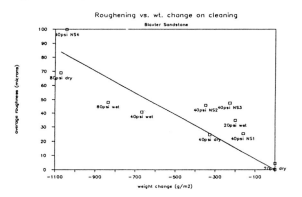

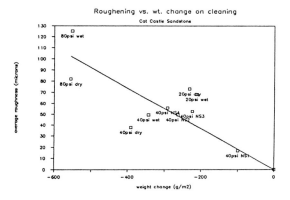

Figure 3a,b Average surface roughening vs. weight change on sandstones after cleaning. R^2 values for regression lines are shown below Figure 3e.

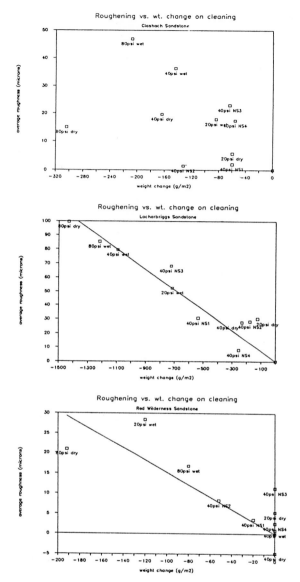

Figures 3c-e Average surface roughening vs. weight change on sandstones after cleaning. R^2 values for regression lines are shown below.

Sandstone	R^2
Blaxter	0.55
Cat Castle	0.44
Clashach	
Locharbriggs	0.85
Red Wilderness	0.62

CONCLUSIONS

Higher grit blasting pressures cause greater degrees of erosion and roughening. Doubling the grit blast pressure approximately doubles the amount of surface erosion.

Wet grit blasting, at least at lower blasting pressures appears to be more erosive than dry grit blasting. The extra erosion may be due to the addition of water into the grit blast jet or to the pressure water jet used to rinse off the stone following wet grit blasting.

Neither changing the size of the grit blast particles (over a range of 200μm to 1600μm diameter) nor changing their hardness (from 5-6 to 7 on Mohs' scale) had any effect on the average weight loss or roughening during dry grit blasting at 40psi.

There is, in most cases, a linear relationship between weight loss and surface roughening. This may not apply with sandstones containing calcite cements since, being preferentially eroded, this can lead to greater degrees of roughening where the calcite cements are irregularly distributed.

Sandstones containing patches of calcite cements with loosely compacted grains suffer surface pitting during grit blasting due to the preferential erosion of the softer calcite patches.

Loss of material from the sandstone surface occurs by detachment of individual grains rather than by shattering of grains.

It can be concluded that blasting pressure is the significant factor in erosion and roughening (although operator control is also a major factor) and neither grit size nor grit hardness (in the ranges studied) appear to have any major impact on the outcome of grit blasting.

Acknowledgements

The authors are grateful for the financial support from Historic Scotland and Scottish Enterprise and the assistance of Stoneguard Ltd.

References

1. BRE Digest 280, 1976, Cleaning external surfaces of buildings.

2. Boyer, D.W., 1986, Masonry Cleaning - The State of the Art, in 'Cleaning Stone and Masonry', ASTM STP 935, J.R. Clifton, Ed., American Society for Testing and Materials, Philadelphia, 25-51.

Plate 1. Block of Clashach Sandstone after dry grit blasting at 40psi. Pitting of the surface was not present before cleaning. Pits are due to erosion of calcite cemented patches in the sandstone. .

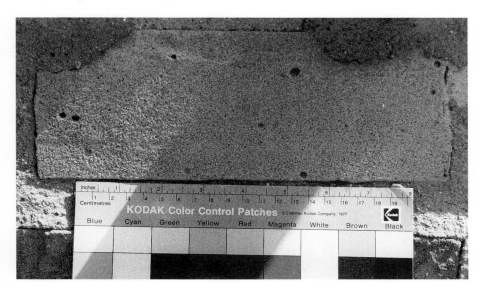

Plate 2. Clashach Sandstone in thin section showing a calcite cemented patch to the lower left with loosely compacted detrital grains. To the upper right is the typical texture of the bulk of the sandstone - grains are more compacted and cemented by silica. Width of photograph is approximately 1mm.

Plate 3. SEI image, gold coated. Cat Castle Sandstone before cleaning. Shows quartz grain with extensive overgrowth surrounded by well crystalline kaolinite.

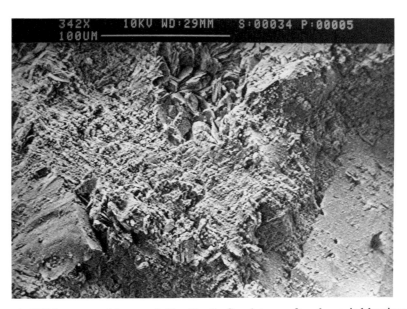

Plate 4. SEI image, gold coated. Cat Castle Sandstone after dry grit blasting at 80psi. Kaolinite has been pulverised where it was exposed to impact. It remains well crystalline where it was sheltered from impact. There is a good deal of surface debris.

12 Research on cleaning methods applied to historical stone monuments

MARTIN WERNER and CLAUDIA NEUWALD
Institut für Baumaschinen und Baubetrieb Rheinisch-
Westfälische Technische Hochschule, Aachen, Germany

INTRODUCTION

This paper briefly describes the reasons for cleaning historical monuments made of sandstone and the aims of cleaning them. The cleaning methods investigated can be sub-divided into three groups, and they are dealt with in this sequence:

1. Cleaning methods using pure water;
2. Cleaning methods using chemical substances;
3. Mechanical cleaning methods.

In all, the effects of 12 different cleaning methods were investigated. These are basically physical and chemical investigations, most of which are standardized.

The main emphases of the investigations were the changes of the capillary water absorption, chemical changes dependent on the depth profile, changes of colour, and the determination of the loss of substance.

The investigations were carried out on four standard varieties of sandstones, ashlars which had to be changed anyway during the course of the restoration.

THE PROBLEM

The physical, chemical, and mineralogical characteristics of sandstone surfaces are changed by depositions of dusts as well as depositions of gaseous and liquid pollutants from the air or from rainfall which react with the dusts or with the substrate. Measurements of immission rates of the single pollutants (1) as well as investigations of crust from different historical monuments (2) show that physico-chemical as well as chemical-biological processes are set in motion by the concentration of pollutants, which destroy or change the original surface of the sandstone in a negative way. This can be seen from the changes in colour, surface structure and the outer appearance. In order to stop the weathering process, the detrimental substances have to be removed and further measures have to be taken.

AIMS OF CLEANING

The aims which have to be taken into account for the cleaning of the sandstone of historical monuments are manifold and partly contradictory. On the one hand the aims comprise the improvement of the outer appearance, the opening of the capillary pores for a subsequent application of consolidants, and the restoration of the physical characteristics. On the other hand the loss of substance which is caused by the cleaning should be minimized. In order to achieve these aims different methods are used in practice.

INVESTIGATED CLEANING METHODS

According to their respective types, three different groups of cleaning methods can be differentiated:

1. Methods using water without chemical additives;
2. Methods using water with chemical cleaners;
3. Wet and dry mechanical methods.

From the methods using water without chemical additives the following ones were investigated:

1. Pressureless sprinkling with cold water;
2. Ceaning with jets of warm water at various degrees of pressure and temperature (60 bar/60°C, 90 bar/60°C, 150bar/60°C, 60 bar/90°C, 90 bar/90°C);
3. Cleaning with steam jets (30 bar/150°C).

Due to the diminishing significance of the cleaning method using chemical additives, the effect of only one standard cleaner containing hydrofluoric acid was investigated. From the mechanical methods sandblasting using solid, dry or wet, abrasives for blasting was investigated. Abrasives for blasting were used with diameters from 0.1mm to 0.7mm, with different graduation and made of different materials.

SANDSTONES

The investigations were carried out at four historical monuments which have been undergoing large-scale restoration and from which square stone had to be taken and changed due to the restoration measures. These square stones are made of Sander Schilfsandstein, Schillingsfürst Castle; square stones made of Werksandstein from the residence of Würzburg; square stones made of Franconian Rhaetic sandstone from the Kolb brewery, Bayreuth; and square stones made of Franconian new red sandstone of Plassenburg Castle, Kulmbach. The varieties of stone will not be described in detail. The forms of pollution or of weathering are, however, symptomatic of the investigated varieties of sandstone.

One can find further information on the four mentioned varieties of sandstone in Grimm et al. (3).

METHODS OF INVESTIGATION

The evaluation of the effects of different cleaning methods was based on an interpretation of physical and chemical investigations as well as on a subjective description of the microscopic and macroscopic changes of the state of the object. This included in detail:

1. Water absorption capacity under normal pressure and under vacuum pressure according to the German Industrial Standards (DIN) 52103;
2. Capillary absorption coefficient W, in $kg/m^2/sec$, according to the German Industrial Standards (DIN) 52615;
3. Capillary elevation (water penetration coefficient B in m/sec, according to the German Industrial Standards (DIN) 52615;
4. Water penetration according to Karsten (with the Karsten testing equipment);
5. Water vapour permeability coefficient μ_{50-100} ('WET CUP');
6. Water soluble parts dependent on the depth profile;
7. Acid soluble parts dependent on the depth profile;
8. Colour according to the German Industrial Standards (DIN) 5033 and 55981 as well as according to CIELAB EAB;
9. Roughness according to the German Industrial Standards (DIN) 4768 and (4).

The above mentioned parameters were measured before and after cleaning. During and after an attempt at cleaning respectively, the following parameters were measured:

1. The depth profile of temperature for methods using water;

2. The space co-ordinates of the water horizon for methods using water;
3. The loss of substance and the organical parts contained therein.

RESULTS

For reasons of space, only the conclusions from the results of the investigations can be presented. According to their effect the cleaning methods can be sub-divided into four groups:

1. Pressureless sprinkling;
2. Cleaning with jets of warm water without chemical additives;
3. Methods using chemical cleaners;
4. Mechanical methods.

Basically, it has to be emphasized that the state of the weathering at every single spot of a square stone or of a figure influences the single investigation characteristics to a much greater extent than the used cleaning method. One exception is the method of pressureless sprinkling by which substrata with crusts containing gypsum can be cleaned well, and which does not have any effect on other substrata apart from a partially thorough saturating. Another exception is the chemical cleaning method. After its application, residues of the cleaner could be found in all absorbent, porous sandstones, partly up to a depth of 20mm. The methods of cleaning with jets of warm water do not differ from each other with regard to their effect, because the pressure of the impact and the impact temperature is very much dependent on the distance between the jet and the surface of the treated object, and thus the operator can easily change the decisive parameters of the different methods by handling the jet skilfully. Apart from the blasting pressure, the choice of the abrasives for blasting (granular material of glass, quartz sand, pulverized limestone, granular material of wood) and the size of the abrasives for blasting are the decisive parameters of the sandblasting methods, independent of the choice of wet or dry abrasives.

Satisfying results can be obtained by an appropriate choice, even on sensitive surfaces. In any case, long-term damage caused by the use of chemical cleaners or by too much saturating due to sprinkling can almost be excluded for the mechanical cleaning methods. It is recommended – and this could be an important result of our investigations – to prepare one or several surfaces for different cleaning methods at the respective object, because on the one hand the state of weathering plays an important role – as mentioned above – and on the other hand the decisive parameters can be strongly influenced by the operator. The relevant parameters which describe the cleaning effect can then be determined relatively easily at these test surfaces. These parameters are the following:

1. The capillary water absorption, as a measure of the opening of the pores;
2. The colour as a directly visible feature;
3. The roughness as a measure of the loss of substance.

These three characteristics describe relatively well, quickly and cheaply the respective success of cleaning – the capillary water absorption according to the German Industrial Standards (DIN) 52615 can be replaced by the capillary water penetration according to Karsten (5).

These investigations were supported by a grant from the Ministry of Research and Technology (BMFT) as part of a joint venture research project.

References

1. Danneker, W. (1986) 'Einsatz eines neuartigen PassivSammlersystems an Kulturbauten zur Messung sauer reagierender Schadgase in der Atmosphäre.' Sonderheft Bautenschutz und Bausanierung. Köln: Müller, S.46-49.
2. Krumbein, W.E.(1988) 'Biology of stone and minerals in buildings'. Proceedings of the VIth International Congress on Deterioration and Conservation of Stone. Ed. Nicholas Copernicus University, Torun 12.-14.09.1988.
3. Grimm, W.-D. et al.(1990) 'Bildatlas ausgewählter Denkmalgesteine der Bundesrepublik Deutschland'. München: Arbeitscheft 50 Bayerisches Landesamt für Denkmalpflege.
4. Grimm, W.-D.und Völkl, J. (1983) 'Rauhigkeitsmessungen zur Kennzeichnung der Natursteinverwitterung'. Zeitschrift der deutschen geologischen Gesellschaft 134, S.387 - 411.
5. Snethlage, R.(1986) 'Messungen zur Dauerhaftigkeit von Hydrophobierungen an Sandsteingeb äuden'. Sonderheft Bautenschutz und Bausanierung. Köln: Müller, S.16-19.

13 Experience with cleaning and consolidating stone facades in Hungary

MIHÁLY ZÁDOR
Institute of History and Theory of Architecture,
Technical University, Budapest, Hungary

INTRODUCTION

In Hungary during the last 20 years, interest in the preservation of monuments has focused on that of stone monuments and facades exposed to rapid destruction. This problem is prevalent in Hungary because of the peculiar climatic conditions - a yearly average of 40 to 50 freeze/thaw cycles, fast growing air pollution, and the use of poor, rather porous coarse limestone and tuff as building materials.

Unfortunately, the stone material most widely used for the first stone buildings in Hungary from about the 11th century, such as important Romanesque churches, as well as for monumental stone buildings of the powerful turban development in the last century, such as the Opera House and Parliament Building, up to family houses and holiday homes, has been porous, coarse limestone from Sóskut, with little or no frost resistance.

In the last 50 to 60 years, the decay rate of our limestone, tuff and sandstone materials has increased by five or ten times. This accelerated rate of decay, and the growing international interest in preserving Hungarian monuments, led to a number of steps being taken to further investigation of the decay mechanisms at work:

1. Active participation in relevant international forums and membership, together with Professor Dr Pál Kertész, in the ICOMOS-RILEM Stone Committee since 1972;
2. Establishment of the technical-scientific research base for Hungarian monuments preservation at the Technical University of Budapest, focusing, in the last decade, on finding a consolidation/repair, completion method for domestic, weathered coarse limestones instead of perpetual stone replacements, with special consideration given to diagnostic tests prior to reconstruction, as reported at the 1976 Athens Symposium;
3. Establishment of the National ICOMOS Conservation Committee;
4. Our research work and a number of monument reconstructions endeavoured to test as many materials and methods as possible, from preventive water repellent treatment of sound stone – 1971: Roman Mithras relief in Aquincum (Budapest); 1973: pylon of the Chain Bridge in Budapest; 1975–1976: the Turkish 'King' Bath in Budapest; a new experimental house systematically tested since 1972 to the actual integer system of diagnostic tests –up-to-date cleaning methods – conservation with consolidation/completing, with self-bond new part;
5. In conformity with a regulation issued by the competent minister, elaboration of rules and technical specifications for cleaning and consolidating stone facades;
6. In recent years, several research institutes, the National Monuments Inspectorate, and several enterprises concentrated activities on saving decaying stone facades and carvings.

OBSERVATIONS

A summary of our findings with regard to stone cleaning and correlated consolidation works, as outlined above, is given below:

1. An ulterior survey of cleaning made in the past two decades, mainly by moist sand blasting, mechanical and manual cleaning, and ion-exchange paste cleaning, indicated that most of the procedures used suited a given area, but it is debatable whether or not they were applied to the most suitable areas and in the most appropriate manner.

   Grey dirt on facades proved not to be an aesthetic problem–increasing the historical value of the monument–but rather an accumulation of stone destroying matter.
2. Instrumental testing, or sometimes, simple macroscopy of cleaned surfaces after some years, shows cleaning–a costly exercise–to be meaningless without consolidation.

   Four or five years after cleaning, a simple, hard limestone ashlar abutment wall (Mount St.Gellért) shows marked grey pollution.
3. Consolidation is also imposed by the fact that stone surfaces, mostly exposed to war damages, have been repaired by grey cement mortar–mostly destructive to the stone–which match the surfaces that are turning grey but emerge as grey spots after cleaning. (Similarly, grey surfaces

repaired in white, become spotted like hyenas.) These grey spots have to be removed, imposing repair of the stone surface.The same refers to the repair of joints, crucial elements in the destruction of stone facades, in conformity with statements made in Hungary and by the International Stone Committee. Destructive moisture usually enters masonry across joints. Accordingly, cleaning, stone repair, completion and consolidation have to be treated as an integral system.

4. The structural, physical and chemical aspects of a building's masonry should also be treated as an integral system. These aspects have to be known and taken into account, bearing in mind that we are talking about whole buildings, rather than single stone carvings. Facades cannot be taken to laboratories or stone carving workshops, dipped in water tubs or in conserving agents, nor taken to pieces in diagnostic tests prior to cleaning, an essential difference in approach and methodology between museum conservers and building restorers, or between cleaning and preservation.

5. Following actual building examination, the resumption of facade destruction, often soon after cleaning and consolidation may be attributed to the omission or incorrect performance of a careful, up-to-date diagnostic test. In any case, in-depth in-situ instrumental and laboratory tests have to be made prior to cleaning in order to determine the correct cleaning and consolidation methods (studied from 1972 to 1978 by the ICOMOS-RILEM Stone Conservation Working Committee headed by Mr Marc Mamillan, which presented its findings at the 1978 Paris Conference), while the surface itself has to be subjected to trial cleaning and consolidation prior to formulating the final technology specification.

EXPERIENCE WITH CLEANING PROCEDURES

Our experience of cleaning procedures in Hungary, primarily in Budapest, seems to be rather similar to that abroad, so only a few special cases are outlined below:

Water cleaning

Water cleaning is undoubtedly the simplest, cheapest method available and may be effective in small dosages. However, practical observations indicate that the hard crust of pollution, mostly overlying weathered stone material, cannot be removed from porous stone by simple washing, even if warm water is used.

Increasing the pressure or the water volume, either by soaking or by spraying, may lead to a case similar to that of an Hungarian enterprise which, having cleaned the building of the Ministry of the Interior, flooded the rooms of officials and the archives and had to resort to using another method, to be outlined later.

It must be borne in mind that masonry soaking may introduce a wide range of destructive factors:

1. Among physical causes, frost – about 10% expansion in pore volumes;

2. Chemical damage: efflorescence or a volume increase in pores, of soluble salts (by about 200-300%);
3. Biological damage: the appearance of algae, lichens;
4. Aesthetic damage due to, for example, salt efflorescences.

Serious damage can be caused to the inner linings of buildings, electric wiring, not to mention invaluable murals, ornaments and mosaics.

The overwhelming enthusiasm accompanying the advent of water–based technologies a few years ago, has much receded. However, it has led to the development of another technology: with the Basilica of Budapest in mind, a piece of equipment combined with a computer was developed at the Department of Building Constructions of TUB, for continuously metering wall moisture during water cleaning and during drying. It should, however, be emphasised that it is better to avoid the possibility of masonry soaking before the operation is carried out.

Mechanical methods

For decades manual and mechanical methods of physical cleaning have been continuously applied to buildings and monuments in Hungary. Concomitant problems are breaking of surface crystals; stone dust caulking pores; and alteration of the original, typical surface texture–typically mainly of porous rocks, e.g. Hungarian coarse limestones.

However, it should be remembered that physical cleaning is needed only as a supplement to other methods in any case and one may ask why originally applied stone carving tools are not used instead to work over the surface and so clean it.

Chemical cleaning

In Hungary, chemical cleaning was attempted mainly in the 1970s but with little success. Alkaline materials were shown not to remove pollution, while using acid cleaners, neutralization by rinsing proved ineffective–pores retain acids sufficiently to cause damage to the stone. It has even been shown that neutralization causes the damaging agent to penetrate the stone. These agents may also damage mortar joints.

Paste cleaning

Better results were obtained recently using paste cleaning in its ion exchange form, where the paste, applied after preliminary washing, reacts only with the surface pollution, rather than damaging the stone.

However, the advantages of this method must be weighed against its low productivity and high cost, making it economically viable perhaps only for cleaning sculptures and monuments.

Wet and dry sand blasting

Wet or dry sand blasting of weathered coarse limestone may be rapid and productive especially on richly decorated facades, but it may 'shave' the surface (e.g. Opera House, trial surface of the Parliament Building etc.). As an early example, in 1973, faces of lions on the Chain Bridge abutments were, literally, shaven, and even suffered deep cuts, so the work had to be stopped and the lions restored by sculpture restorers.

These methods are not suitable for every type of building or monument and a separate examination is necessary in every case. Effective wet sand blasting has several precedents, mainly for hard limestone and granite, and even dry sand blasting has been applied–albeit cautiously and using the proper technology, for the large stone facade of the Sopron Post Office.

Obviously, none of these methods is exempt from problems, prompting the monuments preservation enterprise, ANTIKART, to look for a new procedure– the JOS (patented) method introduced in 1987, after about 15 years successful application in Germany, e.g. on Regensburg Cathedral, several office buildings in Munich, monuments and statues.

After the failure of the wet cleaning of the building of the Ministry of the Interior, this procedure was applied with success, to the Hungarian Academy of Sciences. Its essential tool is a special nozzle spraying little water and amalgam in a turbulent flow –rather than normally to the surface–at an angle favouring dirt removal by turbulent water, air and detergent.

Comparing this method with water cleaning, it was shown that 200–300 litres of water were required for cleaning, compared with 6 litres/m^2 of wall using the JOS method. Drying is therefore faster using the latter method, consolidation may follow after a few days rather than weeks, and scaffolding may soon be removed. Indeed, cleaning and consolidation may even be done without scaffolding.

A JOS 'mini-nozzle' was applied by a conserver colleague for cleaning part of the facade of the National Theatre in Pécs, a fine Baroque doorway at Buda Castle, and several buildings in Austria.

Among six competitors, the firm applying the JOS method won the commission to clean the Academy building. In trial cleanings, water meters were distributed among the competitors to check respective water consumptions in trial cleanings.

Consolidation

Cleaning must be followed by consolidation. However, the requirements for agents to consolidate Hungary's weathered coarse limestones were not met by any of the consolidants available from abroad. These requirements are as follows:

1. A unified, homogeneous system of consolidation where the agent consolidating the natural stone contributed to the stone completion by intrinsic bind (without adhesive), the system being solely made up of the original stone and the consolidant, enabling them to 'co-act';

150

2. In addition to the generally required water repellency, vapour diffusion of at least 15% in the consolidated part, conforms to 'domestic' standards. In other words, the consolidated, water repellent part of the weathered stone remains porous;

Brunswick Castle, lion sculptures before and after cleaning and conservation.

3. Penetration upon inherent suction without pressure, to a depth equal to that of water, crossing the weathered part as thick as 10 to 15cm;
4. Increase of, mainly bending, strength of the consolidated layer (even from dust condition) up to that of the original stone, referring also to completions: high-grade reconstructed stone from grindings of the original stone and the consolidating agent;
5. An elastic bond between stone crystals overcoming the effects of temperature fluctuations and of dynamic stresses, safeguarding the bond between the weathered layer and the sound stone parts, a requirement increasingly stressed in German specialist literature;
6. Outstanding frost resistance under climatic conditions in Hungary–a minimum of 50 freeze/thaw cycles in laboratory tests;
7. In addition, leaving colour, texture and dullness unaffected, although a minor tone darkening of the stone seems impossible to avoid, e.g. the appearance after rain. Anyway, stone facades exhibit heterogeneous shades or even colours.

In the absence of such an agent, the ZKF stone consolidant is available, which has been efficiently applied in Hungary and in Germany for about six years, e.g. Post Office in Sopron; Brunswick Castle in Martonvásár; facade of a house at 13a Donáti u. Budapest; the secondarily bricked-up doorway of the one-time 'Zeughaus' in the Buda Castle, etc.

This procedure meets the strict requirements outline above and may be demonstrated on request.

References

Dr Zádor, M. (1983) 'Müemlék konzerválásának új módszere'.('New Methods on Monuments Conservation'). Budapest.

Dr Zádor, M. (1985) 'Moderni Metodi di Reintegrazione dei Centri Storici ... Conservazione e restauro in Ungheria'.Restauro, 77-78. Napoli.

Dr Zádor, M. 'Recent Methods of (coarse) Limestone Consolidation in Hungary. Vth International Congress on Deterioration and Conservation of Stone. Lausanne, 1985 Proceedings II.

Dr Zádor, M. 'Problems of Actual State of Stone Conservation'. Periodica Polytechnica Vol.30. No.1–4. 1986.

Dr Zádor, M., Orcsik, É, Kertész, P.,Marek, I.,Varga, T. 'Observation on the alteration and Conservation of limestone'. XVth Czeshoslovak Conference on Electron Microscopy, Prague, 1977.

Tonk,V. 'Makro és mikroklíma hatása a hazai müemléképületek köanyaganak korróziója. Kézirat'. ('Macro and micro influences on the corrosion of Hungarian building stones'. Dissertation Manuscript, Budapest), 1991.

Session III

THE CLEANING OF CARBONATE STONE

14 Stone cleaning by the inversion of gypsum back into calcium carbonate

THEODOR SKOULIKIDIS and
PARASKEVI PAPAKONSTANTINOU
Department of Materials Science and Engineering, Faculty of
Chemical Engineering, National Technical University of Athens

INTRODUCTION

It is well known that atmospheric SO_x, with humidity, transforms the marble and stone surfaces of monuments which do not come in contact with rain water, into gypsum. Gypsum is also produced between two rains on surfaces that are not protected from rain water. It is also known that, for reasons of geometry (roughness of the surfaces) and due to the sorptive properties of gypsum, suspended particles coagulate preferentially on the sulphated surfaces, causing changes to their colour and appearance (1).

We have found that on the surfaces of gypsum films details of statues and ornaments are preserved and that, beyond a certain limit of film thickness, the details on the marble-gypsum interface are eliminated, due to the mechanism of sulphation (1-6).

For this reason, to consolidate the gypsum films and to save the details we found a method, by spraying a solution of potassium carbonate (K_2CO_3) on the gypsum surfaces, to inverse gypsum back into $CaCO_3$ (7, 8, 9).

This method was first of all applied to samples from pentelic marble (from the same quarry that supplied stone for the Acropolis Monuments) sulphated in an artificial atmosphere of 50% sulphur dioxide (SO_2) + 50% water vapour saturated air at 25°C.

The method was then tested on flat sulphated surfaces on the Acropolis Monuments.

In the latter case we observed that as well as the inversion of gypsum into $CaCO_3$, the surface was cleaned.

The object of this work is to present this new method of stone cleaning, that at the same time transforms gypsum into $CaCO_3$ and consolidates the details of statues and ornaments. This method is different from the already known cleaning methods, i.e. water (hot or cold, under pressure or not, vapours), acidic or alkaline or soap or surfactants solutions, with pastes (complex formation, adsorption), mechanical cleaning (sand blasting,micro-sand blasting, ultrasounds, lasers etc.).

EXPERIMENTAL

The experiments were carried out in situ on dirty sulphated surfaces. A 0.3M K_2CO_3 solution with $CaCO_3$ solution (to facilitate the crystallization of $CaCO_3$) was sprayed on the surfaces. Because the rate of the reaction $CaSO_4.2H_2O \rightarrow CaCO_3$ is very slow, it was necessary to spray the gypsum surfaces many times during a three month period (9).

The transformation was followed by our method of liquid crystals (10); it was stopped when all gypsum film was transformed into $CaCO_3$ (EPMA measurement for S in small samples). In all cases we observed that the marble was also cleaned. In Figures 1a,b we see surfaces before and after the inversion of gypsum.

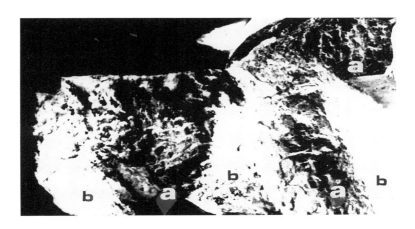

Figure 1 (a) Before and (b) after inversion of gypsum.

From a surface before and after inversion, samples were taken and were analysed by atomic absorption for Fe, Cu, Zn, and Pb. These are constituents of substances that we have found (6) in several coagulated suspended particles on the surface of Acropolis Monuments. The results are shown in Table 1.

Table 1   Fe, Cu, Zn, Pb Content (%) of Marble Samples from Sulphated Surface Before and After Inversion of Gypsum Back into CaCO$_3$

Element	Before inversion	After inversion	Reduction (%)
Fe	0.0700	0.0252[*]	64
Cu	0.0021	0.0004	81
Zn	0.0020	0.0011	45
Pb	0.0060	0.0020	66

* Marble contents also Fe, that was also analyzed.

The cleaning results are more satisfactory if some hours after spraying the surface with the K$_2$CO$_3$ solution and after drying, a flow of air was directed on to the surface in order to remove the loosened particles.

DISCUSSION

The cleaning of the surfaces by inversion of gypsum into CaCO$_3$ is an experimental fact. We can explain this by the rearrangement of the ions during the reaction CaSO$_4$.2H$_2$O $\rightarrow$ CaCO$_3$ and the decrease in the volume, that loosens the particles that colour the surface. This explanation is evident, but a further investigation is necessary.

The only case where this method cannot be applied is where a gypsum film is not present on the surface. This is possible when the rain water makes soluble dirty gypsum films and transports the particles to surfaces, usually horizontal, where the water stagnates and evaporates. In this case a precipitation of CaCO$_3$ also occurs and the particles are included between the crystals. The only possible means of removing the particles is by mechanical means or by micro-sandblasting or by laser beams.

CONCLUSIONS

From the above mentioned it follows that:

1. Where gypsum films exist a preferential coagulation of suspended particles takes place making the surfaces dirty. It is therefore possible to clean these surfaces by the inversion of gypsum back into CaCO$_3$. In this case the rearrangement of the ions during the reaction and the decrease of the volume

loosen the particles;

2. The inversion can take place by spraying the surface many times with a 0.3M K_2CO_3 solution. After some hours of spraying and drying of the surface a flow of air must be directed on the surface and thus the loosened particles are more easily removed;

3. This method cannot be used for dirty surfaces that are not sulphated.

References

1.   Skoulikidis,Th., Papakonstantinou,P., and Charalambous, D.(1976). 'Attaque atmospherique (marbres) et mesures prendre'. 2nd International Symposium on the Deterioration of Building Stones (Athens): 327-342.

2.   Skoulikidis,Th., and Papakonstantinou-Ziotis,P. (1981). 'The mechanism of sulphation by atmospheric SO_2 of limestones and marbles of the ancient monuments and statues. I. Observations in situ and measurements in the laboratory; activation energy'. British Corrosion Journal. 16:63-69.

3.   Skoulikidis, Th., and Charalambous, D. (1981). 'The mechanism of sulphation by atmospheric SO_2 of limestones and marbles of the ancient monuments and statues. II. Hypothesis and proofs on the rate determining step; galvanic cell model'. British Corrosion Journal. 16:70-77.

4.   Skoulikidis,Th.,Charalambous,D.,and Papakonstantinou, P. (1982). 'Preuves supplementaires pour le modele de la pile galvanique, valable pour la sulphatation des marbres'. 4th International Congress on the Deterioration and Protection of Building Stones (Louisville). 307-310.

5.   Skoulikidis,Th., Charalambous,D., and Papakonstantinou–Ziotis,P. (1983). 'Mechanism of sulphation by atmospheric SO_2 of the limestones and marbles on the ancient monuments and statues. III. Further proofs for the galvanic cell model'. British Corrosion Journal. 18:200-202.

6.   Skoulikidis,Th., and Charalambous,D. (1985). 'Preuves pour le modele de la pile galvànique du mecanisme de la sulphatation des marbres'. Vth International Congress on Deterioration and Preservation of stone (Lausanne). 547-551.

7.   Skoulikidis,Th.,and Beloyannis,N.(1981). 'Inversion de la sulphatation du marbre; reconversion du gypse forme sur les surfaces des monuments et des statues'. International Symposium on Conservation of Stone (Bologna). 545-558.

8.   Skoulikidis, Th., and Beloyannis, N. (1984). 'Inversion of marble sulphation – reconversion of gypsum films into calcite on the surfaces of monuments and statues'. Studies in Conservation. 29:197-204.

9.   Skoulikidis,Th., Georgopoulou,E., and Adamopoulou,P. (1990). 'Oriented inversion of gypsum on the surface of ancient monuments into calcium carbonate back'. 2nd ASMOSIA Meeting (Leuven-Belgium).

10.   Skoulikidis,Th., Koui,M., and Kostoudi,A. (1991). 'A new non-destructive method to differentiate in situ marbre from gypsum and

CaCO$_3$ from inversion of gypsum; use of liquid crystals'. Molecular Crystals, Liquid Crystals.

15 Removal of sulphated-crust from marble using sulphate-reducing bacteria

K. LAL GAURI[1], **LAWRENCE PARKS**[2], **JOHN JAYNES**[1] **and RONALD ATLAS**[2]

Department of Geology[1] and Department of Biology[2], University of Louisville, Kentucky, USA

INTRODUCTION

Marble ($CaCO_3$) surfaces exposed to sulphur dioxide air pollutants form crusts of gypsum ($CaSO_4.2H_2O$) which exfoliate from the surfaces of marble statues, destroying their sculpted forms (1,2). The anaerobic, sulphate-reducing bacterium *Desulphovibrio desulphuricans* can carry out dissimilatory sulphur metabolism in which lactate, pyruvate or ethanol is oxidized to acetate and carbonate while sulphate serves as an electron acceptor and is converted to sulphide (3, 4, 5). However, in this calcification reaction, hydrogen sulphide (H_2S) is produced which can react with environmental iron (Fe) to form a black iron sulphide (FeS) precipitate as shown in previous experiments in our laboratories (6). In the present work, we sought to improve the physiological conditions for sulphate depletion by these bacteria and to develop methods to apply broth cultures to self-standing outdoor statues.

MATERIALS AND METHODS

Growth of Bacteria

Desulphovibrio desulphuricans ATCC 29577 was grown in Postgate's Medium C (5) (KH_2PO_4, 0.5g; NH_4Cl, 1.0g; Na_2SO_4, 4.5g; $CaCl_2.6H_2O$, 0.06g; $MgSO_4.7H_2O$, 0.06g; sodium lactate, 6.0g; yeast extract, 1.0g; $FeSO_4.7H_2O$, 4mg; sodium citrate.$2H_2O$, 0.3g; sodium ascorbate, 1.0g and sodium thioglycollate, 0.1g per litre) in which the iron concentration is reduced to 0.014 mM. Medium C was modified by the addition of Lcysteine (0.1 g/l) and resazurin (Sigma Chemical Co, 1.5mg/l) immediately prior to autoclaving. Growth of *D. desulphuricans* in Medium C at 30°C produced only a very slight amount of FeS precipitation, usually not seen until four or five days after inoculation. For field trials, Medium C was further modified by omitting Na_2SO_4 and replacing $MgSO_4.7H_2O$ and $FeSO_4.7H_2O$ with $MgCl_2$ (0.06g) and $FeCl_2$ (4.0 mg) respectively (sulphate-free Medium C).

Cultures of *D. desulphuricans* containing approximately 10^8 cells/ml were incubated anaerobically for three to four days at 30°C in an Anaerobic System Model 1025 incubator (Forma Scientific) with an atmosphere containing 5% CO_2, 10% H_2 and 85% N_2. In the field study, additional deoxygenation of the medium to protect the desulphovibrio was achieved by adding Oxyrase EC–100 (Oxyrase, Inc., Ashland, Ohio), which is a preparation of frozen, partially-purified bacterial membranes that removes dissolved oxygen from aqueous environments.

Sulphate determination

Sulphate concentration was assayed by the turbidimetric method using barium chloride essentially as previously described (7) except that all volumes used were decreased 10–fold. Turbidity was measured with a Spectronic 20 spectrophotometer using Na_2SO_4 as a standard.

Field trial

A field trial was performed using a 115-year old, gypsum-encrusted marble statue located in Cave Hill Cemetery in Louisville, Kentucky. To prevent disintegration of areas with partially or completely exfoliated crust during bacterial treatments, such areas were selectively treated with 5% Fluoropolymer-Elvacite to consolidate them (8). The statue was then enshrouded in a sheet of 20 mil polyurethane plastic. The bag was filled with water and drained two times to ensure its integrity and to measure the volume of medium which would be required. In this field trial, sulphate-free medium C was utilized so that the only source of sulphate was from the gypsum-covered statue. Eighty five litres of sulphate-free medium C were then added together with 100 ml of Oxyrase EC–100. After 30 min. to permit removal of residual

O_2 from the medium, 10 litre of a *D. desulphuricans* culture grown for three days in Medium C, centrifuged at 5000 x g, for 10 min and resuspended in an equal volume of sulphate-free medium C were added. The culture was allowed to incubate for four days at ambient temperature between 13°C and 28°C and then drained out of the bag by siphon.

RESULTS AND DISCUSSION

Laboratory experiments

In order to determine the rate and extent of sulphate depletion from the solution by *D. desulphuricans*, 500 ml of Medium C were inoculated with 50 ml of a late phase culture of these bacteria. Ten ml aliquot portions were removed periodically and assayed for sulphate concentration as described above. Figure 1 shows the depletion of sulphate from Medium C by *D. desulphuricans*. Under the conditions described, *D. desulphuricans* removed more than 80% of the available sulphate (from 32 to 0.06 mM) within 60 hours after inoculation of the culture. Sterile controls incubated under identical conditions showed no sulphate removal. Previous experiments in our laboratory had utilized an alternate medium which produced a copious black FeS precipitate as *D. desulphuricans* converted sulphate to sulphide. Use of Medium C eliminated this problem.

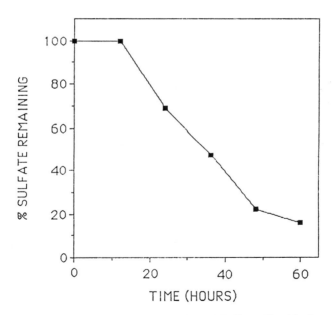

Figure 1 Rate of depletion of sulphate from Medium C with decreased iron concentration by *D. desulphuricans*. Initial concentration of sulphate was 32 mM.

162

Further, marble slabs measuring approximately 2 cm x 1.5cm x 3mm were coated with calcium sulphate by exposure to 10 ppm SO_2 at 100% relative humidity and 20°C as described previously (9, 10). These slabs were immersed in beakers containing sulphate-free Medium C and *D. desulphuricans* and incubated as described above. The bacteria were capable of growth under these conditions as evidenced by increase in turbidity of the culture, production of H_2S, and utilization of lactate.

Field trial

A field trial was performed on a marble statue that had weathered for more than one hundred years under a dome in the Cave Hill Cemetery in Louisville, Kentucky. This statue was the subject of an earlier study (6) when efforts were made to clean the surface selectively by flowing a bacterial culture over it (Figure 2A).

A   B

Figure 2 A 115 year old marble statue in Cave Hill Cemetery, Louisville.
(2A) with black crust, partically exfoliated on the face and arms, the lips, thumbs and left forearm. Notice the streaking along the face and neck caused by a previous treatment with a culture of *D. desulphuricans* (1988).
(2B) After treatment by immersion in *D. desulphuricans* broth (1990).

The head, the upper torso region, and arms had black surfaces since they had been protected from rain. As common to marble weathered under domes, the black region consisted of the external carbonaceous layer with tightly adherent particles of atmospheric soot and dust presumably cemented by gypsum, and an internal layer composed of gypsum; this gypsum layer is somewhat brownish in colour due to a small quantity of occluded soot.

As stated in the methods section, a water-tight membrane had been devised to contain the desulphovibrio broth around the statue. The two washings with water performed as a trial to create this water-tight membrane (during which time the statue was immersed for 24 hours) did not clean the statue. However, the treatment with *Desulphovibrio desulphuricans* in broth removed the blackness almost completely (Figure 2B). This substantiates our earlier observation (6) that the surface of the statue was cleaned largely due to the role of the bacteria.

The treated marble surface, though clean of the black soot, is still brownish in colour revealing that the gypsum layer was not completely calcified in this trial; previous field and laboratory experiments, referenced above, indicated that a partial calcification of the gypsum layer had occurred. An effort was not made to immerse the statue again in a fresh broth to achieve the calcification for fear of the damage due to mechanical stresses that our experiment might produce.

In summary, the field trial shows the potential for using *D. desulphuricans* as a biotechnological tool for cleaning marble which has been disfigured by exposure to environmental pollutants such as SO_2 and soot. Further research is needed to facilitate the application of the methods described here to larger marble structures as well as regulation of physiological conditions such as anaerobiosis and temperature to improve bacterial growth. Future studies should focus on achieving optimal sulphate depletion *in situ* with simultaneous calcium carbonate deposition for facilitating the application of this system to outside exposures (9).

Acknowledgements

We thank Russell Henning for assistance in field trials and the Samuel H. Kress Foundation for their continued financial support of our research on monumental stones.

References

1. Gauri, K.L., 1978. 'The preservation of stone.' *Scientific American.* **238**:126-136.
2. Gauri, K.L., Chowdhury, A.N., Kulshreshtha, N.P. and Punuru, A.R. (1989). 'The sulphation of marble and the treatment of gypsum crusts'. *Studies in Conservation.* **34**:201-206.
3. Grossman, J.P. and Postgate, J.R. (1955). 'The metabolism of malate and certain other compounds by *Desulphovibrio desulphuricans*'. *Journal of General Microbiology.* **12**:429-445.

4. Pfennig, N. and Widdel, F. (1982). 'The bacteria of the sulphur cycle'. *Philosophical Transactions of the Royal Society of London B*. **298**:433-441.

5. Postgate, J.R. (1984). *'The sulphate-reducing bacteria'*,2nd ed. (Cambridge University Press: New York).

6. Atlas, R.M., Chowdhury, A.N. and Gauri, K.L. (1988). 'Microbial calcification of gypsum-rock and sulphated marble'.*Studies in Conservation*. **33**:149-153.

7. Rand, M.C., Greenberg, A.E. and Taras, M.J. (1976). *'Standard Methods for the Examination of Water and Wastewater '*,14th ed. (American Public Health Association: Washington, D.C.).

8. Gauri, K.L. and Apparo, M.V. (1978). 'Certain epoxies, fluorocarbon-acrylics and silicones as stone preservatives.'*Geological Society of America. Engineering Geology Case Histories* **11**:73-79.

9. Gauri, K.L., Kulshreshtha, N.P., Punuru, A.R. and Chowdhury, A.N. (1989). 'Rate of decay of marble in laboratory and outdoor exposure'. *Journal of Materials in Civil Engineering*. **1**:73-85.

10. Kulshreshtha, N.P., Punuru, A.R. and Gauri, K.L. (1989). 'Kinetics of reaction of SO_2 with marble.' *Journal of Materials in Civil Engineering*. **1**:60-72.

16 Geochemical considerations in the cleaning of carbonate stone

RICHARD LIVINGSTON
Building and Fire Research Laboratory, NIST,
Gaithersburg, USA

INTRODUCTION

Carbonate stones such as limestone, marble and calcareous sandstone pose a special class of problems for stone cleaning. These materials have been very widely used for sculpture and architecture. However, they are much more readily dissolved in cleaning solutions than silicate-based stones like granite. Also, the soiling and discolouration of these surfaces is often more than simply a layer of dirt, or possibly an organic film, physically adhered to the surface. Chemical reactions can occur, such as the formation of gypsum, that more tightly bond the soiling agents to the surface. Green stains from copper or red stain from iron compounds are also the result of chemical reactions.

Many types of solutions have been specified for cleaning carbonate stone. These include distilled or deionized water, acidic solutions, solutions saturated with calcite and solutions containing chelating agents such as EDTA (1, 2). However, the use of a chemically incompatible cleaning solution could, at best, be ineffective and, at worst, could cause extensive damage to the stone. Predicting the effect of a given solution is complicated by the fact that in contact with carbonate stone, the solution will change its pH and ionic composition through interactions with the stone itself and with atmospheric carbon dioxide.

Understanding the interactions between solutions and minerals is a major focus of the field known as geochemistry. Therefore, the purpose of this paper is to review the principles of geochemistry as they apply to carbonate stone. Although this involves a certain amount of mathematics, the product of the analysis is a set of phase diagrams that make it possible to show graphically the various processes that take place during stone cleaning. It is hoped that this visual presentation will help to clarify the issues involved.

CARBONATE EQUILIBRIA AND CALCITE SOLUBILITY

In the simplest stone cleaning situation, there are no chemically bound substances such as gypsum or iron stains. In this situation, the solution may contain a detergent. The concern is to minimize the amount of stone dissolved during the cleaning process.

The most critical factor determining the amount of the stone that will be removed is its solubility. However, the literature on calcium carbonate solubility can be confusing, since there can be several values, each one valid for different solution pHs and carbon dioxide pressures.

The dissolution of calcium carbonate begins with the reaction:

$$CaCO_3 \rightleftarrows Ca^{2+} + CO_3^{2-} \qquad \qquad \textbf{1}$$

The solubility product for this reaction is then:

$$K_{calc} = \gamma_{Ca}[Ca^{2+}]\gamma_{co_3}[CO_3^{2-}] \qquad \qquad \textbf{2}$$

where the brackets indicate molarities and the γ's are the activity coefficients. For simplicity, it will be assumed that the calcium carbonate is the crystalline form of ideal calcite, which has the solubility product K_{calc} of $10^{-8.52}$ at 25°C (3).

However, the carbonate anion, CO_3^{2-}, produced by the calcite dissolution can also react with water to yield the bicarbonate ion, HCO_3^-:

$$CO_3^{2-} + H_2O \rightleftarrows HCO_3^- + OH^- \qquad \qquad \textbf{3}$$

Moreover, if there is a gas phase present, the bicarbonate anion can break down into carbon dioxide gas and water:

$$H^+ + HCO_3^- \rightleftarrows H_2O + CO_2\uparrow \qquad \qquad \textbf{4}$$

The equilibria among these ions in solution and carbon dioxide can be derived from chemical thermodynamics. The derivation can be found in standard textbooks on physical chemistry, for example, Butler (3). The concentrations of carbonate and bicarbonate are functions of H^+ concentration and carbon dioxide pressure, P_{CO2} :

$$\gamma_{CO_3}[CO_3^{2-}] = 10^{-18.15}\frac{P_{CO_2}}{\gamma_H^2[H^+]^2} \qquad\qquad 5$$

$$\gamma_{HCO_3}[HCO_3^-] = 10^{-7.82}\frac{P_{CO_2}}{\gamma_H[H^+]} \qquad\qquad 6$$

Then substituting Equation into the calcite solubility product, Equation 2, gives the Ca^{2+} concentration in terms of $[H^+]$ and carbon dioxide pressure:

$$\gamma_{Ca}[Ca^{2+}] = 10^{+9.63}\frac{\gamma_H^2[H^+]^2}{P_{CO_2}} \qquad\qquad 7$$

The numerical coefficients in Equations 5–7 are all for 25°C. Also, under usual conditions, the ionic strength of the solution is so low that the γ's can all be regarded as approximately equal to one.

It is then possible to eliminate $[Ca^{2+}]$ in Equation by using the electroneutrality condition, or the charge balance, of this solution, which can be written:

$$2[Ca^{2+}] = [HCO_3^-] + 2[CO_3^{2-}] + [OH^-] - [H^+] \qquad\qquad 8$$

The righthand side of Equation 8 is defined as the carbonate alkalinity, or the variable Alk for short. Hence, Equation 8 can also be written as:

$$[Ca^{2+}] = \frac{1}{2}Alk \qquad\qquad 9$$

The variable Alk can be stated as a function of the two variables $[H^+]$ and P_{CO2}, using Equations 5 and 6 together with the equilibrium constant for water. Note that when $[Ca^{2+}]$ is zero, Alk must also be zero. However, this does not mean that $[CO_3^{2-}]$ and $[HCO_{3-}]$ must be zero as well. In fact, under atmospheric conditions where $P_{CO2} = 10^{-3.5}$ bar, the total carbonate content would be about

$10^{-5.65}$ mol/L, and the pH would then be 5.65.

To solve this set of equations, Equation 8 or 9 can be used to eliminate $[Ca^{2+}]$ in Equation 7. This yields an equation in $[H^+]$ and P_{CO2} that can be solved numerically using iterative computation.

The results of the numerical solution are plotted in Figure 1. This curve represents the saturation line of calcite. That is, any solution with pH and P_{CO2} coordinates that plot below this line will be undersaturated with respect to calcite and hence will dissolve it. Conversely, a solution that plots above this line is oversaturated and will precipitate calcite. This diagram also indicates that at pressures of carbon dioxide less than 10^{-13} bar, calcite is unstable relative to calcium hydroxide and will tend to be converted to the latter.

The $[Ca^{2+}]$ concentration is equivalent to the calcite solubility since, according to Equation 1, each mole of dissolved $CaCO_3$ gives one mole of $[Ca^{2+}]$. Also, the molecular weight of $CaCO_3$ is almost exactly 100 gm/mol. Hence, one mmol/L of $[Ca^{2+}]$ equals 100 mg/L of dissolved $CaCO_3$.

The $[Ca^{2+}]$ concentration does not appear explicitly in Figure 1. In fact, it would vary continuously along the calcite saturation curve. However, its value at any point on the curve can be calculated from the pH and P_{CO2} coordinates using Equation 7.

Alternatively, the calcite saturation curve can be presented explicitly as a function of $[Ca^{2+}]$ and P_{CO2} by manipulating the set of Equations 5–9 to eliminate the variable $[H^+]$. This is plotted in Figure 2. This diagram shows that $[Ca^{2+}]$, and hence calcite solubility, reaches a minimum at a P_{CO2} of 10^{-6} bar. From the version of the saturation curve shown in Figure 1, it can be seen that each P_{CO2} value corresponds to a unique pH. This correspondence makes it possible to add a pH scale to Figure 2, which indicates that the $[Ca^{2+}]$ minimum occurs at a pH of 9.9.

This pair of diagrams then demonstrates why there can be more than one value for calcite solubility. It is the P_{CO2} that essentially determines the solubility. Consequently, discussions of carbonate equilibria in the geochemical literature always involve specifying the P_{CO2} conditions.

Applying this approach to stone cleaning, we find that there are three likely possibilities for carbon dioxide exposure. The most common case is a solution in contact with calcite and also open to the atmosphere, such as a thin layer of cleaning solution lying on top of a stone surface. In this open system the amount of carbon dioxide gas is essentially unlimited, and hence its partial pressure will not be affected by the dissolution or precipitation of small amounts of calcite. Under these conditions, P_{CO2} is constant at $10^{-3.5}$ bar. This point is labelled on the curves in Figures 1 and 2. The pH is then also constant at a value of 8.3, and $[Ca^{2+}]$ is then found to be 0.43 mmol/L. This is equivalent to a calcite solubility of 43 mg/L.

Another possible case is a system which is closed to the atmosphere, but still maintains a fixed gas volume and also contains solid calcite. An example would be a sealed bottle partially filled with water and chunks of marble. In this case, the supply of carbon dioxide gas in the air space of the bottle is limited and therefore the amount absorbed or released during the precipitation or dissolution of calcite will influence its partial pressure. This system should eventually

169

stabilize at the minimum solubility point shown in Figure 2. At this point, the solubility is 11 mg/L.

In the third case, there is no gas phase. An example of this would be a sealed bottle entirely filled with water and marble chunks. In this case, Equations 4 - 7 would not apply. The mathematical solution of this problem is straightforward, and is given by Butler (3). The result is a pH fixed at 9.9 and a solubility of 11 mg/L, which is essentially the same result as for the previous case of a sealed bottle with an air space.

This analysis reveals that in a pure water solution the calcite solubility is a function only of the pressure of carbon dioxide. Therefore, pH is a dependent variable under these conditions. Obviously, this would not be true if acids such as oxalic acid or bases such as ammonium carbonate were added to the solution. Nevertheless, it would still be possible to calculate the carbonate equilibria, provided that the amount of added acid or base is known.

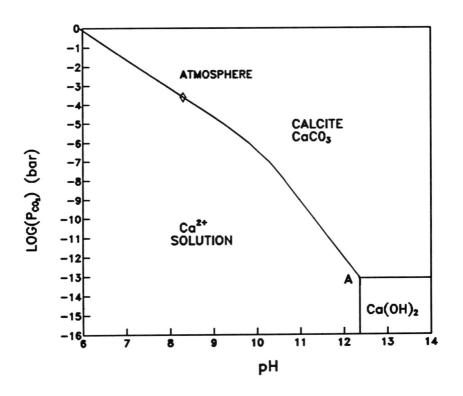

FIGURE 1. CALCITE SATURATION AS A FUNCTION OF pH AND P

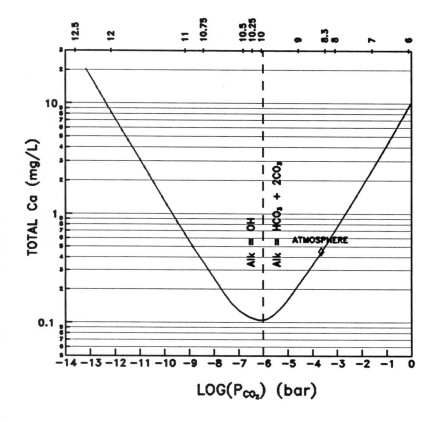

FIGURE 2. CALCITE SATURATION VS CO₂ PRESSURE

IMPLICATIONS OF CARBONATE EQUILIBRIA
FOR STONE CLEANING

These results can then be used to evaluate the effects of various stone cleaning practices. For instance, conservators sometimes specify distilled or deionized water as the cleaning solution. The intent is to minimize the deposition of any residual salts from the solution that could cause further damage to the stone. However, distilled or deionized water contains no Ca^{2+}. Consequently, it is undersaturated with respect to calcite. Such a solution in contact with the stone would dissolve calcite until saturation is reached. Figure 2 indicates that, assuming an open system, 43 mg of calcium carbonate would be dissolved for every litre of distilled water used. The research of Lauffenberger et al. (4) shows that this is enough to produce measurable change of gloss on polished

171

marble. However, this effect may not be as noticeable on rougher limestone or marble surfaces.

A more sophisticated approach would use a solution pretreated so that it is already saturated with respect to calcite. This can be achieved by soaking limestone or marble chips in the solution. However, the efficacy of this approach depends upon the exact procedure. If the pretreatment takes place in an open container, then the resulting solution should be in equilibrium with atmospheric carbon dioxide. Since the same condition applies on the stone surface, the solution would also be in equilibrium with the stone, and no calcite dissolution would occur. On the other hand, if the pretreatment takes place in a closed container, the solution would then contain only 11 mg/L of dissolved calcium carbonate. Thus it would be considerably undersaturated with respect to the stone surface, and some dissolution and etching of the stone would take place.

Another possibility for a cleaning solution is simply tapwater which often contains significant amounts of Ca^{2+}. This can occur naturally in limestone regions. It can also be result of treatment of the water supply with lime. Lauffenberg et al. (4) showed that tapwater in the Washington DC area did not cause significant etching of polished marble. However, the chemistry of tapwater varies significantly from one location to another, and may also include other anions such as Cl^-, SO_4^{2-} or NO_3. that may leave behind residual salts. Therefore, the use of tapwater for cleaning solutions cannot be recommended as a general practice.

The cleaning solutions considered so far all have alkalinities ≥ 0. However, acidic solutions, often containing hydrofluoric acid, are sometimes specified (1). As shown above, the equilibrium pH for a solution in contact with calcite is 8.3. Therefore, to achieve this, any acid present in the solution must be neutralized by reaction with the calcite. The stoichiometry involved shows that one mole of $CaCO_3$ must react for every 2 moles of H^+ of acid. Thus any amount of acid added to the cleaning solution creates a proportional amount of stone damage. This process does not improve the selectivity of the cleaning solution for removing the soiling deposit. Instead, it effectively strips off the surface of the stone, along with any dirt that may be present. In this respect, it is a very effective method for cleaning, but it also destroys polish and sculptural fine detail. Therefore, it should be avoided for carbonate stone.

The method of applying the cleaning solution is also important. There are several options including high-pressure water washing, water soaking and poultices (1). From the perspective of carbonate equilibria, these methods differ primarily in the degree of calcite saturation that the cleaning solution reaches during contact with the stone. High-pressure water washing directs large quantities of water on the surface for short contact times. The degree of saturation that is achieved depends upon the rate of dissolution of the stone. However, these kinetic aspects cannot be determined from equilibrium considerations. In principle, high-pressure water cleaning can achieve effective removal of soiling at a low degree of calcite saturation. However, even though the solution may be greatly undersaturated after contact, it is the product of the degree of saturation and the total volume of water that determines the amount of stone dissolved. If large volumes of water are used, it is therefore possible to remove significant quantities of stone. The water soak method can reduce the total amount of water used, but the longer contact time makes calcite saturation more likely.

The poultice method provides a fixed volume of water in contact with the surface at any given time. A typical poultice consists of a very water absorbent material such as methylcellulose or attapulgite clay (2). It is soaked with the cleaning solution and then placed on the surface to be cleaned. Soluble salts from the surface migrate into the poultice until the solution reaches equilibrium. The poultice is then removed and a new one put into place. This cycle continues until the surface is judged to be sufficiently clean.

Given the typical contact time, on the order of 24 hours, it can be assumed that the solution in the poultice becomes saturated with calcite. However, unlike high-pressure washing or water soaking, the solution in the poultice may not be open with respect to atmospheric carbon dioxide. In fact, it would be desirable to make the poultice as airtight as possible, according to Figure 2, in order to minimize the solubility of calcite and hence the stone loss.

Making the poultice air tight would rule out the practice, sometimes employed, of letting it dry out before removal (4). In fact, letting the poultice dry out could actually be detrimental. Since the solution is saturated, any evaporation would require the precipitation of some calcite to maintain equilibrium. This would lead to the growth of new crystals on the surface that could change the stone's appearance. Lauffenberg et al. (4) found that there was a significantly greater loss of gloss for polished marble in the case when the poultice was allowed to dry out versus when it was removed after 24 hours.

CALCITE/GYPSUM SOLUBILITY

A very common problem encountered in the cleaning of carbonate stone is the removal of 'black crust'. This is a characteristic layer of gypsum ($CaSO_4.2H_2O$) formed on the stone surface by reaction with sulfur dioxide air pollution (5).

The objective of the cleaning of gypsum-encrusted marble or limestone is to dissolve a maximum amount of gypsum while removing a minimum amount of the carbonate substrate. It is therefore necessary to take into account the solubilities of both gypsum and calcite and their interrelationship.

Gypsum dissolves according to the reaction:

$$CaSO_4 \cdot 2H_2O \rightleftharpoons Ca^{2+} + SO_4^{2-} + 2H_2O \qquad \textbf{10}$$

This has the solubility product of the form:

$$\textbf{11}$$
$$K_{gyps} = \gamma_{Ca}[Ca^{2+}]\gamma_{SO_4}[SO_4^{2-}]$$

The solubility product, K_{gyps} has a value of $10^{-4.6}$ at 25°C.

Unlike calcite, gypsum dissolves as a simple salt, which means that its dissolution does not affect the pH of the solution or its carbonate equilibria. On the other hand, the solubility of gypsum is high enough to give a ionic strength of 0.04. This means that the activity coefficients $_{Ca}$ and $_{SO4}$ are significantly less than unity. Also, there is a considerable amount of the ion pair $CaSO_4^{\circ}$ formed in the solution. Hence the measured solubility of gypsum, 2.08 g/L, is about one-third greater than would be calculated using the solubility product alone (6)

The electroneutrality condition for a solution containing both dissolved calcium carbonate and gypsum can be written as:

$$[Ca^{2+}] = \frac{1}{2}Alk + [SO_4^{2-}] \qquad\qquad 12$$

This can then be substituted for $[Ca^{2+}]$ in the calcite solubility product, Equation 2. A numerical solution can be found. This is presented in Figure 3, which plots the saturation of calcite and gypsum as a function of $[SO_4^{2-}]$ and alkalinity for $P_{CO2} = 10^{-3.5}$ bar (atmospheric carbon dioxide partial pressure).

Below a SO_4^{2-} concentration of 9.8 mmol/L, calcite is the stable phase. In other words, gypsum will dissolve and calcite will precipitate. The saturation line of calcite decreases as $[SO_4^{2-}]$ increases. The presence of SO_4^{2-} in the solution depresses the solubility of calcium carbonate through the common ion effect.

At the SO_4^{2-} concentration of 9.8 mmol/L, the solution becomes saturated with respect to both gypsum and calcite. This point, marked by the letter I in Figure 3, is an invariant in this system. The practical implication of this for stone cleaning is that whenever both solid gypsum and calcite are present, the solution will eventually equilibrate at the composition of point I.

At this point the solubility products of calcite, Equation 2, and gypsum, Equation 11, both apply. Dividing one by the other to eliminate the variable $[Ca^{2+}]$ gives:

$$\frac{\gamma_{SO_4}[SO_4^{2-}]}{\gamma_{CO_3}[CO_3^{2-}]} = \frac{K_{gyps}}{K_{calc}} = 10^{3.92} \qquad\qquad 13$$

which implies that the ratio of dissolved gypsum to calcite is fixed and very much greater than one.

Moreover, inspection of the phase diagram, Figure 3, shows that at Point I, Alk $<<$ $[SO_4^{2-}]$ (0.30 vs 9.8 mmol/L). Consequently, the electroneutrality condition, Equation 12, can be approximated by:

$$[Ca^{2+}] \approx [SO_4^{2-}] \qquad\qquad 14$$

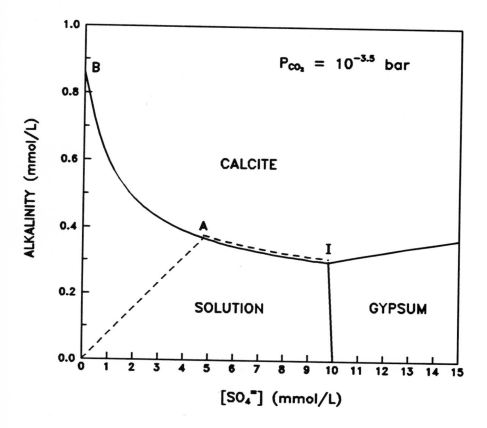

FIGURE 3. CALCITE/GYPSUM STABILITY

Combining this with Equations 2 and 13 ultimately gives:

$$[CO_3] = \frac{K_{calc}}{\gamma_{CO_3}\sqrt{K_{gyps}}} = 10^{-5.88}$$

15

This indicates the $[CO_3^{-2}]$ at the invariant point is determined by the thermodynamic constants of gypsum and calcite. Nevertheless, the alkalinity, and hence the calcite solubility, is still a function of pH and P_{CO2}.

For a system at the invariant point open to the atmosphere, $P_{CO2} = 10^{-3.5}$ bar and from Equation 5, pH = 7.73. This then gives a value of $10^{-3.5}$ mol/L for the alkalinity. This in turn means a calcite solubility of 16 mg/L under these conditions.

The total amount of dissolved calcium, Ca_T, is the sum of three terms:

$$Ca_T = \frac{1}{2}Alk + [SO_4^{2-}] + [CaSO_4^o] \qquad\qquad \textbf{16}$$

The gypsum contribution is the sum of the last two terms and is 15 mmol/L (6). The dissolved calcite is equal to the 1/2 Alk term, or 0.16 mmol/L under atmospheric conditions. Therefore, dissolved calcite makes up only 1% of the total dissolved calcium. Thus, a cleaning solution consisting simply of water would have the desired effect of dissolving mainly gypsum crust rather than the calcite substrate.

The effect of the initial state of saturation of the cleaning solution under these conditions is somewhat more complicated. An example of the dissolution process starting with a deionized or distilled water solution is illustrated by the dashed line in Figure 3. The alkalinity of pure water is by definition zero, although the pH depends upon P_{CO2}. Consequently the reaction path starts at the origin. Assuming that both calcite and gypsum are dissolving, $[SO_4^{2-}]$ and alkalinity will be added to the solution, and thus the solution chemistry will move along the dashed line segment from the origin to Point A. At this point the solution is saturated with calcite, but still undersaturated with respect to gypsum. To reach equilibrium with both these phases, the solution must further increase its $[SO_4^{2-}]$ content. As this increases, the solution chemistry is constrained to move along the calcite saturation curve toward the invariant point I. However, this means that the alkalinity must decrease, which is done by reprecipitating some of the dissolved calcite.

In contrast, a cleaning solution pre-saturated with calcite would begin at Point B. As gypsum is dissolved, the solution would move down the calcite saturation curve, precipitating calcite, until the invariant point is reached.

Reducing the P_{CO2} of the system would reduce the alkalinity and thus shift the calcite saturation curve downward. However, the gypsum saturation would not be affected. In the extreme case of no gas phase, the $[CO_3^{2-}]$ would still be fixed at $10^{-5.88}$ mol/L according to Equation 15. This results in a pH of 8.8 and an alkalinity of $10^{-5.11}$ mol/L or a dissolved calcite content of 3.9 μmol/L. This is only about 2.4% of the amount that would be dissolved under open system conditions. This suggests that an airtight poultice would be desirable.

Finally, if the solution is allowed to dry out, the result will be the simultaneous precipitation of both gypsum and calcite. This occurs because the solution composition is maintained at the invariant point even during the process of evaporation.

EFFECT OF EDTA

The chelating agent EDTA (ethylenediamine tetraacetate) is sometimes recommended for stone cleaning solutions (2). However, the rationale for this is not clearly stated.

In solution, EDTA forms complexes with metal cations such as Fe^{3+}, Cu^{2+} and Ca^{2+}. The nature of the complex depends upon the pH of the solution. In the range of pH under consideration here (6 <pH <10), the EDTA forms two major complexes with calcium (7). Thus the total calcium in solution is given by:

$$Ca_T = [Ca^{2+}] + [CaHL^-] + [CaL^{2-}] \qquad\qquad \textbf{17}$$

where L represents the EDTA molecule. The total Ca constitutes the sum of the dissolved calcite and gypsum. However, the saturation condition is determined by the cation Ca^{2+}, not Ca_T, in the solubility products in Equations 2 and 11. In the absence of EDTA, $Ca_T = [Ca^{2+}]$, but if it is present, Equation 17 shows that $Ca_T > [Ca^{2+}]$. In other words, by permitting the solution to contain more Ca_T for a given $[Ca^{2+}]$, EDTA increases the solubility of both calcite and gypsum. A discussion of the EDTA solution equilibria is beyond the scope of this paper, but it can be shown that in such a solution Ca_T can be orders of magnitude greater than $[Ca^{2+}]$ (7).

On the other hand, EDTA does not affect the selectivity of the cleaning solution for gypsum relative to calcite. This can be seen from Equation 13 in which the ratio of the gypsum and calcite solubility products does not involve the variable $[Ca^{2+}]$. Consequently, the main effect of EDTA is to increase the capacity of a given volume of cleaning solution. In practice, this means that a gypsum crust could be removed with fewer poulticing cycles, but the same amount of calcite would still be removed. However, this holds true only if there is still enough solid gypsum left to maintain the solution composition at the invariant point I in Figure 3. With only a limited amount of gypsum initially present, after it is completely dissolved, the EDTA solution could still dissolve much more calcite. Therefore, EDTA solutions should only be used where there is a thick gypsum crust.

Another justification for using EDTA could be to remove iron or copper stains, which are usually insoluble in carbonate stone. In principle, EDTA increase the solubility of these metals by orders of magnitude. However, this selectivity effect is dependent upon pH and there is competition for the EDTA among Fe^{3+}, Cu^{2+} and Ca^{2+}. For example, at pH = 5, essentially all the EDTA in solution would be tied up as FeL^-, but at pH = 7.5, it would be mainly in form of CaL^{2-}, with less than 1 % as FeL^- (8). Since the solution in contact with carbonate stone would eventually equilibrate at this higher pH, this means that a large amount of calcite would be lost in the process of removing the iron stain.

If the objective is to remove metal stains, there are other organic compounds such as crown ethers, cryptands and calixarenes that are much more selective than EDTA (9).

EFFECT OF CARBONATE LITHOLOGY

The varying susceptibility of the carbonate stone itself must also be taken into account. For example, it has been assumed for the sake of discussion that the solubility of the carbonate stone can be represented by that of ideal calcite. However, this is unlikely to be true in practice. The great variability in observed solubilities is a vexatious problem for carbonate petrologists.

One explanation is that real carbonate stone never consists of pure calcite. There is generally some substitution of magnesium for calcium in the crystal structure, which significantly affects the solubility (10).

Another factor is the microstructure of the stone, which involves its porosity, grain size and crystallinity (11). This in turn is a function of the specific sedimentary process that formed the stone especially whether it was the stone was deposited inorganically or organically (12).

Nevertheless, even if the bulk solubility of the carbonate stone in question departs considerably from that of ideal calcite, the general findings presented here will still be valid.

CONCLUSIONS

The general problem in cleaning carbonate stone is to remove the maximum amount of soiling deposits while dissolving a minimum amount of the carbonate substrate. Although the calcium carbonate solubility depends in a complex way on the pH and the supply of carbon dioxide gas, the relationships can be visualized with an appropriate set of geochemical phase diagrams.

The use of distilled or deionized water, or acidic solutions, should be avoided. The water used for cleaning should be pre-treated by soaking with limestone or marble chips in containers open to the atmosphere. Also, poultices used for cleaning should be as airtight as possible, and should not be allowed to dry out.

Gypsum crusts are much more soluble in water than the calcite substrate and the solubility of gypsum is essentially independent of the pH of the solution. The ratio of dissolved gypsum to calcite can be increased by keeping the poultice air tight. The chelating agent EDTA does not affect the ratio of the solubilities of gypsum to calcium carbonate, but it does increase the total amount of material a given volume of cleaning solution can hold. It should be used with caution and only where there is a heavy gypsum crust.

Finally, the solubility of carbonate stone can vary significantly, depending on its chemical composition, particularly with its magnesium content, and on the sedimentary processes that formed it.

References

1. Boyer, D.W. (1986) In 'Cleaning Stone and Masonry', STP 935, p.25-51, ed. J.R.Clifton. (ASTM: Philadelphia).
2. Lazzarini, L. and Tabasso, M.L. (1986) 'Il Restauro della Pietra' (CEDAM: Padova, Italy)p. 119-121.
3. Butler, J.N. (1982) 'Carbon Dioxide Equilibria and Their Applications', (Addison-Wesley: Reading, MA).
4. Lauffenberger, J.A., Grissom, C.A. and Charola, A.E. (1992) Changes in gloss of marble surfaces as a result of methylcellulose poulticing. *Studies in Conservation*.**37** (in press).
5. Camuffo, D., Del Monte, M., Sabbioni, C. and Vittori, O.(1982) Wetting, deterioration and visual features of stone surfaces in an urban area. *Atmospheric Environment.* **16**:2253-2259.
6. Nordstrom, D.K. and Munoz, J.L. (1985) 'Geochemical Thermodynamics' (The Benjamin/Cummings Publishing Co.: Menlo Park, CA) p. 372-375.
7. Stumm, W. and Morgan, J.J. (1981) 'Aquatic Chemistry' (John Wiley & Sons: New York) p.357-363.
8. Lindsley, W.L. (1979).'Chemical Equilibria in soils' (Wiley:New York) p.239-250.
9. Chartier, D.R. (1991) In 'Materials Issues in Art and Archaeology II' Vol.185 p.73-82. eds.P.B.Vandiver, J.Druzik, and G.S.Wheeler (Materials Research Society: Pittsburgh).
10. Mackenzie, F.T., Bischoff, W.D., Bishop, F.C., Loijens, M., Schoonmaker, J. and Wollast, R.(1983) In 'Carbonates: Mineralogy and Chemistry', p.97-144, ed. R.J.Reeder. (Mineralogical Society of America: Washington, DC).
12. Scoffin, T.P. (1987).'An Introduction to Carbonate Sediments and Rocks'. (Chapman & Hall: New York) p.248-261.
11. Walter, L.M. (1985) In 'Carbonate Cements', p.3-16, eds. N. Schneidermann and P.M. Harris (Society of Economic Paleontologists and Mineralogists: Tulsa OK).

Session IV

URBAN CONSERVATION ISSUES

17 'Acid rain': the cleaning and conservation of stonework in Bath

DAVID McLAUGHLIN
Conservation Architect, Department of Environmental Services,
Bath City Council, UK

INTRODUCTION

Residents and visitors to the Circus can't help but have noticed the extensive scaffolding that surrounded numbers 3, 12, 15, 21, 22 and 23 Circus during 1989. These six buildings are all owned by the City Council and they were among the first buildings to be cleaned and repaired under the Bath Town Scheme which started in 1955, the first town scheme in the country. Now, some 35 years later, further careful cleaning and conservation work has been carried out. Why is this?

Next time you have a cup of tea, while the tea is still steaming hot, lift the cup up and blow across the top of the cup and watch what happens to the steam still within the cup. You will see that the steam can't rise above the cooler air being blown across the top of the cup, but rather that the steam swirls round on itself forming a small rolling current all around the edge of the cup.

With winds blowing from the west, the cooler air would cause the same type of effect over the small contained area of the Circus, admittedly a very large 'teacup' with a diameter of 97 metres, but nonetheless a very similar situation.

Now imagine the Circus in the days when fires were burnt in all the fireplaces. To start with, think of the thirty-three houses of the Circus each with their two chimney stacks of seven or eight flues. That leads to over 400 flues creating a potential encircling rim of smoke. This smoke is a key component in the formation of 'acid rain'. So while the term acid rain may sound like a new piece of jargon, in fact one must look at the question of 'historic acid rain', that is to say the pollution damage from the past.

Alistair Cooke writing 'A Letter From Bath' in 1961 recalled,

> The first time I was in Bath after the war, the Roman baths, the great Abbey, the crescents built by John Wood and his son were black with grime and pitted with rot. In the last year or two Bath has wakened up with a bang to what is unique about its heritage: an eighteenth century town built in a single style out of local stone that abounds in nearby quarries. As they have done in so many other old towns of England ... they have blasted away the centuries of dirt that had added more grime than bloom, and today you can see the two great crescents and the Circus as they were in the seventeen-sixties and -seventies. Great lyrical arcs of a light biscuit colour, gay and graceful as they were meant to be (1).

With winds and cooler air blowing over the ridges of the hills encircling Bath, the city nestles down below in the bottom of the Avon valley basin with its hot springs. The steeply sloping hills with their many cold springs then act like the rim of another, larger 'teacup' containing a very hot brew and in this case that hot brew is acid rain.

This is what is happening in Bath on a series of different scales. At one level, the topography of the city as a whole allows smoke generated in the valley bottom to be trapped by the cooler air and winds above. This is undoubtedly a significant factor in enabling acid rain to cause the decay of the beautiful oolitic limestone of the city's historic buildings. At a second level, the same principle can be applied to much smaller areas such as the Circus.

Why is it that these particular buildings were so very much more decayed than their neighbours? After all they were built with the same type of stone, with the same type of construction, and within a very short space of time of their neighbours.

What differs is their more elaborate detail with much undercut and projecting elements as well as their varying orientations because of their circular plan form and, because of that circular plan form, their ability to act as a container or teacup.

Sir John Soane (1753-1837) prepared an exquisite watercolour of the Circus within the Colosseum to illustrate a lecture to Royal Academy students in 1809. Soane commented that the Circus,

> may please us by its prettiness and a sort of novelty, as a rattle pleases a child ... the area is so small and the height of each of the orders is so diminutive that the general appearance of the building is mean, gloomy, and confined (2).

Writing about the Circus in 1771, Tobias Smollet recorded,

> In blowing weather, I am told, most of the houses in this hill are
> smothered with smoke, forced down the chimneys, by the gusts of
> wind reverberated from the hill behind, which (I apprehend likewise)
> must render the atmosphere here more humid and unwholesome than
> it is in the square below; for the clouds, formed by the constant
> evaporation from the baths and rivers in the bottom, will, in their
> ascent this way, be first attracted and detained by the hill that rises
> close behind the Circus, and load the air with a perpetual succession
> of vapours: this point, however, may be easily ascertained by means
> of a hygrometer, or a paper of salt of tartar exposed to the action of the
> atmosphere (3).

This problem is not unique to the Circus. In 1987 the West Front of Bath
Abbey was scaffolded to inspect the condition of the stonework there. It was
found that the restoration work and new carvings completed during 1960 were
similarly affected. Within 27 years a problem had occurred or, indeed, re-
occurred.

'ACID RAIN'

'Acid rain' is the generic term for air pollution which increases the acidity of the
environment either through wet forms like rainwater or snow or dry forms like
dust or as mists like fogs or low cloud. While the term 'acid rain' has
increasingly come into use, the problem of acid rain is not a new phenomenon.
The damage caused by 'acid rain' to buildings was recognised as long ago as
1858 when Robert Smith in a paper to the Chemical Society noted,

> it has often been observed that the stones and bricks of buildings,
> especially under projecting parts, crumble more readily in large towns,
> where much coal is burnt, than elsewhere. Although this is not
> sufficient to prove an evil of the highest magnitude, it is still worthy of
> observation ... I was led to attribute this effect to the slow but
> constant, action of the acid rain (4)

One must consider the concept of 'historic acid rain', that is to say the pollution
damage from the past. Just as one might use the expression 'there's no smoke
without fire', so too one might equally say 'there's no smoke without pollution,
and no pollution without decay'.

Undoubtedly the soft coals from the North Somerset and South
Gloucestershire coalfields burnt in the myriad fireplaces of eighteenth and
nineteenth century Bath gave rise to high levels of smoke containing sulphur
dioxide within the city. Acid rain, therefore, is not a new phenomenon but a
continuing problem.

The erosion of limestone surfaces is just one of the results of this continuing
problem. A study of Portland limestone at St Paul's Cathedral, London (5),

highlights this erosion by illustrating the differential weathering between the Portland stone copings and their lead plugs over the period 1727 to 1982. One can see very similar evidence of such damage over the period 1837 to 1990 between the Bath stone copings and their lead joggles on the Church of St Michael with St Paul, Broad Street, Bath.

HISTORIC ACID RAIN AND THE MEMORY EFFECT

Writers and artists alike have recorded their concern about acid rain over the centuries.

The miniature painter Nicholas Hilliard (1547-1619) wrote in the 1600s of the connection between sulphurous pollution and the deterioration of some pigments, 'the culers themselves may not endure some ayers, especially in the sulphirous ayre of seacole' (6).

In 1734 Alexander Pope (1688-1744) was at Bath with Bolingbroke ... but he was not complimentary to the place 'to prefer racks and dirt to flowery meads and lovely Thames, and limestone and fogs to roses and sunshine. When I arrive at these sensations I may settle at Bath, of which I never dreamt, further than to live just out of the sulphurous pot, and at the edge of the fogs at Mr Allen's for a month or so. I like the place so little that health itself could not drag me thither, though friendship has twice or thrice' (7).

The artist Thomas Gainsborough (1727-1788) wrote in 1763 'I have taken a House about three quarters of a mile in the Lansdown Road; tis sweetly situated and I have every convenience I could wish for; I pay 30 pounds per year, and so let off my House in the Smoake except my painting room and best parlour to show pictures in' (8)

In the 1800s Jane Austen recorded that as she crossed the old bridge to enter Bath, one of her characters, Anne Elliott, 'caught the first dim view of the extensive buildings, smoking in rain, without any wish of seeing them better ...' (9). Even in fine weather Jane Austen noticed this smoke. She wrote to Cassandra on Tuesday, May 5th 1801,

> The first view of Bath in fine weather does not answer my expectations; I think I see more distinctly through rain. The sun was got behind everything, and the appearance of the place from the top of Kingsdown was all vapour, shadow, smoke and confusion.

One hundred and fifty years later things had not improved. Under the headline 'Saturday "Soup Surprise": Bath Becomes "City of Ghosts"', the local paper reported:

> The 'pea soup' fog which took Bath by surprise on Saturday afternoon was the thickest for very many years and caused considerable traffic chaos ... The low-lying portions of the city – the bottom of the 'bowl' – had the worst of it. On most of the hills leading out of the centre one had only to proceed a few hundred yards before emerging into the 'clear', with a starry sky above. In recent fog spells

affecting most of the country, Bath has been fortunate, so Saturday's 'blanket' was an unwelcome surprise. For several hours it was a 'city of ghosts', the thousands of shoppers being mixed up with the crawling traffic and all wondering how they were going to get home. (10)

Some of the continuing decay of historic buildings may be attributable to their past exposure to much higher levels of pollution, that is to say historic acid rain, than those that are experienced today. During that time, limestone surfaces reacted with sulphur dioxide to form calcium sulphate. Even if the stone has subsequently been carefully washed with low-volume, low-pressure mists of water, it is still only the apparent surface of the stone that has been cleaned. The decay mechanisms caused by the effect of historic acid rain can still be found at depths of several millimetres or even centimetres into the stone (11).

Furthermore, these hidden decay mechanisms can easily be activated by wetting and drying cycles and the action of heat, such as sunshine. These factors reinforce the need for the most careful and sensitive washing of stonework. Some of the decay that is seen today is therefore attributable to past pollution levels rather than current levels, and may well continue for several decades. This phenomenon is known as the 'memory effect' (12).

Figure 1 Looking across Bath in the early 1950's before the impact of the 1956 Clean Air Act, one can just make out the towers of the Bathwick Street Fire Station and the churches of St John the Baptist, Bathwick and, further in the distance, St Mary, Bathwick. Photograph, circa 1950, of the Snow Hill (No. 1) Clearance Area with backs of Weymouth Buildings and fronts of Upper Pleasant Place in foreground. (Copyright Bath City Council).

187

SCIENTIFIC OBSERVATIONS

In 1978, in London, road traffic accounted for 46% of smoke emissions, while power stations contributed 26%. In a 1962 London smog the acidity of acid droplets was one thousand to twenty thousand times higher than natural rain water (11).

Sulphur dioxide levels have been recorded at Bathwick Street, Bath, since 1962 as part of the National Survey of Smoke and Sulphur Dioxide. Sulphur dioxide levels for Bath between 1962 and 1988 are set out Table 1. They are recorded as the annual arithmetic mean of micrograms of sulphur dioxide per cubic metre of air. Smoke levels are also recorded over the same period for this site. The recording equipment for the survey was relocated on the same site in 1981, reflected in the records for that year.

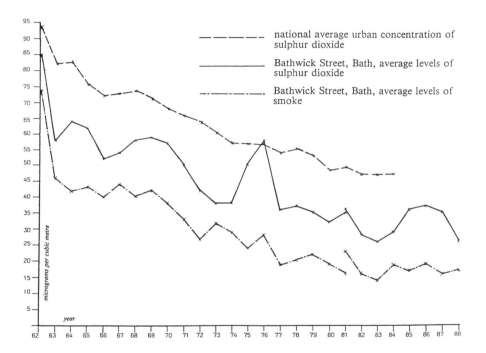

Table 1 Comparison of national urban concentrations of sulphur dioxide to levels for Bath. Bath data source: *Warren Spring Laboratory, Department of Trade and Industry. National Survey of Smoke and Sulphur Dioxide.* Print-out of readings between 1962 and 1988 for Bath. UK data source: (5)

The sulphur dioxide levels for Bath are compared to UK average urban concentrations of sulphur dioxide between 1962 and 1984. The national monitoring sites numbered 500 initially, increasing to about 1200 by 1966. At present 450 urban sites are in operation. (5)

It was not until 1956 that the Clean Air Act was introduced. Since then smokeless zones have been steadily introduced throughout Bath. The air may now *appear* to be cleaner but, as smoke emissions and sulphur dioxide levels have decreased, so road traffic and its pollutants, oxides of nitrogen and particulates, grow. Readings of levels of oxides of nitrogen have only recently commenced in Bath and comparative figures are therefore not yet available.

BATH ABBEY SURVEY, 1987

A major campaign of stone cleaning and restoration of Bath Abbey was undertaken between 1948 and 1960 culminating with the carving of the angels climbing Jacob's ladder on the West Front during 1960. In 1987 the West Front was scaffolded to inspect the condition of the stonework. The survey was undertaken by Nimbus Conservation Group on behalf of the Parochial Church Council of Bath Abbey.

The survey highlighted the damage done to the angels carved in 1960 in Box Ground stone, an exceptionally durable and hard-wearing stone, now sadly worked out and no longer available. In this case, the dry deposition of acid-laden dust on horizontal ledges and surfaces had already resulted in the break-up of the stone surfaces over a period of only 27 years. The continuing damage to the medieval and Victorian stonework of the West Front was also noted.

A campaign of cleaning and lime-based conservation of the West Front by the Nimbus Conservation Group under the direction of the PCC's architect, Alan Rome, began in the spring of 1991. The work will be carried out over two seasons.

THE CIRCUS

The 1987 survey of Bath Abbey West Front confirmed that the acid rain problem had not yet been solved. As the 1960 replacement stone could be clearly identified, the West Front survey rang the alarm bells about the possibility of stonework continuing to deteriorate elsewhere in the city although it had already been cleaned and repaired. A preliminary investigation of the north side of the Circus with the Research and Technical Advisory Service of English Heritage during the summer of 1987 confirmed the probable need for conservation work within the Circus during the preparation of the 1988/89 budgets.

With the buildings fully scaffolded for the 1988 painting contract on the six houses owned by the City Council (numbers 3, 12, 15, 21, 22 and 23) it was possible to inspect the stonework in detail. This confirmed that further conservation work was indeed necessary. As a result, from June to December 1989 the ornate stonework of these six houses was carefully cleaned and conserved using lime-based conservation techniques by Nimbus Conservation Group.

This work in the Circus highlights the continuing problems of stone conservation in Bath following damage by historic acid rain. For it was these same six houses that were among the first to be cleaned and repaired under the town scheme starting in 1955.

The Circus was built by John Wood and his son between 1754 and 1767. In his *Essay Towards a Description of Bath*, John Wood extolled the merits of Bath stone, 'a most excellent Building Material, as being Durable, Beautiful and Cheap; ... in Truth, [it] is fit for the Walls of a Palace for the Greatest Prince in Europe' (13).

Bath stone is a beautiful building material but, like all natural materials, it needs to breathe. Stone, like other building materials, absorbs moisture in and breathes it out in a natural cycle of wetting and drying. But if the pores of the stone get clogged up, it can't breathe and the surface of the stone begins to break up.

Figure 2 (left, above) In this 'before' photograph of 14 Circus, circa 1955, one can clearly see the extensive damage resulting from the effect of acid rain in the Circus. While the metopes and triglyphs have survived practically unscathed, the mutules of the Doric cornice have been decayed almost beyond recognition. The volutes of the Ionic capitals have disintegrated and both the upper and lower beds of the Ionic cornice have been severely eroded. The Corinthian order is similarly affected. (Copyright Bath City Council).

Figure 3 (right, above) Photograph, circa 1974, of 14 Circus after repairs during 1973/1974. Comparison with the 'before' photograph emphasises the phenomenal amount of decay that had been caused by the effects of acid rain. (Copyright Bath City Council).

CONCLUSIONS

Heavy soiling of buildings is not simply an aesthetic problem; it is also a major cause of decay. Sulphur dioxide in the atmosphere reacts with Bath stone forming a skin of calcium sulphate, causing the stone to spall and blister. Other compounds in the atmosphere can have similar effects.

It is noticeable that buildings abutting heavily trafficked roads are becoming heavily soiled again after comparatively recent conservation work. On the London Road, 1 and 2 Fountain Buildings (grant-aided 1979), Hay Hill Baptist Chapel (1986) and Hay Hill House (1978) are all rapidly becoming badly stained. Pollutants generated by road traffic are suspected to be the primary cause of this further damage (14).

There is also recent evidence in Bath of the deterioration of stone surfaces over the period 1975 to 1990 on the east-facing ornately carved facade of John Wood the Elder's 1727 Town House for Ralph Allen. This three-storey building is located in a quiet courtyard just south of York Street in a relatively traffic-free environment, right in the bottom of the Avon valley basin. Pollutants generated by road traffic are again suspected to be the primary cause of this damage. But in this case it is not an immediately abutting road that is the problem but the fact that traffic elsewhere within the city centre is generating sufficient pollution to be held in place by the inevitable effect of the 'teacup' of the city's steeply sloping hills.

The Corinthian capitals on this building which were renewed in Westwood ground stone in the spring of 1975 were found to show early signs of deterioration by the summer of 1990. Nimbus Conservation Group carried out careful cleaning using intermittent nebulous water sprays followed by lime water consolidation, lime mortar repairs and shelter coating during the late summer and early autumn of 1991 under the direction of Bath City Council's Department of Property and Engineering Services.

The Corinthian capitals on this building which were renewed in Westwood ground stone in the spring of 1975 were found to show early signs oif deterioration by the summer of 1990. Nimbus Conservtion Group carried out careful cleaning using intermittent nebulous water sprays followed by lime water consolidation, lime mortar repairs and shelter coating during the late summer and early autumn of 1991 under the direction of Bath City Council's Department of Property and Engineering Services.

As a result of the recent work in the Circus and the evidence of continuing decay on previously cleaned and repaired historic buildings, the City Council are considering incorporating stone cleaning into the regular maintenance programme for their historic buildings and historic building housing stock. With the present 5-yearly cycle of external painting and repairs, subject to available funding, it is proposed to carefully wash down the stonework of the City Council's historic buildings and the historic building housing stock once every 15 years in areas where heavy soiling persists.

The recent cleaning and conservation work in the Circus and the survey of the West Front of Bath Abbey both highlight the importance of regular careful cleaning of stonework by washing down with low-volume, low-pressure mists of water as the first stage of a carefully prepared campaign of conservation. Part of the present problem has been that interventions have been too far apart and that need for the *maintenance* of stone has not been fully appreciated. In certain cases it has therefore been necessary to make a *major* intervention, the *conservation process itself*, and then get the maintenance cycle back onto a proper footing.

References

1. Cooke, A. (1961) A Letter From Bath: Reflection on the City and Frank Lloyd Wright. *The Listener*. 6 July 1961.
2. Holburne of Menstrie Museum. (1975) *Circle Square and Crescent: an exhibition for European Architectural Heritage Year*. 8-9, illustration B28.
3. Smollett, T. (1771,1977). *Humphrey Clinker*. 64- 65.
4. Smith, R.A. (1858). cited in Smith, R.A., (1872) *Air and Rain - The Beginnings of a Chemical Climatology* in GLC Scientific Services Branch, (1985) *'Acid Rain''and London*. 3.
5. Building Effects Review Group. (1989) *The Effects of Acid Deposition on Buildings and Building Materials in the UK*. 4-6, 22 and figure 2.3 facing 48.
6. Murdoch, J. et al (1981). *The English Miniature*. 12.
7. Bath in the Eighteenth Century. (1905) *Edinburgh Review*. 179-180.
8. Woodall, M. (ed.) (1963) *The Letters of Thomas Gainsborough*. 157.
9. Austen, J. (1818). *Persuasion*. 290-291.
10. *Bath Weekly Chronicle and Herald*. (1949). Saturday 5 February. 7.
11. GLC Scientific Services Branch. (1985) *'Acid Rain' and London*. 6.
12. English Heritage. (1988) *Conservation Bulletin*, 5:4-5.
13. Wood, J. (1765, 1969) *An Essay towards a Description of Bath*. 338, 425.
14. Bath City Council. (1990) Survey results of pollution in Bath are detailed in the report of the Director of Environmental Services *Air Quality in Bath* to Environment Committee on 22 October 1990.

18 Conservation and planning considerations in stone cleaning

CHRIS ANDREW
The Robert Gordon Institute of Technology and
EMMA CRAWFORD
The Architectural Heritage Society of Scotland

INTRODUCTION

The cleaning of stone buildings has attracted much attention from within the architectural conservation world, with opinions both for and against. This paper looks at the background to this situation, and at stonecleaning from the point of view of the architectural conservator and in addition at the planning implications of recent research conducted by The Masonry Conservation Research Group at The Robert Gordon Institute of Technology, Aberdeen.

CONSERVATION CONSIDERATIONS

Until relatively recently grants for stonecleaning have been readily available, and in some areas cleaning has been actively encouraged. The generally perceived benefits of stonecleaning can be considered to be:

1. Stonecleaning results in an improvement in the visual appearance of buildings;

2. Stonecleaning contributes to a sense of urban renewal;
3. Cleaned buildings encourages greater interest in the built environment;
4. Stonecleaning contributes towards a broader trend of reinvestment;
5. Stonecleaning might contribute towards increased property values.

The debate within the conservation movement has hinged upon whether the undoubtedly positive effects of an increased interest in the built environment which is stimulated by cleaned buildings can really be approved while the long term results of cleaning upon the fabric of buildings is uncertain.

A great deal has been done in Glasgow in the area of urban renewal, including major programmes of refurbishment of historic buildings, and returning previously redundant buildings to new and useful life, such as warehouse to flat conversions in the Merchant City. Such schemes, whether they are conversions, refurbishments, restorations, or mere facade retentions, have almost invariably involved cleaning the external elevations. This has been treated as a symbolic signal to the buildings owners, users and developers of the development/refurbishment work being completed. It has therefore become almost invariably expected as a part of any refurbishment programme.

Following from this is the belief on one side of the conservation movement that while cleaning buildings may carry some long term risk, this argument pales to insignificance when considered against the possible fate of many historic buildings, for whom restoration without cleaning would simply not proceed. Demolition, or continued neglect would mean the buildings would be lost sooner or later. Those funding restoration schemes 'need' the incentive of a building which, at the end of the period of work, visually appears to have been restored. At the same time, these newly cleaned buildings have the richness of detail and quality of materials, massing and styling that is usually only found in historic buildings.

The other side of the argument in conservation circles is that while cleaned buildings may enjoy greater attention or prominence, some cleaning processes have caused damage to elevational masonry. Much of the cleaning carried out in the 1970s and early 1980s was done with abrasives, frequently on rotary disks. This method was quite extensively used, and sometimes even on buildings which had elaborate tooled ashlar surfaces, such as horizontal or diagonally droved. In such cases, the sophisticated surface treatment was simply ground off, representing a most unfortunate loss of original skilled workmanship, as well as an intervention resulting in a net loss in the quality of the building as a whole.

In more recent programmes of work, chemical methods of cleaning have become more common. This has brought different problems. The process brings about dramatic changes to the fabric of the building the effect of which to some extent at least are unknown. The processes are so relatively new in comparison to the life of the buildings on which they are being used, which may be several centuries old, that conservationists cannot feel that the processes are without risk. The long term effects on buildings simply cannot yet be ascertained. Stone is one of a number of constituents of a whole building, and the whole unit must be considered when an intervention is planned: the external masonry shell simply cannot be isolated from the structural functions and decorative qualities of the building.

With buildings, a thorough understanding of masonry structures, and their construction technologies is very important if processes affecting the entire construction materials (stone) are being considered. Buildings are complicated, and experience has shown that cleaning and other processes are too often undertaken on Historic Structures without an adequate understanding of how the structures work as a whole. The behaviour of a stone in a parapet wall in which a lead-lined wallhead gutter has developed a leak will be vastly different to a stone mid elevation on a sheltered south facing facade. Victorian buildings tend to be embellished with finials, usually fixed with iron rods in the stone. These corrode, frost action occurs, and spalling of the stone can often result. An understanding of the local climate is also important to interpreting a building, wind and weather erosion vary considerably in different areas.

Little new building is currently constructed in stone in present times. More commonly stone is used as 'geological wallpaper'. This has a consequent effect on recently trained building professionals, who having little experience of specifying stone for structural purposes, are naturally less familiar with its inherent properties. The suitability of stone for particular purposes, such as finials, and the way it will behave in particular weathering conditions are also less well understood among recently trained building professionals. Therefore there is a net decrease in knowledge and understanding of stone as a building component. If the trend to clean increases, and there is a parallel net decrease in working knowledge of stone and masonry structures, then clearly this is likely to be to the detriment of the building stock.

Cleaning buildings actually covers many processes, so in order to safeguard historic architecture against incorrect processes, and uninformed interventions, a thorough understanding both of these processes, of building stones, and of the architecture involved must be demonstrable in the agent wishing to clean a building. This isn't the case at present, although much cleaning is going on. Again, the loser is the historic fabric of our towns, cities and villages.

While there is considerable debate on the ethics of cleaning, conservationists are also opposed to cleaning because of the framework in which cleaning takes place at present. There appears to be inadequate legislative framework to regulate stone cleaning practitioners, and there is certainly no standard training for operatives. The losers in a system so open to the learning curves of the untrained and the dealings of the unscrupulous are inevitably the buildings and their fabric. A survey conducted of Agents involved in stonecleaning work by The Masonry Conservation Research Group in 1991 (1) showed damage to stone to be the major perceived technical drawback to cleaning. In addition, particularly with some abrasive cleaning methods, the operatives and supervisors have motives to increase the pressure of abrasives, allowing the contract to be completed quicker. This will probably result in financial gain for the cleaning firm, while the masonry will have undergone an irreversible intervention to its surface. In some refurbishment schemes the proportion of the budget allocated to stonecleaning is often very small and with a tendering system often the lowest bid will be accepted. Coupled with this can be very loose specifications for the work, all in all not a recipe designed to lead to good quality workmanship. Recently less damaging abrasive methods have been introduced which work at much reduced pressure which may well overcome many of the problems of early abrasive techniques, however these are likely to be much more expensive. Many building owners are simply unaware of the potential damage which can be caused by cleaning. If the mistakes made in the 1970s and 1980s are not to be repeated, then clearly the care, time and financial resources devoted to both stonecleaning research, practice, and training will need to be increased.

Another view on cleaned buildings in the conservation field, which assumes that a process could be found which could be guaranteed to have no harmful effects on buildings at all, is concerned with the ethics of cleaning buildings. It hinges on whether or not the soiling, as evidence of the passage of time should actually be removed from buildings.We actually should remove the evidence of the passage of time from buildings by complete removal of soiling from buildings. Research by The Masonry Conservation Research Group (1) has shown that the perceived age of buildings is significantly altered by cleaning. The research shows that stonecleaning has the effect of making building appear younger. This might lead to a false sense of the age of an area as well as removing part of the history of the building.

The question of retaining buildings in their soiled condition has to be set against other considerations including scientific evidence (2) which suggests that heavy soiling on stone leads to moisture build up behind the patina which may react with the stone to cause it to break down. In addition there is evidence (1) that stonecleaning is very favourably received in tenement areas where it has the perceived effect of lessening the oppressive nature of some tenements. Clearly it is necessary to examine a whole range of factors closely before any decision is taken on stonecleaning. In addition to considerations at the level of the building and its fabric are the wider planning implications.

PLANNING CONSIDERATIONS

In the case of historic buildings, the process of listing buildings theoretically affords them protection. If alterations are to be made that would materially affect the character of a listed building, then listed building consent must be obtained before such work can be carried out. Many authorities process Consent applications at the same time as applications for planning permission. While cleaning is considered as a process for which Listed Building Consent must be obtained, there is little standardisation among Scottish Planning authorities on how such applications are received, and what information must be submitted to the authorities when applying for consent. As far as processing the applications is concerned, there is certainly no standard view among Scottish planning authorities as to whether consent should be granted. For example, in Dundee the view is that no listed building should be cleaned, and no consents have been granted there for some time. In Glasgow on the other hand, the process is welcomed as a constituent of a larger process of rediscovery and regeneration. Clearly the lack of any guidelines based on research evidence has lead to these inconsistencies.

The ethics of cleaning urban buildings has also caused some debate in conservation circles. In squares for example, there is an architectural unity of storey height, fenestration, detailing, building material, which was clearly meant to be read as a whole. If some buildings are cleaned, this unity of architectural expression is compromised. The same is true of terraces, crescents and even of some semi-detached houses, where the change in colour destroys the previous harmony of detailing, massing and texture. Research evidence from The Masonry Conservation Research Group shows widespread dislike of this effect from both professionals and public alike.

Arguments usually advanced in support of this piecemeal approach to cleaning are centred around two main issues. Firstly, the right of individuals to do as they wish with their property includes their right to remove soiling from its surface. The counter argument to this however, is that given that planning permission is required before changes can be made to many other visual aspects of buildings it seems logical to include cleaning in this category in view of the dramatic visual effect it has not only on the building itself, but on neighbouring buildings as well. The second argument raised is that individual cleaning encourages others to clean their properties and this will eventually lead to the complete cleaning of whole urban areas. This argument presupposes that wholesale cleaning is advantageous, a view which, in itself, is open to question. Also this type of cleaning policy has the considerable disadvantage that the result of cleaning adjacent buildings at different times (particularly with chemical cleaning) leads to differences in stone colour and texture.

There are widespread examples where individual stones, being part of two adjacent properties, are of two very different colours following cleaning. It is difficult to maintain consistency of colour and texture when entire terraces or crescents are cleaned as a complete unit, at one time and using a single method. When terraces are cleaned piecemeal using different methods (or even the same method on different occasions) and different contractors, etc. it becomes almost impossible to obtain consistency over the entire terrace. Piecemeal cleaning also means that different properties will be at different stages in their cycle of resoiling adding to the problem. At present the way in which cleaning grants and planning policy operates tends to encourage piecemeal cleaning activity. Not only does cleaning need to be planned at the level of individual streets, but at the neighbourhood and city level as well. A move towards a more systematic approach to planning would have implications for the way in which stonecleaning is funded.

Planning authorities have tended to be reactive rather than proactive in their approach to cleaning, responding to, and having to make decisions on individual cleaning applications without any clear end result in mind. What is required is a systematic audit of the urban building fabric and, based on research evidence, cleaning policies formulated for entire urban areas. Once a properly formulated policy, based on some understanding of the intended result has been formulated a more systematic approach to cleaning can be adopted. This may mean (as in areas of Edinburgh New Town) that no cleaning is permitted. In this way at least urban areas have the benefit of some measure of unity. Planning policy must be based on sound conservation, aesthetic and scientific research if mistakes too commonly made in the past are to be avoided in the future.

References

1. Masonry Conservation Research Group, RGIT, Aberdeen (1991), Stonecleaning in Scotland Report to Historic Scotland & Scottish Enterprise.
2. Bluck, B.J. and Porter, J. (1991) 'Sandstone buildings and cleaning problems'. Stone Industries Vol 26, (2) March 1991, 21-27.

19 Stone cleaning in urban conservation

DENNIS RODWELL
MA (Cantab), FRIAS, FSA Scot, FRSA

There are some people for whom stone cleaning is an emotive issue. Otherwise sane and well-balanced, they suddenly become agitated even at the mention of the term. A missionary zeal takes over, casting all rational debate aside.

A small, but regrettably vocal, minority is opposed to stone cleaning as a matter of principle, on 'moral' grounds. One argument, for example, which is presented by one of the co-author's of the Edinburgh New Town Conservation Committee's 'Maintenance Manual', is that stone cleaning does not benefit the appearance of old buildings or the ability to appreciate their form and detail, and that they actually look better when they are dirty. He does not admit to any exception to this generalisation. Justification is attempted along the lines that degrees of dirtiness help to describe the age of a building, and that to clean old buildings is somehow a subversion of history.

Personally I find this a thoroughly eccentric point of view, but one which highlights much of the ambiguity and confusion that surrounds issues related to the techniques and purpose of stone cleaning, especially in the context of urban conservation.

I took issue recently with the wording on a questionnaire sent to me, one item of which read: 'Philosophy of Conservation in relation to stone cleaning: What, in your view, are the ethical (sic) issues involved in attempting to make an historic building "look new"?' Equally, I take issue with the oft repeated view that stone cleaning, as such, can be equated with giving an ageing lady a surgical face-lift, with the deliberate intent to mislead. We are trafficking here in terms that are applied with emotive and adversarial undertones. They serve to anticipate a negative case, and obscure a considered assessment of the most appropriate technical methods of stone cleaning, and the beneficial result that can accrue to the appreciation of our urban environments. This moralistic hyping attracts ridicule to a fringe element of the Conservation Movement – quite deservedly so in my view. Most unfortunately, however, it tars others of us with the same brush.

There is no virtue in filth, and to confuse the process of cleaning with that of contrived rejuvenation, as opposed to evolutionary regeneration, is as unhelpful as it is unconvincing.

I am quite happy here to found on my dictionary's definition of the verb 'clean', namely 'make free from dirt or filth'. Thus a more appropriate analogy with our ageing lady is taking a periodic bath, not a 'face-job'. This interpretation is surely what André Malraux, that most cultured of men, had in mind when in 1959 he resuscitated the Paris Cleaning Order, with dramatic result to the major monuments and streetscapes of the French capital.

I am also quite happy to agree with the Prince of Wales, unfashionable though it may be, when he wrote in his 'A Vision of Britain': 'The Houses of Parliament look particularly wonderful since they've been cleaned – you see the full glory of them now'.

Dirt, irrespective of whether or not it is of itself harmful to their fabric, makes old buildings look uncared for and unvalued. It symbolises neglect. It encourages the view that maintaining old buildings is an insurmountable problem, that they have a finite life, and that conservation is an anachronism. It is a passive form of vandalism, that inspires the active.

Much of the quality of historic buildings, both in design and construction, derives from the articulation of form and the intricacies of detail. Observation of these qualities is rendered difficult and sometimes impossible if the enriching effect of the passage of light and shade is suppressed by filth. A modulated facade becomes just a silhouette on the skyline, just as I would maintain the old North British Hotel had become before it was cleaned. The blackened Scott Monument, disguised now by its protective enclosure, had become even more of a silhouette.

This reduction of three dimensional architecture to two dimensional flats may represent some people's idea of preservation, as stage set facadism unrelated to the structures and the functions of the buildings behind. But it has little to do with the concept that the protection of our heritage is an integral component of evolutionary change in our towns and cities, which to me is what urban conservation is all about.

Urban conservation, in the broad sense, is not therefore restricted to the major monuments of our heritage. These are the high points, the structures which first catch the eye of a visitor and which distinguish one city from another in the travel brochures. These highlights, whilst retaining a symbolic importance, are largely taken for granted by local people and do not impact on the daily lives of the inhabitants of our established cities in the same way as do the lesser buildings, many of which are not historic in the sense of being Listed. It is these that collectively establish the distinctive urban grain and provide the

Signal Tower, Leith – restoration and stone cleaning of an historic landmark

backdrop to the living and working environments of the majority. Their qualities are equally disguised by dirt.

To the Edinburgh folk of Gorgie and Dalry, Tollcross and Easter Road, their established communities and their architectural environment is just as valuable, and certainly far more extensive, than are the architectural set pieces of the New Town, or the substantially de-populated Old Town.

Urban conservation, taken as a general concept and not simply cordoned off into Conservation Areas, has established a chord with a broad spectrum of opinion, and not simply with those architectural historians who would like to monopolise the Conservation Movement and dictate their terms over how other people should react to the circumstance that they live in historic towns.

The fact of the matter is that the whole concept of urban conservation is now so widespread in cities such as Edinburgh that it encompasses large tracts of the city, and impinges directly on the living environments of perhaps as high as half the population, and the working environment of an even greater proportion.

The complementary role which sustaining and improving the environmental quality of this city's huge extent of Victorian and Edwardian tenemental housing, and other building uses, plays in reinforcing the public perception of the value of conserving the more historical central areas should not be underestimated.

This also, necessarily, means that the whole question of the cleaning of stone buildings has a far wider relevance than simply to such landmark structures as the church of St John's West in Princes Street, to take another example, and that the context for the need to devise appropriate technical solutions is general, not selective. Bad cleaning techniques are just as damaging to a tenement in Caledonian Road as they would be to one in Heriot Row, and we as professionals have a responsibility to ensure that we do not inflict defective cleaning treatments on any stone buildings, at whatever end of the architectural scale they happen to be.

I can see no merit in disagreeing with the public perception that dirty buildings look uncared for, just as do unpainted ones. I am also quite happy to recognise that stone cleaning has a very important role to play in reinforcing people's confidence in their environment. Indeed I am delighted that the restoration and cleaning work which I carried out a few years ago to the Grade A Listed Signal Tower at Leith was used in some promotional literature as symbolising the re-vitalisation of Leith. This in turn has served to support the re-use, better maintenance and cleaning of other less historic, and often un-listed, buildings that comprise the overall established environment of this seaport. Indeed part of the justification for the composite public funding that was involved in the Signal Tower restoration was the knock-on effect that was anticipated, and the perception that a broadly conservationist approach is beneficial to the people of Leith, in contrast to the policies of 30 years ago.

Confidence, pride and sometimes showmanship, are very much involved here, and if we are really concerned to ensure that conservation is with us to stay, and not just a passing fad, then all of these positive sentiments should be admitted and recognised. They are not antipathetic to conservation, they are highly supportive.

I have lost count of the number of buildings, mostly in Edinburgh, and mostly residential tenements, that my practice has cleaned over the last twenty years. These have included buildings in the Lawnmarket and St Mary's Street, certain ones in the New Town, and properties in most of the principal tenemental areas of the city. In none of these cases was stone cleaning forced

Figure 2 Lawnmarket, Royal Mile, Edinburgh – restoration, stone cleaning and painting as part of a Housing Improvement Scheme

upon the owners, and indeed with quite a number of our repair and restoration projects stone cleaning has not, for one reason or another, been carried out.

I like to think that none of the buildings we have cleaned has been damaged by the techniques we chose, which have varied from brushing, to low pressure sand and hydrofluoric acid. But whereas I take issue with the 'moral' opponents of stone cleaning, I have no argument at all with those who have, quite rightly, questioned the technical methods that are most commonly used.

It is expressly not my purpose here to attempt any duplication of the several specialised presentations which others, whose advice I both respect and depend upon in my practice, are giving as part of this Conference.

My purpose is rather to underline the guiding principles which I consider we should observe and reinforce.

Firstly, I no more perceive stone cleaning as a one-off 'final solution' than do I adhere to the view that all buildings have a finite life. Cleaning, in the proper sense, is periodic: even if it were only to take place every 50 years it would still be periodic. It is important to recognise it as such in order to avoid an over-enthusiastic approach to the application of method. This can be achieved if one makes it clear in specifications, and more especially on site, that it is the removal of surface and not ingrained dirt that is the objective. A partial clean, say an 80% clean, is largely indistinguishable from a total clean, and it achieves more than adequate environmental gain. It is the attempts that are made to remove the last 20% or so that in my experience cause damage. Without question, a great deal of irreversible damage has been done to stone faced tenements, most notoriously in Glasgow in recent years, arising from a mis-guided attempt to over-clean buildings. But it is wrong to over-react to this and to conclude that stone cleaning of itself is wrong. It is important therefore to get away from the notion that the purpose of stone cleaning is to make a building 'look new'.

Secondly, stone cleaning must be seen in townscape terms, and I fully agree with the policy in this city that insists that sporadic cleaning in Listed terraces is not approved. An extension of this policy to all areas might be justified, although at present no mechanisms exist that would enable such a policy to be adopted. Conversely, group cleaning should be encouraged, including to Listed terraces that are dirty.

Thirdly, and I know that people like James Simpson disagree with me on this point, I have little doubt that in the generality of the cases where one is dealing with central urban buildings, cleaning makes restoration much easier. It helps greatly to identify defects, and it aids the site technicians. It is of course partly a question of degree, but with buildings which have heavy deposits of dirt, especially soot, much of which covers over and conceals fractures or lamination in stone facework, cleaning is of major assistance to the achievement of satisfactory maintenance and long-term repair.

Fourthly, no distinction should be drawn in practice between the techniques applied to Listed or non-Listed buildings. Irrespective of whether it is historic or simply old, the external envelope of any building is of equivalent importance to the people who own it and occupy it, and there should be no gradation of treatment simply on the basis of whether or not one perceives a particular building or group as having more architectural importance than another.

Fifthly, the imperative requirement which we must seek to satisfy is to research and determine the method or methods that are safe, to establish the parameters within which they should be employed, and to promote their adoption only by skilled site operatives. One of the most frustrating things about practising as an architect is that whereas we are expected to be trained,

Figure 3 St Mary's Street, Edinburgh – restoration and stone cleaning as part of the Regeneration of the St Mary's Street Area

qualified and experienced, none of these attributes are an essential prerequisite for site operatives. Some form of licensing of firms engaged in stone cleaning should be considered, to counter-balance the catalogue of disasters that has given stone cleaning a bad name.

In conclusion, I have heard it suggested that the present enthusiasm for stone cleaning is a transient fashion that has been generated by such bodies as the Scottish Development Agency (especially Glasgow) or the District Council here in Edinburgh, as though these were imposing the idea rather than responding to public demand. This I cannot agree: the input of these bodies has reflected, not originated, the demand.

Buildings do not need to be cleaned simply because they are old, but in our polluted urban environments cleaning has a vital role to play in sustaining the principles of conservation, and in ensuring that the fabric and vitality of our cities is never again compromised by ill-conceived destruction and re-development. It is vital therefore that we should direct every endeavour towards satisfying the demand, and not seek to deny or oppose it.

20 Building cleaning – process or procedure, an industry view

CRAIG LIDDLE
The Stone Federation

INTRODUCTION

With the growing emphasis on conservation of our heritage, the building cleaning and restoration industry has grown at a remarkable rate during recent years to an estimated annual market value in excess of £100m. During this period of market expansion many new companies have been formed and established companies have diversified to include cleaning and restoration in their services. Unfortunately this has given rise to a situation where purported specialists with little knowledge of the industry have employed equally unskilled operatives and buildings have been damaged as a result.

The Stone Federation has been aware of the potential problems for several years. It has been far too easy to enter the industry and the ability to purchase aggressive cleaning systems and agents virtually over the counter must be considered a contributory factor.

The number of cleaning contractors in Federation membership is a very low percentage of those now trading, making control and education very difficult. There is a definite need for a recognised central body available to all parties involved in a cleaning programme.

The Federation feels this is a role it can play and has welcomed the recent research that has been carried out which can only help the industry at large.

The Stone Federation is the leading body in the natural stone industry with some 200 member companies engaged in the preparation, use and restoration of natural stone buildings.

Stone Federation members operate quarries, supply and fix masonry and cladding in the complete range of natural stone types, including limestone, sandstone, slate, marble and granite, and provide comprehensive cleaning, repair and restoration services.

The Federation provides information and technical advice, produces publications and films, and organises courses on the use of stone in building.

The Federation strives for the attainment of the highest standards and actively promotes training and the development of technical standards. High standards of membership are maintained and members are required to abide by a Code of Conduct.

THE STONE FEDERATION – COMMITTEES

Committees within the Federation cover:

1. Membership;
2. Marble and Granite;
3. Promotions;
4. Quarries;
5. Technical;
6. Training;
7. Stone Cleaning and Surface Repair.

The Federation's view is that it is essential that control be brought to the industry and this must start with communication between all concerned in the cleaning programme. Without the help of specifiers and the professionals the situation can only get worse.

Failings have occurred through adoption of a system under the illusion that it was a 'miracle cure' or 'magic wand'. Regrettably this never has or will be the case despite what some of the manufacturers' astute marketing may claim.

A number of criteria must be considered to give a contract the best chance of success.

STONE CLEANING CONSIDERATIONS

Firstly, it is necessary to ask 'Why is the building being cleaned?' – is it for aesthetic considerations, to arrest decay mechanisms, or as part of a larger restoration programme?

Secondly, have competent specialists been identified and consulted?, and has the substrate been identified, often varying throughout the facade of the building?

Other considerations include:

1. Have the surface contaminants been identified and the soiling pattern taken into consideration?
2. Have test panels been carried out to ensure that expectations are possible?. It would be unusual for one technique or system to be suitable throughout a facade, so it becomes important to categorise areas to appropriate systems.
3. Have the necessary protection requirements been considered? Apart from possible damage to the fabric being cleaned, it is far too often the case that neighbouring fabrics are damaged often beyond repair.
   Depending on the cleaning system that is being considered, differing amounts and types of protection will be required.
   Polished marble and granite can be etched or burned beyond repair. Glass can similarly be ruined.
   Some chemicals must be contained within certain areas of the facade, as a system that may be sympathetic to one fabric may attack another.
   Paintwork is very susceptible to damage from alkalis. Windows, vents and doorways will require thorough sealing to avoid dust, water or fume ingress.
4. The method of access for the works must then be considered. Scaffolding cradles or hydraulic platforms may be options for varying situations, and depending on the system, containment of overspray to the working area must be addressed.
5. Has a time programme been prepared?
6. Have all the site constraints been evaluated?

Having found satisfactory answers to all of these questions, we should now be in a position to design a cleaning programme.

TECHNIQUES AVAILABLE

The number of techniques available has grown dramatically and tremendous advances have been made in the use of abrasive chemical and water systems.

To avoid commercially biased recommendations, specialist contractors should provide a more impartial view than manufacturers. In the past it has often been the case that a complete specification has revolved around one manufacturer or range of products. In practice a combination of techniques is more often the most efficient answer.

A typical example would be on a High Street bank, with elaborate details at high levels, ashlar stone at lower levels, with marble columns and a polished granite plinth.

Upon first inspection the sandstone is not particularly dirty and shows some sign of moss and lichen growth. On the main portico heavier accumulations of soiling are present.

The stone will generally respond to a mild alkali/acidic wash but the high level stone will require a light abrasive blast which can be used in a very localised manner.

Protection is going to be a critical factor throughout the operation. The polished marble columns will first of all be washed down with very mild detergent and rinsed with cold water. The surface would then be leathered off and left to dry. A protective roll-on peel-off latex coating 'tak guard' can then be applied. This needs to be done with care by experienced operators, as one mistake can result in thousands of pounds worth of damage. Without careful checking of the film thickness and total coverage it is easy to leave areas open to exposure by the cleaning agents. Alternative methods of protection to the columns would be by the use of waterproof tapes and polythene sheeting, but this tends to be more problematical with chemicals, as penetration can occur through joints etc.

The same process will have to be carried out to the polished granite plinth. Also the window glazing will be coated with tak guard and all openings sealed with waterproof tapes.

Any illuminated signs, facia signs, etc. would preferably be removed or completely shrouded in polythene and tape.

Having assessed the full extent of protection required to the building, consideration must now be given to the public and building owner. In most town centre situations, the cleaning operation will be carried out outside normal working hours to minimise inconvenience and comply with highway regulations. However, the scaffolding should be closely sheeted to contain any dust or overspray to the working area.

Before the cleaning process begins, we have already seen that we are in the hands of the specialist and his operatives who need to be familiar with differing fabrics and certainly have a knowledge of the reaction that differing processes will have upon them.

The fact that a lot of stone cleaning is carried out outside normal working hours by necessity, puts a further responsibility on the specialist as it will be unlikely that outside supervision will be present.

It must be in everybody's interest to consider discussion with a proven specialist essential, before documenting the specification, as already we have covered critical areas without even establishing exactly what system is to be deployed.

Small sample panels can now be undertaken, to establish the minimum chemical strength required to clean the stone and also establish that our expectations are possible. The sample can also be left as a reference point. Abrasive blasting samples can also be conducted on more heavily soiled areas, although access may be limited.

Now a considered and detailed specification can be formulated. It should be noted, however, that throughout the operation tremendous responsibility lies with the specialist especially as most of this work will take place 'under wraps' or out of hours making supervision difficult or non-existent.

This makes it essential that the operatives are thoroughly trained in all aspects of their skills including the very important Health and Safety aspect of what to do should there be an accident.

Unfortunately it is all too common an occurrence to see this typical job undertaken by the 'cheapest contractor in town' using totally unskilled operatives with no prior experience; protection is shabbily done and falls off as soon as a water lance or abrasive gun comes near. The results are etched glass, burnt marble and granite even before we consider the areas we were intending to cover. The stone that is being cleaned is treated with a proprietary cleaning system in ignorance and when the expected result is not achieved, more and more coats, more and more concentration of chemicals and more and more pressure is applied.

THE STONE CLEANING AND SURFACE REPAIR COMMITTEE

The stone cleaning and surface repair committee of The Stone Federation comprises members from contract, manufacturing and supply companies.

With the major chemical companies and abrasive blasting equipment manufacturers among its members, the Committee has a firm grasp of new techniques, problems etc.

The contracting side is represented by companies operating throughout the United Kingdom, once again giving a solid base of experience and expertise.

It should be noted that this committee covers the cleaning and restoration of all external materials, which vary dramatically through the UK.

The committee covers the following matters:

1. Membership: although there is a main membership committee, every stone cleaning and restoration contractor that applies, has their application referred to the surface repair committee. Strict criteria have to be met before acceptance.

   An interview is conducted at the applicant's premises to establish the manner in which the business is run, the type of business, the attitude to training, what type of labour is used, and what numbers are employed.

   Checks are carried out on insurance cover and accounts have to be submitted for the preceding two years.

   A safety policy also has to be submitted, and finally, some of the projects undertaken by the company are visited and references taken up.

2. Technical: the committee is kept abreast of all changes in legislation and has an input into all technical standards. Testing and research carried out by the Building Research Establishment (BRE) and other independent bodies is reported and covers all types of stone, marble, granites, brick and terracotta. New cleaning techniques or adaptations are also evaluated.

3. Health and Safety: this is an important aspect of the Committee's workload, where recently a lot of work has been carried out in connection with COSHH. Data sheets have been formulated for all relevant activities.

   New regulations are considered and input given to the Health and Safety Executive, who often give draft documents for consideration and comment. Consideration is also given to the future where perhaps increased legislation emanating from Europe is going to dramatically change the industry.

QUALITY ASSURANCE

With the growing emphasis on BS 5750, the committee has undertaken work with the help of the Federation's Technical Officer to consider an industry standard which can help members in the formulation of a system that can be implemented in individual companies wishing to seek accreditation.

PROMOTIONAL EVENTS

Two seminars were held last year to put over the Federation's case, highlighting the fact that some of the bad press the industry has received in recent years has perhaps been inaccurate and alarmist. These seminars also served to show the Federation's commitment to working with all concerned and to bring some control to the sector and hopefully gain the respect of the professionals whose co-operation is necessary if any inroads into future control are to be made.

All aspects of the Federation's workload were also illustrated and discussed.

TRAINING

Probably the most important aspect of current workload has been the formulation of a training manual, which hopefully will be adopted by a training agency.

This document is in five sections:

1. Health and safety: including safe operation and care of equipment, protective clothing, safety policy, safety rules, reporting and emergency procedures, causes of hazards and accidents in a working environment, safe working practices including good housekeeping, safety signs and symbols and their meanings, responsibilities under the Health and Safety regulations, safe lifting techniques including load distribution, reporting procedures, COSHH requirements.
2. Site preparation: types of stone used in construction:- sandstones, limestones, slates, marbles and granites; types of brick used in construction:- glazed, faced, rustic, common; engineering surface conditions: corrosion spalling, damage; surface discolouration: algae, grease/oil, carbon, graffiti; types of scaffolding and their restrictions; types of protection required and the knowledge of the reaction of cleaning systems on differing fabrics.
3. Machinery operation: knowledge of typical items of plant and machinery; maintenance of the units; fault finding and correction; safe working tolerances; frost precautions.
4. Surface cleaning: ability to recognise differing fabrics and faults; knowledge of cleaning techniques and their safe usage; site and surface preparation; testing;
5. Site clearance: the safe preparation of all plant and equipment for removal from site; checking and documentation of any faults, etc.; ensuring that the site is left completely free from hazards; removal of all protective coatings; re-fixing.

CONCLUSION

It has not been the intention to go into the varying techniques and their respective advantages and disadvantages in this paper. However, it must be recognised that no matter how detailed the research prior to a cleaning programme and no matter how thorough a specification is written, one must be very careful to ensure that a capable proven specialist is contracted to execute the work, if possible from a recognised central body such as the Stone Federation.

Session V
CHEMICAL AND MICROBIOLOGICAL STUDIES

21 Chemical cleaning of sandstone – comparative laboratory studies

JOHN MacDONALD, BRUCE THOMSON and KEN TONGE
School of Applied Sciences, The Robert Gordon Institute of
Technology, Aberdeen, UK

INTRODUCTION

In previously reported laboratory studies (1) it was shown that freshly quarried sandstones, which are sulphate-free, can absorb applied chemicals to depths of more than 10mm. This absorption was observed in each of four standardised techniques based on popular chemical stonecleaning processes. These respectively, make use of:

A. Alkaline degreasing and hydrofluoric acid cleaning;
B. Alkaline degreasing and mixed hydrofluoric/phosphoric acid cleaning;
C. Alkaline poultice cleaning and hydrofluoric/phosphoric acid neutralization;
D. Ammonium hydrogen fluoride gel cleaning.

In each case washing with high pressure water is carried out at appropriate stages.

In complementary field studies (1) it was found that aged sandstone from an urban building (Barony Church, Glasgow, Scotland) was heavily contaminated with soluble sulphate to depths of 15-20mm. After commercial cleaning (acid washing) of the building it was found that the soluble sulphate content of the stone was increased down to a depth of about 8mm. It was speculated that this increase was due to reaction of insoluble sulphate with the applied acid absorbed in the cleaning process.

Other cases, where the chemical analysis data were less complete, could be explained in the same way.

It seemed desirable to complement the above field and laboratory studies with the laboratory cleaning of aged, dirty stones using the same standard cleaning regimes as those which had been used in the investigations of fresh sandstones (i.e. A,B,C and D above). Work has thus been carried out on stone taken from the demolition of Leith Railway Station, near Edinburgh, Scotland.

The Leith Station stone is a buff coloured sandstone. The outer surfaces of the recovered stones are blackened with pollution. The surfaces are not smooth, but are decorated by indented tool marks.

EXPERIMENTAL

The four standard cleaning methods (A,B,C and D, described fully in (1) were applied to four separate stones, numbered 1,2,3 and 4. Stone 1 was sampled as a 'before cleaning' example. A fifth stone (no.5) was also sampled as a 'before cleaning' example.

The following tests were applied to the stones and cleaning systems:

(i) Colour analysis of the stones before and after cleaning using the Minolta Colormeter CR-200b. Measurements were made at several points over the surface of each stone and averaged;

(ii) Visual observation of the physical behaviour of the cleaning agents during the cleaning processes;

(iii)Retention of chemicals was determined by difference from the measured quantities of chemicals applied and the quantities found by analysis in the wash waters collected during the cleaning;

(iv)Depth profiling of the stones. This is the determination of soluble ion concentrations at various depths below the surface of the stone.

RESULTS

(i) Colour analysis

Table 1 shows the values of the three quantities recorded by the chromometer before and after cleaning each of the four stones selected for treatment.

The quantities representing the colour (Hue) and vividness (Chroma) of the stone appear to be affected only insignificantly by cleaning but the lightness (value) is markedly improved in each case. Although methods B and C appear to give the best results it should be noted that the cleaning regimes were not optimized to give the best possible cleaning effect but were simply standardized laboratory simulations of typical methods devised for comparative purposes only.

Table 1   Effect of cleaning on the colour of the stones

Cleaning method	Stone number	Before/ After	Value	Hue	Chroma
A	1	Before	14.0	0.346	0.352
		After	17.6	0.358	0.356
B	2	Before	12.8	0.352	0.367
		After	24.8	0.342	0.347
C	3	Before	11.0	0.350	0.352
		After	22.7	0.358	0.354
D	4	Before	25.1	0.352	0.358
		After	34.4	0.345	0.348

(ii) Visual observations

The tendency of the stones to absorb or retain chemicals was noted. In methods A and B, despite very thorough prewetting the applied chemical solutions were seen to soak into the stone after brushing on.

In method C, although the poultice material was largely scraped off after its 24 hour dwell period under plastic sheeting and its texture seemed unchanged, nevertheless a certain amount remained on the inaccessible parts of the surface, namely the tooled indentations. These residues of the poultice were dislodged by the high pressure water spray.

In method D the gel was completely absorbed by the stone during its 60 minute dwell time.

(iii) Chemicals retained

Table 2 summarises the results of measurements made of the quantities of chemicals applied and the quantities collected in the wash waters.

In methods A and B the was waters containing applied chemicals are collected after degreasing and after acid cleaning. The first washings were analysed for sodium, the second for sodium, and fluoride (and phosphate in B).

In method C wash waters are collected during the rinsing off of residual poultice and after neutralization rinse. The first washings were not analysed as most of the poultice was scraped off and still contained a very large excess of alkalis. The second washings were analysed for fluoride and phosphate.

In method D only one wash water was collected, that is after washing off the residue of gel. This was analysed for fluoride.

Table 2   Amounts of applied chemicals retained during cleaning

Meth-od	Stone number	Area of stone (cm^2)	Wt.retained $(g\ m^{-2})$			Retention as % of amount applied		
			Na^+	F^-	PO_4^{3-}	Na^+	F^-	PO_4^{3-}
A	1	338	127.4	33.7	-	82	76	-
B	2	216	119.3	19.5	17.0	82	54	35
C	3	297	-	5.0	3.0	-	71	88
D	4	273	-	79.0	-	-	84	-

(iv) Depth profiles of stones

Untreated stones (Figures 1 and 2)

The two untreated stones are quite different, in terms of the sulphate content, from each other and from the previously tested Barony Church sample (1).

Unfortunately the exact history of the stones taken from the Leith Station demolition is not known. Stone 1 has a similar soluble sulphate concentration to that found in the Barony Church but the distribution is different in that the concentration is highest at the surface. Measurements of the calcium concentration in the extracts from the Leith Station sample suggest that the sulphate is principally the calcium salt. The stone may have come from an area of the building protected from the prevailing weather so the sulphate has not been washed from the surface.

Stone 5 shows a similar distribution pattern for soluble sulphate but the concentration of sulphate is only about 1/100th of that in stone 1. Again, it is not known where, exactly, this stone came from in the building.

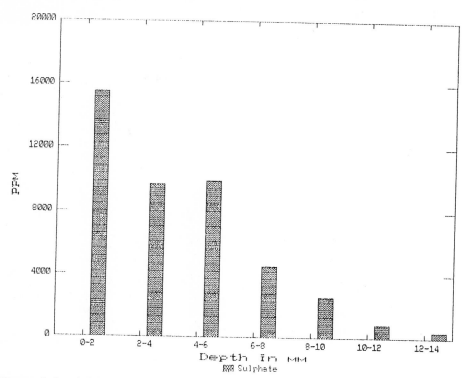

Figure 1 Stone 1 before treatment

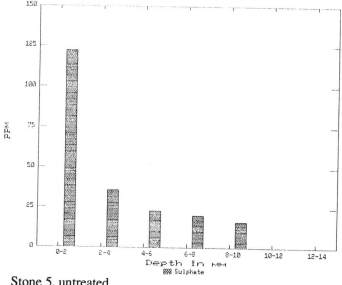

Figure 2 Stone 5, untreated

Treated stones (Figures 3,4,5 and 6)

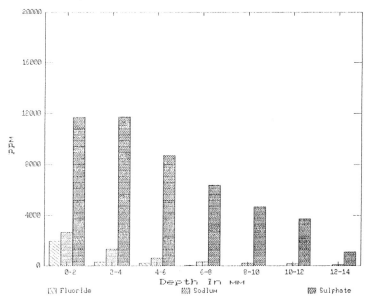

Figure 3 Stone 1 after treatment by method A

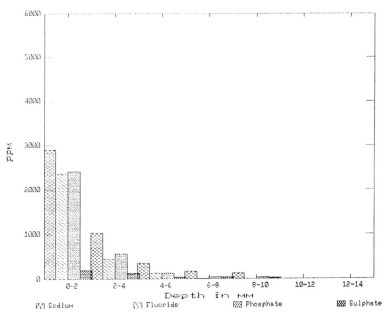

Figure 4 Stone 2 after treatment by method B
The depth profile shown in Figure 3 is that of stone 1 after treatment by method

A. The soluble sulphate has decreased immediately below the surface, but the deeper layers shown an overall slight increase. The small amounts of residual chemicals still present in soluble form are an indicator of the depths to which these can penetrate; down to 12-20mm in this case.

Figure 4 also demonstrates the depths to which the applied chemicals have penetrated, in stone 2. In this case traces of sodium and phosphate are seen down to 8mm depth. The soluble sulphate content is low, perhaps indicating that before treatment this stone may have been similar to 5 in its sulphate content.

The depth profile of stone 3 (Figure 5) after treatment C, the alkaline poultice, shows that sodium has penetrated to 12-20mm. Fluoride from the neutralization is more superficial and is much lower in concentration no doubt because of the short dwell time (5 minutes) allowed in this method. The soluble sulphate is, unlike other cases, more evenly distributed at about 0.4 to 0.5% down to 10-12mm.

Treatment D on stone 4 also results in penetration of fluoride down to 12-20mm with the highest concentration of about 0.5% being found close to the surface. The concentration falls rapidly with depth. The sulphate is at relatively low concentrations in this stone, though not so low as in untreated stone 5 nor as in treated stone 2.

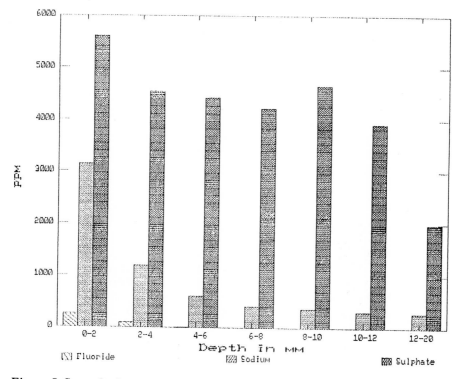

Figure 5 Stone 3 after treatment by method C

223

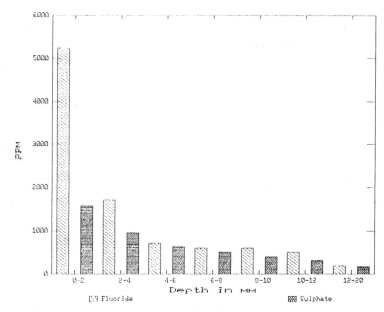

Figure 6   Stone 4 after treatment by method D

DISCUSSION

It is clear from the results presented here that applied chemicals can penetrate to depths of 10mm or more in aged, polluted stones, just as has been found with freshly quarried stone. Similar results have been reported by Werner (2). Short dwell times seem to result in less penetration (e.g. the five minute neutralization wash of method C c.f. the 30 minute cleaning stage of the acid treatments A and B). In practice all methods employ lengthy dwell times at some stage in the procedure. It is not known how the retention of chemicals would be affected by adopting procedures which involved multiple applications and short dwell times.

It was unfortunate that for these series of experiments the stones chosen proved unexpectedly to be so variable in their sulphate content since this makes quantitative interpretation of the data rather difficult given the possibility that the sulphate may play a key role in determining the fate of retained chemicals.

Depth profiles show the concentrations of only the soluble ionic substances present. The fate of an applied chemical may be to:

1. Wash off unchanged,
2. React with stone constituents to form soluble substances, subsequently washed off or retained,
3. React with stone constituents to form insoluble substances,
4. Remain in the stone unchanged.
   From the experimental results the amounts of retained chemicals which have

been converted to insoluble form can be estimated. This is the difference between the total amounts retained (shown in Table 2) and the total amounts extracted in the determination of the depth profiles of soluble salts. The total amount of ions extracted in the depth profiling is easily calculated by integration of the relevant histograms (Figures 1,3,4,5 and 6). Table 3 shows the results of these calculations.

The very wide variation in the total amount of soluble sulphate from stone to stone can be seen. The reduction from 277gm^{-2} to 241 gm^{-2} for stone 1 on treatment is significant. The increase is equivalent to 0.38 mol m^{-2}. This might be due to reaction of HF with $CaSO_4$. The conversion of 1.1mol m^{-2} of retained fluoride into insoluble form would in theory release 0.55 mol m^{-2} of sulphate, which is crudely similar to the increased amount found. Lack of knowledge of the initial sulphate levels in the other stones unfortunately prevents this kind of analysis in the other cases. However, one notes that stone 2 probably had a very low initial sulphate concentration and the amounts of fluoride and phosphate converted to insoluble form are also low. In stone 3 it has already been noted that the short dwell time results in low absorption of fluoride so it is hardly surprising that in this case the insoluble fluoride is also in low concentration.

Stone 4 however, appears to have had a higher sulphate concentration and a greater conversion of fluoride to insoluble form may be the result of this.

Although not conclusively proved, it appears at this stage that the sulphate content of polluted stones may have a major role in determining the fate of absorbed chemical cleaning agents.

Table 3 **The amounts of ions present in cleaned stones, in soluble and insoluble forms**

Method	Stone no.	Amount extracted/g m^{-2} (from depth profiles)				Amount retained in insoluble form/mol m^{-2}		
		Na^+	F^-	PO_4^{3-}	SO_4^{2-}	Na^+	F^-	PO_4^{3-}
A	1	29.0	13.5	-	277	4.3	1.10	-
B	2	24.7	15.9	2.2	2.4	4.1	0.20	0.16
C	3	-		-	191	-	0.17	-
D	4	-	51.6	-	24.6	-	1.40	-
Untreated	1	-	-	-	241	-	-	-

In conclusion we can say that the laboratory regimes adopted appear to be valid in that they yield results comparable to those found in field tests following commercial cleaning operations.

References

1. Masonry Conservation Research Group, The Robert Gordon Institute of Technology, Aberdeen (1991), Report on 'Stonecleaning in Scotland', Research Commission sponsored by Historic Scotland and Scottish Enterprise.
2. Werner, M. (1990) 'Changes of Surface Characteristics of Sandstone Caused by Cleaning Methods Applied to Historical Sandstone Monuments'5th International Conference on Durability of Building Materials and Components, Brighton, England, 7-9 November.

22 Effects of particulate air pollutants on materials: investigation of surface crust formation

BRIAN WHALLEY, BERNARD SMITH and RALPH MAGEE
School of Geosciences, The Queen's University of Belfast

INTRODUCTION AND BACKGROUND

Black crusts (scabs) or stains on buildings and monuments are usually considered as unsightly and require removal, particularly where they occur on buildings or monuments of importance. One difficulty is that, if removed, they may form again; how quickly will depend upon several factors but air quality is not the only control. Locations where crusts and stains occur on buildings depend upon both gross and detail building morphology, the nature of the building material and its finish. The project currently under way is an investigation of the nature of crusts and their impact on natural building stones and involves three main areas of study: crust examination, identification of specific types of crusts, and crust growth simulation, of which the first two are reported briefly here.

Black crusts are complex features and there is no single or simple reason for their occurrence at any location. It is therefore important that their nature is understood before any cleaning is attempted. To this end, we briefly outline:

1. The nature of black crusts;
2. Their relationships to buildings and building stone;
3. Their characterisation;
4. Their material damage potential.

THE NATURE OF BLACK CRUSTS

Crusts form on parts of buildings sheltered from direct rain washing, in areas exposed to more concentrated pollution attack in the form of 'occult' and dry deposition. By definition, they occur in their most extreme form in areas away from rain wash. In many cases such locations may be out of view and crusts may accumulate unobserved and untreated in relation to more exposed areas. The black pigmentation is usually due to a number of factors such as 'smoke' particles in the size range 1-100μm diameter. Smoke here includes all those products of combustion ejected into the atmosphere and includes: domestic, commercial and vehicular sources with coal, oil and diesel internal combustion sources as predominant in the modern setting. In some areas wood or peat may (or may have been) more important [1]. Mixed in with these particles are organic and inorganic particles from various sources. Thus, the black crust on a building is a time integration of the pollution of an area since construction or previous cleaning. However, this does not necessarily mean that the build-up is linear over time.

As well as particulates, crusts may contain the products of alteration of the stones (especially limestones) or mortar. Oxides of sulphur in the atmosphere react with calcareous materials to produce calcium sulphate (gypsum) (e.g.[2, 3]). Where the, rather insoluble, gypsum is precipitated within the pores of building stone it may cause damage, an aspect examined below. Black crusts are most often associated with calcareous stones, perhaps because of the tonal contrast. Surface sulphation of limestone can occur in a matter of months even in 'clean' environments [4]. This rapid alteration can incorporate particulates. Crust formation may also pose a threat to other natural stones. In the case of sandstones, for example, they may enhance the development of features associated with salt weathering mechanisms.

BLACK CRUST RELATIONSHIPS ON BUILDINGS AND BUILDING STONES

The following discussion is necessarily brief and comments upon the general aspects of crust formation rather than the detailed physico-chemical mechanisms involved (qv. ref. 3, chs. 4 and 8).

It is useful to distinguish between crusts on sandstones and crusts on limestones. On limestones, the crusts are invariably located where persistent rain-washing does not occur. Even on broad expanses of buildings some faces may be stained but others may be devoid or partly clear of stains (Figure 1a). Because even pure rainwater is slightly acidic the limestone surface is slowly dissolved and deposition is washed off along with any dissolved calcium carbonate. If there is marked sulphur oxide content of the rain then surface sulphation may give a 'whitewashing' effect which may be of redeposited gypsum or of calcite (3). This is often seen in close proximity to black crust streaking. Even in temperate maritime climates like the British Isles, there can often be long periods of dry weather or when no rain-washing occurs on buildings. If such dry periods coincide with smokiness (winter anticyclonic conditions for example) then this may produce dry deposition which is not removed by subsequent wash (Figure 1a). Architectural detail tends to give marked crusting where it interrupts surface water flow or prevents it where water flow is enhanced. On detail, especially sculptures and balustrades for example, crusts can be very thick and sharply defined. In these cases, the thick crusts are built by airflow (dry deposition) and may be millimetres thick. The local environmental pollution is significant here and it must be remembered that many historic buildings existed in very smokey conditions even before industrialization. Differential crust formation can often be seen even where there appears to be uniformity of the features (Figure 1b). Such anomalies appear to be due to the intricacies of airflow around the detail.

Figure 1
a. Belfast City Hall (Portland limestone) showing large areas of both 'clean' and black crust.
b. Sandstone blocks showing differential deposition of crusts on a rough cut block (centimetre scale, All Souls Church Belfast, Scrabo sandstone).
c. Differential crusts on a balustrade showing the differences between adjacent pillars and on different parts of the central pillar.
d. Lancaster Town Hall (sandstone), showing differential block crusting and the horizontally (wind blown) striping around the pillars.

On sandstone buildings (and this also appears to be true of brick) there tends to be much more uniform deposition of black pigment or staining. This is due to the generally rougher nature of the sandstone surface (at about the level of <1mm) compared with limestone. The surface accumulates the grime but there is no self cleaning effect as the surface is not dissolved. Calcareous sandstones however, tend to behave like limestones. At the scale of ashlar blocks there can still be a variegated discolouration because of inhomogeneities of the surface (Figure 1c) which gives a patchwork appearance to some buildings. If surfaces are left rough textured then some parts of a block can be clean whilst others are dirty. For dry deposition on monument detail, sandstone surfaces can give crusts as thick as limestones.

Persistent rain-washing results in crust-free areas on sandstone buildings as there is little opportunity for deposition to accumulate. A more complex deposition can be seen where there are horizontal or sub-horizontal streaking of black crusts. These are the result of localized airflow around buildings (Figure 1d) and may also be apparent on limestone buildings.

MATERIAL CHARACTERISTICS OF BLACK CRUSTS

Black crusts have four basic components which we may consider as:

1. Inorganic airborne particulates (e.g. soil particles, dust, 'fly ash');
2. Organic airborne particulates (e.g. plant remains, pollen);
3. Inorganic precipitates, perhaps produced in situ (e.g. gypsum);
4. Organic growth in or on the crust (e.g. bacteria, fungae).

Of these, all but 3. may produce or help produce the black colouration but (3) is instrumental in bonding the whole together. Crusts, especially where they are thin, may have considerable mechanical strength which often makes sampling difficult.

A number of techniques have been used to identify these components and help characterize different types of crust. These techniques include: optical and scanning electron microscopy (SEM) but other methods including X-Ray Diffraction (XRD) and Atomic Absorption Spectroscopy (AAS) allow the identification of stone mineralogies together with pollution-induced components of crusts (3, 5). Salts are an important part of a crust, particularly gypsum (calcium sulphate), but others, such as sodium chloride, are present in groundwater, in precipitation in coastal environments or can be leached from certain mortars. Such salts in building stone can aid weathering despite their transient nature.

Although airborne particulates may adhere to an inert surface (such as sandstone) there can still be salts formed which help bond these particulates together and to the substrate. Figure 2 shows micrographs of some of these components. Some fly ash itself contains gypsum or other non-combusted material (6) which can be dissolved and redeposited to give gypsum through the action of atmospheric sulphur oxides. Indeed, the high specific surface of such particulates and their possible catalytic action in the oxidation of SO_2 to SO_3

Figure 2

a. Electron micrograph of a crust on Scrabo Sandstone with (porous) fly ash spheres of various sizes and small solid sphere (arrowed). The well-formed crystals are parts of the sandstone (All Souls Church, Belfast).

b. Electron micrograph of fly ash spheres and irregular organic fragments. The cubic crystal is sodium chloride, not unexpected in a very maritime location in a dockland industrial area. (Sinclair Seamen's Church, Belfast).

c. Electron micrograph showing an open-work system of gypsum laths (All Souls Church, Belfast).

d. Back-scattered electron image of a polished cross section of a crust. The dark area is resin-impregnated pore spaces, the light area is gypsum, itself with small pores (Gloucester Cathedral).

enhance reactions at the crust substrate interface (7). A further source of salts (in both sandstone and limestone buildings) is from mortar dissolved by 'acid rain'. This is particularly important in sandstones as they are (generally) more porous than limestones and can thus absorb the solution containing salts near the surface. Migrating water fronts through a crust to near surface substrate can also provide salt deposition.

MATERIAL DAMAGE POTENTIAL

Acid deposition, in its various manifestations, is generally considered as a potent means of building weathering (8). Black crusts present a further, and long term, problem which induces a 'memory' in the decay process as crusts grow in response to the effects of both past and present pollution attack. They are also often directly associated with weathering processes, particularly salt crystallisation, which cause volume expansion behind the crust (visible as blistering), disaggregation of the stone matrix and ultimately lead to crust and substrate detachment (Figure 3a). Both these effects are as likely with sandstone as with limestone buildings. Material loss is therefore severe, often catastrophic, and newly exposed stone offers less resistance to further weathering or crust re-development in an atmosphere where pollution levels are not reduced (Figure 3b).

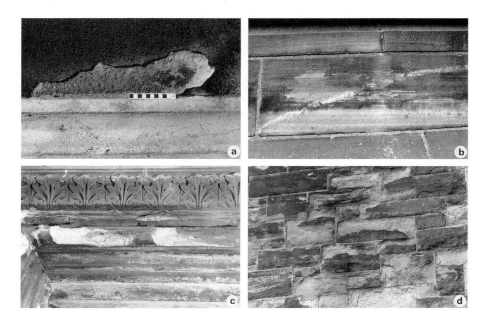

Figure 3 Damage, sandstone and limestone.
a. Crust redevelopment on top of a surface which has already scaled off (Oolitic limestone, St Matthais Church, Budapest, Hungary).
b. Thin scaling on ashlar with dirt adhering to the revealed surface (Sandstone, Liverpool Cathedral).
c. Blistering and scaling on heavily encrusted mouldings (Istrian limestone, Venice).
d. A complex crusting with variable stone quality showing scaling and flaking of stone with differential black crust development. (Scrabo sandstone, St Mathews Church, Belfast).

Surface granular disintegration, flaking and scaling are often evident in association with crusts and exemplify the necessity to examine crust related decay within the broader decay 'context' on any building. It should also be noted that bio-degradation processes occur together with physico-chemical mechanisms, with the result that organic material can and does become incorporated into crusts. Previous work does not always clarify whether there is likely to be damage as a consequence of crust formation, whether crusts act as barriers to stone decay or whether they are neutral. Under some circumstances it may be that all of these are possible in the life cycle of a crust.

Where flaking of black crusts is seen it does not necessarily indicate that the crust itself is the cause. Rather, some other mechanism, for example salt crystallisation a little below the surface of the substrate, may be responding to salt migration and crystallisation from another source (mortar for example). Conversely, the presence of a crust may hide disintegration (especially scaling) the extent of which is not revealed until the crust itself falls off or is removed by cleaning.

To the above discussion, there is a further question regarding the role of crusts in the cleaning of buildings. Here it must be said that once a thick crust forms it may ultimately accentuate decay. Given that the bonding of crusts to substrate is often strong, removing the crust may directly affect the substrate. A further problem concerns salt migration by washing such material into the pore spaces during the washing process. Just as occasional heavy rain may drive salts from a crust into the pore spaces of a stone, so too may this be the case with washing. The stone porosity and permeability may be important here (i.e. it is more significant for sandstones than limestones) but, as yet, we have no data on this. However, we do know that salts crystallizing in the outer few millimetres of a sandstone can produce scaling and blistering. If this material is then subjected to even a single freeze-thaw event, catastrophic scaling may take place overnight. It is notable that with the heavy crusting seen on some Venetian statues, a dry method of cleaning is preferred (9) although for low porosity, durable limestones a water drip method is suitable.

CONCLUSIONS

Black crusts represent the most extreme form of soiling evident on natural stone buildings today. They not only affect the aesthetic value of a building, but may hide on-going decay, the extent of which is not fully apparent until material loss occurs. By then, damage has often progressed beyond that amenable to routine cleaning or conservation. From that point of view, crust removal may be imperative. However, crust removal itself may induce damage potential which may not be evident for some time after cleaning has taken place.

Acknowledgements

This work has been done on Department of the Environment Contract (PECD7/12/08). We would also like to thank the various authorities for access to buildings used in this work and the assistance of the Electron Microscope

Laboratory QUB.

References

1.   Brimblecombe, P. (1987) 'The Big Smoke, a history of air pollution in London since Medieval times.' (Methuen, London).
2.   Cammuffo, D. del Monte, M. and Sabbioni, C. (1983) 'Origin and growth mechanism of the sulphated crusts on urban limestone'. Water Air and Soil Pollution, 19: 351-359.
3.   Amoroso, G.G. and Fassina, V. (1983) 'Stone decay and conservation'. (Elsevier: Amsterdam).
4.   Smith, B.J., Whalley , W.B. and Magee, R.W. (in press a) Stone decay in a 'clean' environment: western Northern Ireland. In 'Proceedings of a Conference on Science and Technology and the European Cultural Heritage'. Bologna.
5.   Smith, B.J., Whalley, W.B. and Magee, R.W. (in press b) Background and local contributions to acidic deposition and their relative impact on building stone decay: A case study of Northern Ireland. In J.W.S. Longhurst (ed) 'Acid deposition: sources effects and controls'. (Elsevier: Amsterdam).
6.   Fisher, G.L., Prentice, B.A., Silberman, D., Ondov, M. Biermann, A.H. Ragaini, R.C. and McFarland, A. (1978) Physical morphological studies of size-classified coal fly ash. Environmental Science and Technology, 12: 447-4512.
7.   Cheng, R.J. Hwu, J.R. Kim, J.T. and Leu, S,M. (1987) Deterioration of marble structures, Analytical Chemistry, 59: 104A-106A.
8.   Building Effects Review Group (BERG) (1989) 'The effects of acid deposition on buildings and building materials in the United Kingdom'. (HMSO: London).
9.   Fassina, V., Armani, E. and Costa, F. (1986) The deterioration of Istrian stone in Ca'Pesaro and the technique of conservation used. In 'Materials Science and Conservation' F.H. Wittmann, ed 445-468. 2nd International Colloquium, (Technisches Akademie Esslingen: Esslingen).

23 The impact of stone cleaning on micro-organisms and microbially influenced corrosion

MARKUS WILIMZIG, WOLFGANG SAND and EVERHARD BOCK
University of Hamburg, Institut für Allgemeine Botanik,
Abteilung Mikrobiologie, Hamburg Germany

BIODETERIORATION BY NITRIFYING BACTERIA

In the last six years about 25 buildings in Germany have been analyzed for contamination by nitrifying bacteria. Two groups of specialised bacteria are responsible for nitrification, which is the two-stage oxidation of ammonia to nitrate. The first reaction, carried out by ammonia oxidizers, is the oxidation of ammonia to nitrite. The second reaction, carried out by nitrite oxidizers, is the oxidation of nitrite to nitrate. Both steps produce salts and/or mineral acids (NO_2/NO_3/HNO_2/HNO_3).

Sandstone with calcareous binding material is the most endangered natural stone with respect to attack by nitrifyers. Both salt stress and acid attack results in stone damage. Nitric acid changes water insoluble calcium carbonate ($CaCO_3$) into water soluble calcium nitrate ($CaNO_3$) which is washed out by rainfall, raising up water (capillary water).

Bacteria are often found to live in micro-colonies in natural stone, which are surrounded by a bio-film consisting of extra-cellular polysaccharides. Thus the bacteria are protected against dryness and/or toxic agents.

ANALYSIS OF CLEANED BUILDING STONES

Analysis of drill cores from the dome of Cologne showed that bacteria are not only living near the surface but also in depths to 30cm. This type of growth is called endolithic.

Mechanical cleaning procedures are usually applied to the surface of the stone, water or particles removing only a thin layer so as not to destroy the surface structure. However, endolithic bacteria are not removed by this means, because they live deep in the stone.

Cleaning fluids like acids or bases have been shown to penetrate into the stone. This may lead to a decreasing concentration gradient of fluid in the depth. Bacteria protected by a bio-film are not harmed by low concentrations of toxic components. Accordingly, toxic fluids will never kill the whole bacterial population.

Typical cleaning procedures involve consolidation, cleaning, and hydrophic treatment. Most agents have little impact on micro-organisms, but may be substrates for them. Buildings treated 20 years ago with these agents show that the surface split off in large areas corresponding to the penetration depth of the agents. Often damage is more severe with treated than with untreated stones.

Analysis of the Leinefassade of the Leineschloß in Hanover before and one year after mechanical, chemical, dry, wet, and heat treatment showed reduced concentrations of ammonia and nitrate, whereas cell numbers of nitrifying, and heterotrophic bacteria, and fungi, remained unchanged.

Similar results were obtained at the gatehall in Lorsch. The mortar in the gatehall was treated with silicic acid or tylosis. Again, differences in cell numbers of nitrifyers before and after treatment were not detectable.

LABORATORY EXPERIMENTS

Laboratory experiments with ground stone showed that 15ppm of isothiazolinone (used for the sterilization of industrial equipment) reduced the cell number of endolythic bacteria from 10^7 cells/g to 10^2 cells/g after one week of treatment. Fungi were reduced from 10^6 cells/g to 10^5 cells/g. The experiments were done under optimal conditions. Building stones are not ground and therefore have little surface area for the application of treatment agents. Thus toxic agents never penetrate a stone totally as is the case with ground stone. The results indicate that endolithic micro-organisms will probably not be killed by toxic agents applied to the surface.

CONCLUSIONS

Before any treatment of building stones is carried out, a microbiological analysis of the stone microflora must be undertaken to evaluate the methods to be used.

24 Microbial interactions with building stones, with special reference to various cleaning conservation and restoration techniques

WOLFGANG KRUMBEIN, JOANNA BRAAMS,
GABI GROTE, MONIKA GROSS, KARIN PETERSEN,
VOLKER SCHOSTAK and THOMAS WARSCHEID
Institut für Chemie und Biologie des Meeres, Universität
Oldenburg, Germany

(ABSTRACT)

In the past years more than 50 architectural objects including buildings, sculptures and mural paintings made of sandstones, limestones and marbles as well as mortar surfaces and mural paintings have been microbiologically analyzed in our laboratory. They included very different types of buildings, problems and climatic regimes.

The monuments have been treated by various methods frequently used by conservators and restorators. The interactions of the following techniques with the natural rock, its indigenous microflora and the changes of the microflora brought about by the treatments have been analyzed: cleaning with water, cleaning by sand-blasting and other techniques, consolidation with silicones, by polyacrylic impregnation under vacuum, hydrophobisations, treatment with newly developed polyurethanes, and anti-graffiti substances.

Special cases included the study of the use of organic solvents and casein from skimmed milk in mural paintings and treatment of the Akropolis marbles with lime water. The changes in the microflora brought about by the treatment techniques, the potential of new damages and of protection as well as the aspects of durability and reversibility of the techniques are discussed.

Our work showed that several of the techniques that have been used in restoration and conservation are of little or no effect, while others had a long-lasting effect which in some cases was very detrimental to the whole architectural surface or the mural painting. A simple procedure such as cleaning with water may largely change the microbial community living on and within the rock and even enlarge the danger of microbial degradation in case the treatment is not done properly. Hydrophobisations may be largely diminished by activities of micro-organisms that grew even better in their presence than in the absence of such substances. Unaesthetic biofilms and biogenic surface deposits may develop as an outcome of hydrophobisation in some cases. The same has been documented for treatments with anti-graffiti substances. Biocides that are very efficient in sandstone treatment may turn out to be completely useless for eliminating a microflora on marble and vice versa.

A conclusion of our work is that microbiological analyses are advised prior to any treatment selected and also preliminary tests have to be made with the materials in question in contact with the original surface (material) and with micro-organisms living normally in the environment of the building material. Microbiological investigations of untreated and treated surfaces as well as the compatability of original material, micro-organisms and materials used for the treatment of the historical material are urgently advised.

25 Microbiological damage to building stone: analysis and intervention

ROBERT PALMER Jr
Institut für Allgemeine Mikrobiologie, Universität Kiel,
Germany

INTRODUCTION

The geological significance of microbial metabolism cannot be debated. Microorganisms play a crucial role in pedogenesis, mineral transformation, and global cycling of elements (ref.1 for review).

The purpose of the present contribution is to briefly summarize microbial community structure and its analysis with respect to weathering of building stone.

Three specific examples will be discussed in detail.

Micro-organisms and microbial community structure

For the purposes of this article, the term microorganism comprises prokaryotic organisms (eubacteria, archaebacteria, as well as cyanobacteria or blue-green algae), all fungi, and the microscopic eukaryotic algae. Lichens (symbiotic relationships between fungi and algae) play a role in stone weathering but will not be discussed here. The reader is referred to Brock and Madigan (2) for a general introduction to microorganisms, and to Syers and Iskandar (3), for a review of lichen pedogenetic activities.

Microorganisms in nature rarely exist in isolation as single species, but rather in interdependence with other micro- and macroorganisms. Several species of microbes form a community which is organized as a nutritional web conceptually similar to that of macrobiological communities. Producers (e.g. eukalyptus trees and algae) use either sunlight or inorganic chemical energy to generate cell material (biomass) from inorganic carbon. Consumers (e.g. koala bears and fungi) break down this biomass as a source of energy and of organic compounds necessary for growth. The community is characterized by energy fluxes with initial energy input normally at the level of the producer. Phototrophic organisms (cyanobacteria and algae) absorb sunlight and chemolithotrophic organisms (nitrifying bacteria, sulphur-oxidizing bacteria) break inorganic chemical bonds; the resulting energy is stored in biomolecules such as ATP and NADH. These molecules, in turn, are used to drive interconversion of other (mainly carbohydrate) compounds necessary for cell growth and maintainance. Consumers (heterotrophic organisms: fungi and 'typical' bacteria) use carbohydrates excreted by producers or they break down producer biomass. In either case, their growth is dependent on a source of preformed, assimilable carbon compounds.

All microbes require an energy source for growth. As described in the previous paragraph, sunlight, inorganic chemical energy, or 'digestable' carbon compounds fufill this requirement. A carbon source is also necessary because carbon is the basic building block of biological material. For autotrophic organisms, CO_2 is the usual carbon source. For heterotrophic organisms, the carbon source is usually the same carbon compound which serves as the energy source; the compound is broken down to release energy, and the resulting smaller molecules are put back together to form other biochemicals. Besides carbon, several other elements are required in relatively large amounts. Nitrogen is obtained from the breakdown of protein and from nitrate. Some microorganisms can incorporate otherwise biologically unavailable N_2 directly. Sulphur is usually obtained from sulphate, and phosphorus from phosphate; for most microbial communities, these elements are normally in abundant supply. Finally, and most importantly, all microbes require a source of water. Bacteria appear to require liquid water and are generally quite sensitive to water stress (4), whereas some fungi (5) and certain algae (6) do not require liquid water and can metabolize at low relative humidity. It should be noted that extreme dryness is rarely encountered in natural systems, that rock matrices seem to increase water availability for enclosed microbes (4), and that many microbes have water-retaining extracellular sheaths which allow them to survive and metabolize during drought.

Types of microbiological damage to building stone

Microorganisms can be responsible for the complete spectrum of building stone deterioration: from relatively benign aesthetic damage to severe disintegration of the substrate resulting in collapse of the structure. The most obvious but least destructive injury is the well known formation of dense green, blue-green, or black carpets of cyanobacteria and algae on building surfaces (e.g. ref. 7). Non-photosynthetic pigmented bacteria, if present in abundance, can also create aesthetic problems. Fungi can produce black/brown reproductive structures which appear as small dark dots, and some fungi have pigmented filaments that, in high concentrations, can be seen with the unaided eye. In addition, many microbes can oxidize manganese and iron, thereby producing a black coating often associated with weathered stone.

More serious is disintegration of the stone proper. Certain autotrophic bacteria, e.g.,*Thiobacillus* spp. and *Nitrosomonas* spp., can excrete large amounts of acid during oxidation of, respectively, sulphur and nitrogen compounds. In the case of sulphur-oxidizing bacteria, acid production can be so high that concrete is degraded to the point of collapse (8). The weathering potential of such sulphur-based microbial communities has been well-characterized in the laboratory (9). Fortunately, these populations are only encountered under rather stringent conditions of pH, oxidation-reduction potential and sulphur sources (9,10). More frequently encountered is an association of nitrifying bacteria responsible for formation of nitrate salts in many types of building stone (11,10). To date, only indirect quantification of nitrifying bacteria and their weathering potential has been published. In contrast to the two previous communities, heterotrophic bacteria and fungi are ubiquitous inhabitants of all building stone types and their presence can be quantified. Many of these organisms excrete organic acids which can chelate metal ions as well as reduce pH. The relative importance of decrease in pH versus ionic chelation is debatable (cf.12,13,14), as is the rate of acid production under natural conditions, but it is certain that excretion of organic acids can occur independent of a large pH decrease (12) and that chelation-dependent metal ion solubility occurs at neutral pH (15,16).

Many microorganisms, especially algae and cyanobacteria, resist drought through production of water-retaining sheaths. This material expands and contracts in response to cycles of wetting and drying. The force generated by this swelling and shrinking has not been quantified, but under certain circumstances it appears to lead to physical deterioration of the stone, similar to crystallization of ice or salts (17). Indeed, because the sheath material acts as a water reservoir, the amount of water present for ice formation is undoubtably greater in colonized than in uncolonized stone.

ANALYSIS AND INTERVENTION

The importance of microbial weathering processes on a specific building can be assessed only by a complete description of the microbial community and proof that this community is mechanistically responsible for deterioration. Classical isolation techniques should be used to determine which microorganisms are present. The organisms should be physiologically characterized under culture conditions that reflect nutrient levels in the stone itself. Quantitative data on numbers of organisms and on their activity is especially important. Biomass can be quantified by counting cell numbers indirectly (dilution-plate counts; e.g. re. 12). This technique has the major problem of medium selectivity (18).

Organisms can be washed off and counted directly after staining, or stained cells can be counted in thin sections (19). These techniques suffer from the problems that organisms are often difficult to remove from stone particles and that staining techniques do not distinguish between living and dead organisms.

Quantitative methods based on biochemical analysis have been developed in the past decade. All active organisms have a membrane consisting of phospholipid. This material is rapidly degraded in nature, thus the amount of phospholipid is a sensitive (nanomolar) indicator of living biomass (20). Fatty acids (molecular components of phospholipids) can be quantified by gas chromatogaphic methods thus providing a 1000-fold increase in sensitivity. Furthermore, many microorganisms have unique fatty acids, so-called biomarkers (21), which can be used to calculate cell numbers (22), or to estimate the ratio of fungi to bacteria (23).

It is important to note that, for any organism, cell number is not a measure of in situ activity. To date, no satisfactory technique exists by which microbial activity can be quantified directly in stone environments. Many indirect measurements have been reported: for example, excretion of amino acids (24), excretion of organic acids (12), uptake of carbon dioxide (4), and nitrifying potential (11). Meaningful calculations of microbial weathering rates must await development of direct in situ activity measurements such as those for aquatic systems.

Abiological weathering occurs on all building stones; biological activity increases the rate of specific weathering processes. Therefore, the weathering mechanisms must be analyzed and understood. The geochemistry and physics of the stone must be understood; mineral composition and strength of weathered and unweathered stone should be compared. The pH of the stone should be determined, and sources of organic compounds (deposition, runoff) should be quantified. These analyses show how the stone is degraded and if microbial influences on deterioration exist. Should it be established that microbes contribute to the weathering, a strategy for intervention can be laid out.

Aesthetic damage is usually combated through a combination of physical and chemical cleaning. These techniques generally are temporary solutions; regrowth of the community normally occurs. The cleaning must then be repeated. Over time, this process can often impair the stone that it should be protecting. Little work performed on inclusion of agents to prevent regrowth (e.g. antibiotics). In addition, it is difficult to attack a broad spectrum of organisms with a single agent, therefore this strategy could only succeed when dealing with a specific microbial population of low diversity.

Physical damage to the stone is even more difficult to combat. In addition to cleaning, the stone matrix must be stabilized. Typical consolidation agents (e.g. polyurethane) can be metabolized by microbes (25), thus leading to regrowth or establishment of a new community. In end effect, it is desired that the rate of weathering be significantly decreased; although cleaning and consolidation are far from perfect solutions, they usually achieve a temporary decrease in degradation. Regrowth of the microbial population and the extent to which treatments must be repeated are the deciding factors in the overall weathering rate.

ANALYSIS OF MICROBIAL COMMUNITIES ON BUILDINGS IN NORTHERN GERMANY

In a study of microbial degradation of a sandstone courthouse, it was shown that phospholipid concentration was low compared to that of other microbial communities, that microorganisms isolated from weathered areas could produce organic acids at low nutrient levels, that the organic acids produced in culture could also be found in the weathered stone in amounts correlated to biomass, and that pH of neither the cultures nor the stone itself was especially low. Also notable was a lack of producers in the community; carbon was most likely obtained from runoff and deposition. For details of experimental conditions and results, see Palmer et al. (12). Concentrations of the chelating organic acid citrate reached 10 nanomoles/gram in the weathered stone. This translates to a concentration of 0.2 millimolar in water-saturated, unweathered stone: a concentration roughly 10-fold lower than that used in geochemical dissolution experiments to date (e.g. 15). In contrast, total organic acid concentration was roughly 1 millimole/gram, or 25 molar in saturated stone! Intervention should include reduction of carbon input through runoff and deposition. Because this community had no producers, microbial activity would thus be reduced and consolidation of the weathered stone could be undertaken.

A much different community occurred on the granite foundation of a rural church. Here, much algal and cyanobacterial biomass was present, therefore carbon input was not a limiting factor for associated bacteria and fungi. Phospholipid concentration was twice as high as that for the courthouse, and was at the lower end of the range reported for soils. The presence of producers supported a high number of fungi and bacteria: 100- to 10,000-fold higher numbers than on the courthouse. For details, see Palmer and Hirsch (17). A similar situation, but with different producer organisms, was found under glazed surfaces of bricks on another church. Primarily cyanobacterial biomass supported high numbers of bacteria and fungi. The cyanobacteria produced a thick slime capsule which was partly responsible for exfoliation of the glaze. Details of this study are also found in Palmer and Hirsch (in press). On both of the churches, the type of stone (granite or glazed brick) and the nature of the microbial community (high numbers of algae or cyanobacteria) contributed to a unique weathering situation in which photosynthetic organisms were directly involved. This presents the opportunity to treat the stone with photosynthesis-blocking agents, the simplest of which is copper. Indeed, copper window sills are present on second church and exfoliation of the glaze is minimal underneath the sills.

PERSPECTIVES ON FUTURE RESEARCH

'...essential [is] a full understanding of mechanisms of deterioration ... not only for laboratory specimens but also for full structures.'
'The mechanism of damage itself is highly complex with many facets: mechanical, chemical, biological.'

These quotations (reproduced from Cooper, ref.26) should be kept in mind during evaluation of weathering investigations and stone cleaning strategies. Much work on the microbiology of weathered stone has been anecdotal and is therefore ridiculed (and rightly so!) by microbiologists. In addition, the work usually sheds little light on weathering mechanisms and is therefore of little practical use for geologists, engineers, or conservators. It is hoped that a more complete understanding of microbial weathering processes can be achieved by bridging the gaps between these fields through interdisciplinary studies. Without a full understanding of the clearly quite complex weathering mechanisms, it is unlikely that treatment or prophylactic measures will succeed.

References

1. Ehrlich,H.L.(1990). 'Geomicrobiology', 2nd edn. (Marcel Dekker: New York).
2. Brock,T.D. and Madigan,M.T.(1991). 'Biology of Microorganisms', 6th edn. (Prentice-Hall, Inc.: Englewood Cliffs).
3. Syers,J.K. and Iskandar,I.K.(1973). Pedogenetic significance of lichens. In 'The Lichens',p.225-248,eds.V.Ahmadjian and M.E.Hale. (Academic Press: New York).
4. Palmer,R.J.Jr. and Friedmann,E.I.(1990a). Water relations and photosynthesis in the cryptoendolithic microbial habitat of hot and cold deserts. Microbial Ecology.19:111-118.
5. Ayerst,G.(1986). Water and the ecology of fungi in stored products. In 'Water, Fungi and Plants', p.359-373, eds.P.G.Ayres and L.Boddy. (Cambridge University Press: Cambridge).
6. Palmer,R.J.Jr. and Friedmann,E.I.(1990b). Water relations, thallus structure and photosynthesis in Negev Desert lichens. New Phytologist.116:597-603.
7. Albertano,P.,Forni,C. and Caiola,M.G.(1987). Characterization of the algal flora growing on ancient roman frescoes. Phycologia.26:387-396.
8. Milde,K.,Sand,W.,Wolff,W. and Bock,E.(1983). Thiobacilli of the corroded concrete walls of the Hamburg sewer system. Journal of General Microbiology.129:1327-1333.
9. Sand,W.(1987). Importance of hydrogen sulfide, thiosulphate, and methylmercaptan for growth of thiobacilli during simulation of concrete corrosion. Applied and Environmental Microbiology.53:1645-1648.
10. Sand,W. and Bock,E.(1991). Biodeterioration of ceramic materials by biogenic acids. International Biodeterioration.27:175-183.
11. Wolters,B.,Sand,W.,Ahlers,B.,Sameluck,F.,Meincke,M., Meyer,C.,Krause-Kupsch,T. and Bock,E.(1988). In 'Proceedings of the 6th International Congress on Deterioration and Conservation of Stone',p.24-31. (Nicholas Copernicus University Press: Torun).
12. Palmer,R.J.Jr.,Siebert,J. and Hirsch,P.(1991). Biomass and organic acids in sandstone of a weathering building: production by bacterial and fungal isolates. Microbial Ecology.21:253-266.
13. Eckhardt,F.E.W.(1979). Über die Einwirkung heterotropher

Mikroorganismen auf die Zersetzung silikatischer Minerale. Zeitschriftfür Pflanzenernährung und Bodenkunde.**142:**434-445.

14.Kuroczkin,J.,Bode,K.,Petersen,K.and Krumbein,W.E. (1988). Some physiological characteristics of fungi isolated from sandstones. In 'Proceedings of the 6th International Congress on Deterioration and Conservation of Stone', suppliment, p.21-25. (Nicholas Copernicus University Press: Torun).

15.Bennett,P.C.,Melcer, M.E.,Siegel,D.I. and Hassett,J.P. (1988). The dissolution of quartz in dilute aqueous solutions of organic acids at 25°C. Geochimica Cosmochimica Acta.**52:**1521-1530.

16.Schenk,D.,Petersen,A. and Matthess,G.(1989). Acceleration and retardation of silicate weathering due to organic substances. In 'Water-rock interaction', p.605-607,ed.D.Miles. (A.A.Balkema: Rotterdam and Brookfield).

17.Palmer,R.J.Jr. and Hirsch,P.(in press). Photosynthesis-based microbial communities on two churches in northern Germany: weathering of granite and glazed brick. Geomicrobiology Journal.

18.Eckhardt,F.E.W.(1988). Influence of culture media employed in studying microbial weathering of building stone and monuments by heterotrophic bacteria and fungi. In 'Proceedings of the 6th International Congress on Deterioration and Conservation of Stone', suppliment, p.71-81. (Nicholas Copernicus University Press: Torun).

19.Greenfield,L.G.(1988). Forms of nitrogen in Beacon Sandstone rocks containing endolithic microbial communities in southern Victoria Land, Antarctica. Polarforschung.**58:**211-218.

20.White,D.C.,Davis,W.M.,Nickels,J.S.,King,J.D. and Bobbie,R.J.(1979). Determination of the sedimentary microbial biomass by extractable lipid phosphate. Oecologia.**40:**51-62.

21.Vestal,J.R., and White,D.C.(1989). Lipid analysis in microbial ecology. BioScience **39:**535-541.

22.Mancuso,C.A.,Franzmann,P.D.,Burton,H.R. and Nichols,P.D.(1990). Microbial community structure and biomass estimates of a methanogenic Antarctic lake ecosystem as determined by phospholipid analysis. Microbial Ecology.**19:**73-95.

23.White,D.C.,Bobbie,R.J.,Nickels,J.S.,Fazio,S.D. and Davies,W.M.(1980). Nonselective biochemical methods for the determination of fungal mass and community structure in estuarine detrital microflora. Botanica Marina.**23:**239-250.

24.Siebert,J.,Palmer,R.J.Jr. and Hirsch,P.(1991). Analysis of free amino acids in microbially colonized sandstone by precolumn phenyl isothiocyanate derivatization and high-performance liquid chromatography. Applied and Environmental Microbiology.**57:**879-881.

25.Kay,M.J.,Morton,L.H.G. and Prince,E.L.(1991). Bacterial degradation of polyester polyurethane. International Biodegradation.**27:**205-222.

26.Cooper,T.P.(1989). The effects of air pollution on historic buildings and monuments. Publication EUR 11626. (Commission of the European Communities: Brussels)

Session VI
STONE DECAY, WEATHERING AND FUTURE PROSPECTS

26 Assessment of building stone decay: a geomorphological approach

BERNARD SMITH, BRIAN WHALLEY and RALPH MAGEE
School of Geosciences, The Queen's University of Belfast

INTRODUCTION AND BACKGROUND

Building stone decay has become the concern of numerous disciplines, ranging from the practical conservator to architects and materials scientists. Each discipline has brought with it its own approaches and terminologies based upon individual priorities and professional training. Pragmatism has dictated that these priorities have centred upon conservation strategies and selection of durable replacement materials, frequently with limited concern for the causes of decay. Geomorphologists, on the other hand, have traditional interests in the natural processes responsible for weathering and erosion of rock. This expertise has been applied to urban stone decay in the belief that decay cannot be successfully treated unless its origins are thoroughly understood and that there are many similarities between natural rock faces and buildings.

In recent years the geomorphological study of weathering processes has resolved itself into increasingly detailed evaluations of the responsible mechanisms (e.g. salt crystallisation and solution) – often involving laboratory simulations. This is combined with a concern for the morphology of the features produced and a realisation that weathering represents complex interactions between form, process and materials. These interactions change as weathering progresses and relationships are frequently complicated by the combined or sequential operation of several weathering mechanisms. Salt weathering, for example, may involve crystallisation, hydration and/or thermal expansion depending upon environmental conditions, salt concentration and mixture and any changes in rock properties induced by earlier weathering.

Through these studies of natural weathering phenomena, several factors have been identified that must influence how one investigates and interprets building stone decay:

1. Weathering features are invariably polygenetic – the result of more than one process;
2. Weathering processes fall approximately into two categories: high frequency/low magnitude events, (e.g. surface dissolution), and low frequency/high magnitude events (e.g. the breaking away of a large surface scale);
3. Weathering is not continuous but is episodic and characterised by periods of relative quiescence interspersed with episodes of rapid change. At one level this may reflect the intermittent occurrence of suitable environmental conditions (e.g. rainfall). At another level, episodic change may represent the crossing of strength/stress thresholds – see below;
4. Physical weathering, in particular, depends upon the balance between the strength of the stone and the magnitude of the stresses to which it is subjected. If stress exceeds strength, weathering will occur. This stress/strength threshold can be breached in a number of ways. Over a long period of time there may be a progressive reduction in strength due to, say, chemical alteration or the cumulative effects of repeated low magnitude stresses (fatigue failure). Alternatively, the stresses to which rocks are subjected may be increased until they exceed rock strength.
   These stresses are a combination of relatively constant stresses (e.g. vertical loading), cumulative stresses (e.g. the build-up of salt within the pores) and periodic and cyclic stressing related to environmental fluctuations (e.g. diurnal and seasonal moisture and temperature changes and occasional high magnitude events such as a severe frost). These relationships are illustrated in Figure 1A, which depicts the conditions under which failure of a stone or stone surface might occur. A consequence of these complex interactions is that decay often proceeds in a 'stepwise' fashion, with significant implications for how rates of decay are assessed (Figure 1B). Measurements of surface loss during periods of relative inactivity could, for example, lead to underestimates of long-term decay rates, whereas observations made during episodes of rapid change might underestimate the long-term durability of a building stone. Similarly, the superficial identification of processes causing decay may be influenced by the stage that stonework has reached in the decay sequence. In particular, care must be taken in interpreting the significance of early surface loss if ultimately the stonework is going to collapse through progressive scaling and flaking.

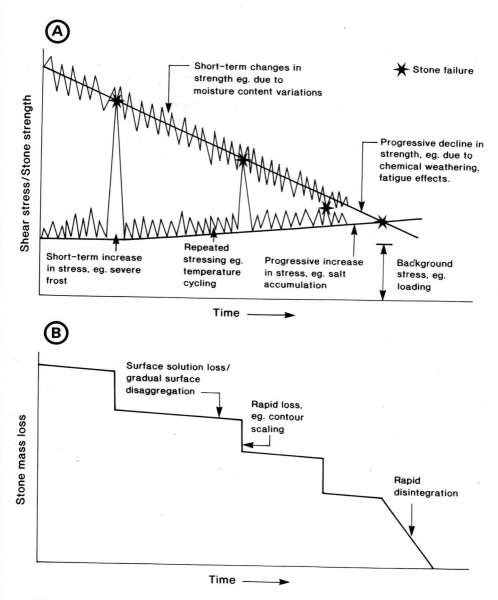

Figure 1. **A.** Rock strength/stress relationships during weathering and conditions when weathering thresholds are breached (adapted from an idea in Finlayson and Statham(1980)). **B.** Mass loss from stonework during weathering.

Such collapse can be extremely rapid and it is not unknown for pre-stressed blocks of stone, which show little outward sign of damage, to be reduced - sometimes literally overnight - to a pile of angular debris if subjected to a severe frost.

5. As well as being concentrated temporally, weathering is invariably concentrated spatially. There are many factors which influence susceptibility to weathering; some are 'internal', related to sometimes very subtle variations in rock properties, others may be related to 'external' controls such as slight differences in microclimate. It is unrealistic, therefore, to expect all areas of a rock face – or building – to be subject to the same weathering processes, or any large surface exposed to the same processes to react in a similar, predictable fashion.

In view of the above observations it is clear that prediction of long-term stone behaviour, especially on the basis of short-term observations, is fraught with difficulties. Geomorphologists have had to learn caution, both when attempting such predictions and when ascribing patterns of decay to a specific process. Nonetheless, the difficulties of measuring process have necessitated that they become adept at inferring process from a combination of environmental conditions, materials (including weathering products) and morphology. It is this skill, together with its associated terminology and interpretations, that comprises the principal contribution that geomorphologists can make to the study of building stone decay. Because of the complexity of weathering mechanisms over space and time it has been found useful to provide a semi-quantitative approach for recording observations. What follows therefore is an outline of how a geomorphological approach can be incorporated into the visual assessment of stone decay.

CHECKLIST FOR THE VISUAL ASSESSMENT OF STONE DECAY

The checklists given in Figures 2 and 3 have been developed over several years during the course of a number of investigations into different aspects of stone decay. These have ranged from specific studies of black crusts and solutional phenomena to general surveys of physical weathering. During these projects it became apparent, on the basis of the processes operating and their products, that there are a number of broad process categories into which weathering features fall. These are: Mechanical Breakdown; Solution; Surface Alteration and/or Deposition, Biological Action and Human Damage/Change. Within each of these there are ranges of individual features, each with their own implications for the weathering mechanisms which operate and also appropriate remedial action. The features are listed in Figure 2, which has blank spaces for new and/or local features to be inserted.

To refine the interpretation of these features, each can be related to other factors or aspects of the building that can influence weathering. These are seen along the horizontal axis of Figure 2 and range from obvious controls such as stone type to subjective assessments of frequency and severity and linkage to

Weathering Features	Code	Stone Type	Severity (Severe, Moderate, Slight)	Frequency (Abundant, Common, Rare)	Architect-ural Features (code)	Sheltered/ Exposed	Bedding (Normal, Edge, Face)	Associated Weathering Features
Mechanical Breakdown								
Blistering	BL							
Flaking (<5mm)	FL							
Scaling (>5mm)	Sc							
Granular Disinteg.	GD							
Honeycombs	Hb							
Caverns (Tafoni)	Cv							
Cracked stones	CS							
Solution								
Surface loss	SL							
Staining	St							
Pitting	Pt							
Scalloping/Fluting	SF							
Recrystallization	X							
Alteration/ Deposition								
Efflorescence	Ef							
Cryptoflorescence	Cf							
Rock Meal	RM							
Alteration Rind	AR							
Case Hardening	CH							
Iron Staining	IS							
Black Crust	BC							
Grey Crust	GC							
Black Encrustation	BE							
Biological								
Lichen	Ln							
Epilithic Algae	EpA							
Endolithic Algae	EnA							
Vegetation	Vn							
Sp.								
Sp.								
Human Damage								
Repair	Rr							
Replacement	Rc							

Figure 2. Visual assessment forms for stone decay features

Stone Type	Architectural Features	Weathering Features	Severity (Severe, Moderate, Slight) % of each	Frequency (Abundant, Common, Rare)	Height Range (m)	

Height Range (m)	Stone Type	Weathering Features	Severity (Severe, Moderate, Slight) % of each	Frequency (Abundant, Common, Rare)	Architectural Features	

Figure 3. Visual assessment forms of stone decay related to stone type and height above the ground.

other weathering features. Of the controls on weathering, three are considered of sufficient significance to warrant special consideration. Aspect is such an important control on environmental conditions that individual forms would be for each elevation of a building. Height above ground and stone type for each aspect are also considered in separate forms (Figure 3); as an aid to identifying causes of decay and, especially, as a guide to future conservation needs.

The value of these forms lies not so much in being able to fill them in, but in the interpretations that can be made from them. These in turn are very dependent upon the experience and expertise of the observer. Space does not permit a full review of the possible interpretations for each category listed, but as an illustration some of the background considerations to mechanical breakdown are given below.

CAUSES OF MECHANICAL ROCK BREAKDOWN

Mechanical rock breakdown, as with all forms of weathering, is the response of rocks formed under conditions of high temperature and pressure to the low temperature, low pressure and chemically variable conditions at the earth's surface. As such, an obvious cause of disruption in some stones, especially granites, is the differential expansion of mineral crystals due to pressure release. This dilatation is responsible not only for the sheeting seen, and exploited, in many granite quarries, but also for microfractures which can be exploited by other weathering mechanisms once these rocks are incorporated in a building.

More typically, mechanical breakdown occurs due to expansion and contraction in response to temperature, moisture and/or relative humidity cycling. This cycling is predominantly diurnal, but seasonal variations, for example related to freeze/thaw incidence, can be significant and there is some evidence that rapid surface changes in temperature occur in response to fluctuations in cloud cover, wind speed and rain falling on heated surfaces.

There has been much debate over the efficacy of temperature cycling alone in causing rock failure, but such debates are academic considering the universal availability of moisture and the inherited stresses and flaws (e.g. through dilatation) that most building stones carry with them. Thermal and moisture cycling combined may instigate breakdown through differential thermal expansion in pores and microfractures. More commonly however, they work indirectly through causing volume changes in salts contained in the stone. These can occur through salts crystallizing out of solution, the differential thermal expansion of crystallized salts and hydration/dehydration as appropriate temperature/relative humidity thresholds are crossed. It is this wide variety of conditions that can lead to salt weathering which makes it such a potent cause of decay; compared to freeze/thaw which requires the crossing of a very specific environmental threshold ($0°C$). Expansion and disruption can also occur in response to volume changes as constituent minerals weather chemically. The best documented example of this is the conversion of biotite to clay in igneous rocks such as granite. This is particularly important where clays can migrate into and exploit any pre-existing microfractures and where they include clays such as montmorillonite and vermiculite that expand as water is absorbed. With all of these mechanisms however, a distinction must be made between those than can initiate fractures and those that are primarily responsible for exploiting pre-existing fractures, weaknesses and pore spaces.

Once armed with an appreciation of how the mechanisms operate and what controls them, it can then be possible to consider why particular weathering features occur in certain areas.

THE LOCATION OF MECHANICAL BREAKDOWN

Mechanical breakdown tends to concentrate in response to a wide variety of controls, knowledge of which clearly assists the interpretation of features found on a building. These locations include:

1. Where temperature and moisture cycling is frequent and preferably intense. For example, areas that are subject to sudden heating and/or cooling;
2. Where salts can accumulate and yet still receive moisture. Most obviously this includes sheltered areas subject to occult deposition, but is also reflected in the tendency for salt weathering to produce hollows (honeycombs and caverns) in which more salt can accumulate – a form of positive feedback;
3. Where stonework has been previously weakened. For example, by chemical alteration, beneath case-hardening or by dilatation;
4. Where stonework is inherently weak. For example, along bedding planes, aligned grained boundaries and pores or where it is susceptible to certain processes. For example, stones with a high microporosity (<5 μm) appear more prone to salt weathering;
5. Where salts are readily available. Because of their background in the study of natural weathering phenomena, geomorphologists are particularly appreciative of background rates of decay as well as the wide range of sources for damaging salts. Within the urban environment these could include: reactions between stonework and acidic deposition; particulate pollutants; sea salts and evaporites as aerosols and in solution; windblow from adjacent buildings; groundwater rise; splash from road deicing salts; leaching from mortars;
6. At certain depths within stonework related, for example, to frequent-wetting depths but also to depths at which outward-migrating salts crystallize during drying phases. Crystallization at depth is instrumental in the formation of contour scales whereas near-surface crystallization encourages granular disintegration;
7. Where weathering can proceed from convergent directions. Corners, edges and protuberances are particularly subject to accentuated temperature and moisture gradients.

Although this list is not exhaustive, it provides an indication of the factors to be considered when interpreting the information collected on the visual assessment forms. Similar considerations could also be applied to information gathered under any of the other broad categories listed in Figure 2. Hopefully, it also demonstrates the value of a 'geomorphological' approach which considers urban stone decay as a specific case within the wider spectrum of rock weathering.

ANALYSIS AND CONCLUSIONS

The visual assessment scheme that has been described does not comprise a comprehensive survey of building stone damage. It does, however, provide a framework which focuses attention upon the weathering processes responsible for decay and identifies the principal parameters that influence the operation of these processes. In itself it is not a substitute for perceptive interpretation by experienced conservators, but it rapidly provides quantifiable information and requires limited training on the part of the field surveyor. In operation it must be supported by supplementary information including, for example, maps showing the distribution of decay, photographs and sketches, assessments of environmental conditions and the sampling and analysis of weathered materials. The procedure is particularly suitable for rapid surveys of building stock where, by selection of appropriate buildings, damage can be related to age, materials and local environment. Acquisition of this information is not a solution to stone decay problems per se. It does, however, allow the extent of the problem to be assessed, and it is self evident that solutions will only be forthcoming once the nature of the decay and its causes are fully understood.

References

Space precludes the full referencing of all the points made in the text; there are available, however, a number of texts in which geomorphological approaches to rock weathering are reviewed and others in which mechanical weathering is dealt with in the context of urban stone decay. Some are given below:

Amoroso, G.G. and Fassina, V. (1983). 'Stone decay and conservation'. (Elsevier: Amsterdam).

Ashurst, J. and Dimes, F.G. (eds) (1990). 'Conservation of building and decorative stone'. (Butterworths: London).

Building Effects Review Group (BERG) (1989). 'The effects of acid deposition on buildings and building materials in the United Kingdom'. (HMSO: London).

Cooke, R.U. and Warren, A. (1973). 'Geomorphology in Deserts'. (Batsford: London).

Finlayson, B. and Statham, I. (1980). 'Hillslope Analysis' (Butterworths: London).

Goudie, A.S. (1989). In 'Arid zone geomorphology' p. 11-24, ed. D.S.G. Thomas. (Belhaven Press: London).

Ollier, C.D. (1984). 'Weathering'. (Longman: London).

Schaffer, R.J. (1972). 'The weathering of natural building stones'. (Facsimile of 1932 edition) (Building Research Establishment: Garston).

Selby, M.J. (1982). 'Hillslope materials and processes'. (Oxford University Press: Oxford).

Trudgill, S.T. (1983). 'Weathering and Erosion' (Butterworths: London).

Trudgill, S.T. (1985). 'Limestone geomorphology'. (Longman: London).

Winkler, E.M. (1975). 'Stone: Properties, Durability in Man's Environment.' (Springer: New York).

27 Decay mechanisms of oolitic limestones in an urban environment: King's College Chapel, Cambridge and St Luke's Church, London

NICK SCHIAVON
Department of Earth Sciences, Cambridge University, UK

INTRODUCTION

Limestone decay in a polluted urban environment has been investigated by several analytical techniques: Optical Microscopy (OM), X-ray Detection (XRD), Scanning Electron Microscopy (SEM), analytical chemistry etc. These studies have indicated the sulphation mechanism, i.e. the replacement of the primary calcite in the limestone by gypsum via the interaction of stone, rainwater and atmospheric pollutants, namely sulphur dioxide (SO_2) ions, as one of the main factors in limestone decay. Growth of black gypsum crusts on the stone surface in areas sheltered from rain wash-outs is well documented (1). The detailed growth mechanism of these crusts together with the contemporaneous chemical attack at the stone surface, however, has not been determined with certainty. Researchers, for example, have first advocated a main inward direction for the weathering front from the stone-crust interface (1), while later noting that in thicker gypsum crusts the distribution of aerosol particles from fossil fuel burning imbedded within the crusts seems to record an outward growth of the crusts during historic changes in main pollution sources (2). Schiavon (3) confirmed the presence of a stratigraphy in the distribution of aerosol particles in some crusts from central London (Westminster Palace) with particles from past coal burning found concentrated near the stone-crust interface and particles from 'present' oil burning common near the crust-atmosphere interface; this 'stratigraphic' distribution, however, while supportive of the outward growth theory, was by no means present in all sections examined.

This paper aims to complement OM with Back-scattered Scanning Microscopy (BSEM) to investigate in more detail the urban weathering behaviour of oolitic limestone in two British monuments: King's College Chapel, Cambridge and St Luke's Church, Chelsea, London.

PETROGRAPHICAL NOTES

The sampled building limestones from both buildings come from the Middle Jurassic Inferior Oolite Series: King's stone from Weldon, near Corby in Lincolnshire, St Luke's stone from Doulting in Somerset. They are both oolitic limestones, their most abundant constituent being oolitic grains; calcite fragments, quartz grains and fossils are also present in varying amounts. The main petrographical difference between the two limestones is the type of cement binding the particles together: in the Weldon stone the cement is mainly composed of microcrystalline calcite (oomicrite) whereas in the Doulting stone the cement is largely composed of coarser interlocking calcite crystals (oosparite). Although subjected to considerable compaction during their geological history (as suggested by extensive intergranular pressure solution) both stones are relatively porous compared to other carbonatic rocks.

OBSERVATIONS

BSEM relates differences in elemental atomic weight of the scanned material to picture brightness. Under BSEM, gypsum appears darker (lower brightness) than calcite so highlighting the depth at which sulphation has proceeded inside the stone. The modality of chemical attack appears to have been slightly different for the two rock types:

St Luke's samples

Calcite oolitic grains are actively subjected to gypsum replacement with the weathering front starting at the stone-crust interface and reaching a depth of several centimeters inside the stone. The presence of calcitic remains and the lower sulphur (S) content (as confirmed by EDAX analysis) at the centre of oolites suggests that the replacement occurs from the outer edges of the oolites towards the centre (Figure 1). Most of the times the oolitic texture is preserved

(Figure 1) suggesting also that gypsification may be a slow process not always involving previous dissolution of the calcite with an intervening void phase before gypsum precipitation. In some cases, however, the oolitic texture is destroyed although a spherical outline is still visible (Figure 2). In one example, the space previously occupied by the oolite is now filled with anthropogenic particles and mineral fragments (Figure 2). The sulphation also affects the sparitic cement but not through a replacement process: gypsum instead crystallises within fractures and cleavage planes splitting calcite crystals apart; the so detached calcite fragments are slowly inglobated into the growing crust (Figure 3).

King's samples

Most of the oolites in King's Chapel weathered stone samples, in contrast with St Luke's ones, do not show extensive gypsum replacement, although crystallisation of gypsum between oolitic layers and within fractures has been observed (Figures 4, 5). The micritic cement is, however, almost completely replaced by acicular gypsum crystals up to a depth of several centimeters underneath the present stone-crust interface (Figure 4). Widespread sulphation of the cement can also be seen in areas of the stone where exposure to episodes of rain wash-out has prevented the development of gypsum crusts. Authigenic dog-toothed calcite is also seen precipitating at the oolite edges as a fringe cement (Figure 5). This type of decay may deceitfully lead to an over-estimation of the stone soundness because of the apparent high degree of cementation. Ready dissolution of this gypsum cement, however, results in the well-known crumbling of this stone into a fine 'oolitic' powder.

In many instances the framework of authigenic gypsum crystals last precipitated near the present stone-crust interface appears to be relatively 'pure' (i.e. free of imbedded anthropogenically produced particles; Figure 6).

In both monuments, the decay leads to the build-up in areas sheltered from direct rain-wash-outs of gypsum crusts. Gypsum crusts may reach up to 1cm in thickness. Thicknesses are higher in the London samples probably in direct correlation with higher degrees of atmospheric pollution. Apart from gypsum other constituents of the crusts include anthropogenic particles, calcite, quartz and felspar particles and fossil fragments. In particular, anhedral calcite fragments are very common and evenly distributed throughout the crusts. Continuous calcitic horizons are also present. Fossil fragments can often be seen near the crust–atmosphere interface. Aerosol particles from fossil fuel burning do sometimes show a 'stratigraphic' distribution with oil-derived carbonaceous particles at the outer edges of crusts and coal-derived aluminosilicate particles near the stone surface. The bulk of the crusts appear, however, rather homogeneous.

One of the most interesting decay features typical of oolitic limestones is the presence within the crust of oolitic 'ghosts', i.e. areas now completely filled with acicular gypsum still retaining a faint spherical outline. These areas again appear free of imbedded particles and clearly represent areas formerly occupied by the stone itself. Under OM, a brown line can be seen marking the present

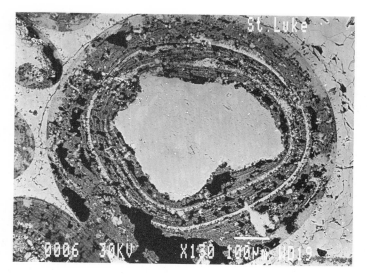

Figure 1 St Luke's Church, London. A former calcite (bright) oolite is being replaced by gypsum (darker). Some oolitic layers and the nucleus are still calcitic. Note the preservation of the oolitic texture after replacement (BSEM micrograph).

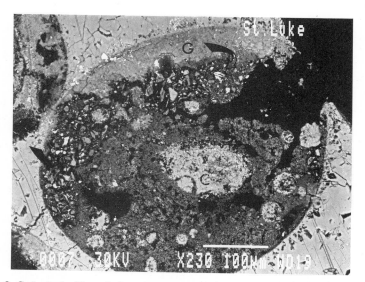

Figure 2 St Luke's Church, London. Weathered oolite with the oolitic texture almost totally destroyed (remnants of the calcitic nucleus – C – are still visible). The secondary gypsum (G) has also been partially dissolved: anthropogenic particles (arrows) and mineral fragments can now be seen inside the void (BSEM micrograph).

Figure 3 St Luke's Church. Stone-crust interface. Gypsum crystals (arrows) crystallising within cleavage planes and intercrystalline boundaries split the calcite cement into fragments (C) which are then incorporated into the crust. Anthropogenic particles from fossil-fuel burning are also visible.

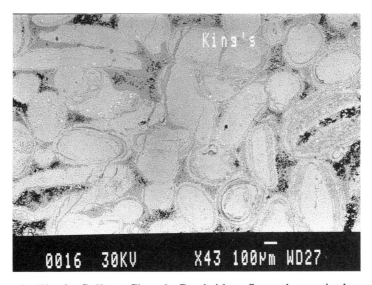

Figure 4 King's College Chapel, Cambridge. Secondary acicular gypsum crystals (brighter) precipitate within the pore spaces after dissolution of the original micritic cement. The decay leads to enhanced porosity of the stone (BSEM micrograph).

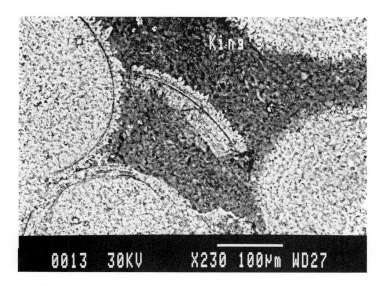

Figure 5 King's College Chapel, Cambridge. Close-up of the secondary gypsum cement, showing detachment of the oolitic cortex due to crystallisation pressure. The isopachous dog-toothed calcite occurring as a fringe cement on the oolites is also interpreted as authigenic (BSEM micrograph).

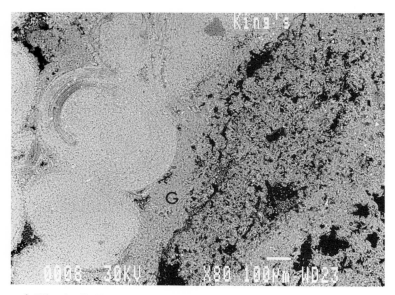

Figure 6 King's College Chapel, Cambridge. Stone-crust interface showing how the gypsum framework recently precipitated (G) does not seem to contain any aerosol particle. Note also how gypsum replacement is starting to affect also the oolites (BSEM micrograph).

stone crust interfaces; similar brown horizons are also present within the weathering crusts.

DECAY MODEL

The ubiquitous presence of authigenic gypsum at the surface and within the pore spaces of the oolitic limestones under study confirms sulphation as the main decay process. The microscopical examination suggests that the following decay mechanisms have affected the building stones:

1. Atmospheric pollutants, namely SO_2 are adsorbed on the stone surface either by dry or wet deposition (the high degree of alteration in areas sheltered from rain favours a dry deposition process);
2. Wetting of the stone causes sulphation to begin and calcite starts to be replaced by gypsum. Through cracks, cleavage and intercrystalline boundary planes, the weathering solutions start to penetrate within the stone. Extensive water circulation leading to deterioration of the stonework has also been reported in an Italian oolitic limestone (4). At this stage, differences in stone microtexture seem to lead to different decay patterns (Figure 7):
i) in the case of the oosparite the oolitic grains are preferentially replaced with respect to the cement; this could be due to the coarse nature (i.e. lower porosity) of the sparite compared to the oolitic layers. The mechanism of replacement can either follow one of two routes: a) dissolution of the calcite followed by precipitation of gypsum in the void thus created; b) slower atomic replacement through a thin film mechanism similar to the transformation from aragonite to calcite occurring in sedimentary carbonatic rocks (5).

The preservation of the oolitic layering texture in many of the oolites (Figure 1) would suggest the latter mechanism to be predominant. However, episodes of dissolution and void creation are present (Figure 2); the presence of anthropogenic particles filling the space and relics of gypsum crystals suggest that dissolution has occurred after the calcite in the ooid had already been replaced. Crystallisation pressures of gypsum within cleavage planes and intercrystalline boundaries cause the cement to split into fragments (Figure 3).

The first stage of incorporation of these fragments into the growing crust is clearly visible in many sections and suggests that most of the anhedral calcite fragments found now imbedded within the crusts are not soil dust or recrystallized calcite but remnants from the cement itself. Quartz grains found imbedded in gypsum crusts in Westminster have also been interpreted as detached stone fragments (3).

ii) In the case of the oomicrite, most of the oolitic grains are still calcitic whereas the micritic cement, despite its low porosity, is almost totally replaced by gypsum (Figure 4). The replacement process, in this case. is likely to have been predated by dissolution of the calcite cement as suggested by the presence of many intergranular microcavities in areas not yet subjected to gypsum precipitation (Figure 4). Recrystallisation of dog-toothed calcite may sometimes precede gypsum precipitation (Figure 5). The fact that most of the oolitic grains have not been replaced might probably reflect the lower degree of pollution-related sulphation in Cambridge compared to London; the dissolution/replacement of the micritic cement is probably a process occurring at a fairly early stage in the decay process; further decay would enable the replacement to occur also within the oolites as seen in the St Luke's samples. Crystallisation pressures from gypsum precipitation, although present (Figure 5), do not seem to cause serious damage.

In both examples the presence of gypsum filled oolitic 'ghosts' and brown horizons within the crusts near the stone-crust interfaces provides clear evidence that the chemically active weathering front is progressively advancing inside the calcitic stone. An inward proceeding decay is then active. Evidence for an outward growth of the weathering crusts is also present, however, in the already mentioned distribution of aerosol particles imbedded in fully formed crusts. The following decay model might explain this contradictory evidence.

In the first stages of decay the framework of gypsum crystals replacing calcite (via either or both mechanisms described earlier) does not probably contain any atmospheric particles as evidenced from recent gypsum precipitation now occurring at the crust-stone interface (Figures 6, this paper). Following the development of this first deterioration layer, aerosol particles are probably entrained on its porous outside surface (1).Their role as catalysts in the oxidation of SO_2 to sulphate (6) and their ability to enucleate gypsum crystals (7) will lead to enhanced decay and thickening of the layer. The build-up of highly corrosive solutions within the growing crust will in time lead to secondary gypsum dissolution; when this happens, some of the anthropogenic particles imbedded in the gypsum framework will be washed away, others will settle inside the stone to fill the new void (Figure 2). Recrystallisation of gypsum either on the particles themselves or by calcite replacement will follow and the cycle (gypsum precipitation-particle deposition-gypsum dissolution-void filling) is repeated several times with the weathering crusts growing in both directions, inwards and outwards with respect to the stone surface. These dissolution-collapse-recrystallisation episodes are not restricted to the stone-crust interface but occur also within the crusts (3). With this mechanism, anthropogenic particles first deposited on the outer surface of the stone could 'follow' the inward movement of the weathering front inside the stone and, theoretically, a 'stratigraphic' distribution of the particles might be preserved. Its preservation, however, will depend on the extent of the dissolution episodes and on the mobility of the particles. The occurrence of fragments clearly detached from the stone (quartz grains, fossils, fragment of the cement) near the present crust-atmosphere interface clearly testify the extent to which redistribution of particles within the weathering crust can occur. The brown lines often seen marking the stone-crust interfaces and occurring also within the crusts probably represent areas where iron oxides precipitate as insoluble residues after the dissolution episodes mentioned above.

CONCLUSIONS

1. The type of cement in oolitic limestones affects the way decay proceeds:
    i) Oosparite: main cause of decay is crystallisation pressures arising from authigenic gypsum precipitation within cracks, cleavage planes and intercrystalline boundaries of the sparitic cement. This eventually leads to the disintegration of the cement into crystal fragments which are then incorporated into the weathering crust,
    ii) Oomicrite: main cause of decay is the dissolution of secondary gypsum cement replacing the original micrite. This leads to loosening of individual oolitic grains into a fine powder.
2. Although in both cases the weathering leads to the eventual partial disintegration of the stone, the oosparite seems to provide better resistance to decay, as evidenced by the overall better state of preservation of the London samples despite the much higher degree of sulphur pollution experienced by St Luke's Church.
3. The growth of gypsum crusts occurs in both directions, inwards and outwards, with respect to the original stone surface. The predominant direction of growth, seem to be the inward one, acting behind the crusts. Urgent removal of these crusts is needed but caution with wet cleaning techniques must be exercised to avoid dissolution of the secondary gypsum framework within the stone pore spaces.
4. Repeated dissolution and particle mobilization episodes might explain the recorded distribution of imbedded anthropogenic particles and stone derived fragments within the crusts.
3. Schiavon, N. (1990) 'Gypsum crust growth and 'stratigraphy' in building limestones: a SEM study of stone decay in the U.K'. Proceedings of the European Symposium 'Science, Technology and the European Cultural Heritage', Bologna, June 1989.

References

1. Camuffo, D., DelMonte,M. and Sabbioni, C. (1983) 'Origin and growth mechanisms of the sulphated crusts on urban limestone'. Water, Air & Soil Pollution. 19: 351-359.
2. Del Monte,M. and Sabbioni, C. (1987) 'Alcuni dati quantitativi nella storia dell'inquinamento urbano'. Bollettino di Geofisica II: 67-78.
3. Schiavon, N. (1990) 'Gypsum crust growth and 'stratigraphy' in building limestones: a SEM study of stone decay in the U.K'. Proceedings of the European Symposium 'Science, Technology and the European Cultural Heritage', Bologna, June 1989.
4. Bernardi, A., Camuffo, D., DelMonte,M. and Sabbioni, C. (1985) 'Microclimate and weathering of a historical building: The Ducal Palace in Urbino' The Science of the Total Environment. 46: 243-260.

5. Pingitore, N.E. (1976) 'Vadose and phreatic diagenesis processes, products and their recognition in corals'. Journal of Sedimentary Petrology. 46: 985-1006.
6. Chang, S.G. and Novakov, T. (1978) 'Soot-catalyzed oxidation of sulphur dioxide'. Report NASA n. 1022: 349-369.
7. Del Monte, M., Sabbioni,C. and Vittori, O. (1984) 'Urban stone sulphation and oil-fired carbonaceous particles'. Science of the Total Environment. 36: 369 -376.

28 The weathering of the statues of Prato della Valle and the criteria used for consolidation

VASCO FASSINA
Laboratorio Scientifico, Soprintendenza i Beni
Artistici e Storici di Venezia, Italy

INTRODUCTION

The 78 statues of Prato della Valle in Padova are located in two rings of elliptic form in one of the largest squares of Italy (see Figure 1A).

They were made between the end of the 18th century and the beginning of the 19th century using a soft limestone from the Berici hills.

The statues of the external ring are mainly made of limestone of fine structure, while the ones of the internal ring are made using limestone of large structure.

In order to properly describe the different forms of decay macroscopically visible a detailed sampling was carried out.

On the statue surfaces we can observe the following forms of decay:

1. Black superficial deposits mainly located on sheltered areas. These deposits are very hard and they are difficult to remove from the underground stone;
2. White superficial deposits located in areas which are exposed to washout. These areas show a rough surface due to a marked erosion caused by dissolution of calcium carbonate by acidic water;
3. Black dendritic crusts mainly located on sheltered areas and characterized by blistering of the surface;
4. Biological growth of algae lichens and mosses due to the presence of trees.

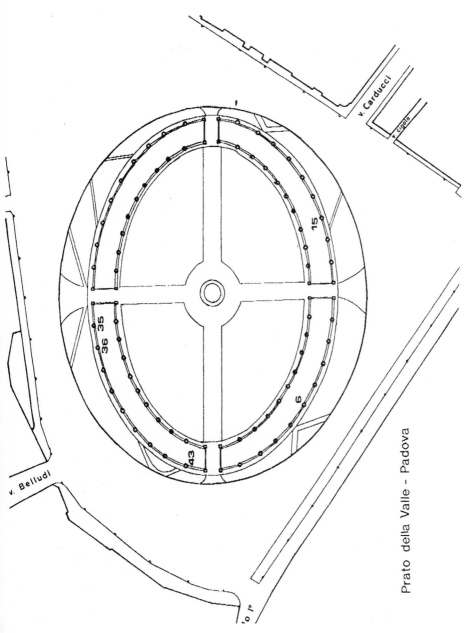

Prato della Valle - Padova

Figure 1A Sketch showing the location of the 78 statues of Prato della Valle

In order to assess the different processes of decay, various analytical methods were carried out:

1. Ionic chromatography to determine qualitatively and quantitatively the anions water-soluble.
2. Scanning Electron Microscopy (SEM) providing structural and chemical information with micrometer or nanometer spatial resolution for different components. In order to obtain more information about the chemical composition SEMs is equipped with a system for detecting characteristic X-rays locally induced in the sample by the electron beam.
3. X-ray diffraction to identify the crystalline phases in the deteriorated products.
4. Cross-section to observe the different layers on the surface.

RESULTS OF THE ANALYSES (of 11 statues)

The SEM observations show mainly the presence of gypsum crystals, carbonaceous particles, spherical particles (1).

From Energy Dispersive System (EDS) analyses the main elements appear to be calcium, sulphur, silicon, aluminium and iron due to deposition of particulate pollutants and transformation of calcite into gypsum.

On the statue surface we can always observe marking patterns with white areas where running water takes place and sheltered areas where dirt can accumulate forming sometimes hard deposits strongly adhering on the stone surface.

The large amounts of sulphates are ascribed to gypsum crystals whose morphological habit was clearly observed at the SEM (Figures 1, 2).

Figure 1 Gypsum crystals completely cover the surface

Figure 2 Typical shape of gypsum crystals

In the black crusts we have found carbonaceous particles which are responsible for the black colour on the sheltered areas of stone surfaces (Figure 3).

The microanalysis on the carbonaceous particles show the presence of large amounts of calcium and sulphur indicating probably the presence of gypsum and the excess amount of sulphur with respect to the stoichiometric ratio between calcium and sulphur could indicate that during the combustion of the fuel an adsorption of sulphur compounds can take place on the surface of carbonaceous particles.

Figure 3 Carbonaceous particles have a spongy appearance thus presenting a high specific surface

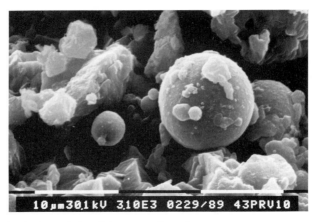

Figure 4 Spherical particle with a smooth surface

In addition to these spongy particles we can observe spherical particles not identifiable by morphological observation (Figure 4). To obtain more information the smooth spherical particles were analysed by microprobe. The main components present are silicon and aluminium and the minor components are iron, calcium and sulphur (Table 1). These particles are formed during the combustion due to the transformation of clay and other minerals present as impurity in the fuel. At the optical microscope these particles show a glassy appearance due to the fusion of earthy compounds during the combustion.

Table 1   Statue 43(Andrea Navagens) - Microprobe analyses on sample no. 10 (see Figure 4)

Component	%
Mg	1.2
Al	30.0
Si	49.9
S	5.0
K	3.2
Ca	5.5
Ti	4.7
Fe	6.4
Pb	1.4

On the surface of statues 87, 6, 15 we have found the absence of gypsum and calcite crystals, commonly observed on all statues. AT SEM the morphological aspect of the surface does not show the typical structure of a limestone. The microprobe analyses seem to indicate an anomalous amount of lead and silicon which could be correlated with compounds perhaps used as consolidants in previous restoration carried out, at the beginning of this century or in the last 60 years.

Table 2 Statue 87(Michele Sactuarole) - Microprobe analyses on sample no.4

Component	%	%
Mg	0.2	0.2
Al	0.8	0.6
Si	2.3	2.1
S	30.5	33.2
K	0.5	0.4
Ca	7.0	5.9
Fe	0.6	0.8
Pb	58.0	56.9

On statue 6, sample 6/2, the surface shows a morphological aspect which could be ascribed to previous treatment (Figure 5).

Figure 5 The surface shows a morphology typical of a treatment

The analysis carried out on the surface shows different amounts of silica which are correlated to the smooth surface (Table 3).

Table 3 Statue 6(Pietro d'Abans) - Microprobe analysis of different areas of decay observed on sample no.2

Component	Scales	Smooth surface
	%	%
Mg	6.8	0.7
Al	-	1.5
Si	14.4	4.7
S	26.6	22.7
K	-	0.6
Ca	14.2	12.7
Fe	0.5	1.3
Pb	37.6	56.0

Another sample (no.3) contains large amounts of lead (Table 4).

Table 4   Statue 6(Pietro d'Abans) - Microprobe analyses of sample 3

Component	%	%	%
Mg	0.4	0.4	1.1
Al	1.0	1.1	1.9
Si	3.8	4.9	6.9
S	24.5	27.4	24.5
Cl	0.2	0.3	0.4
K	0.6	0.6	0.7
Ca	21.4	18.3	15.9
Ti	-	-	1.3
Fe	2.0	2.3	1.6
Pb	45.9	44.7	45.5

On statue 15 in correspondence to a large amount of silicon the sulphation is depressed, on the contrary when silicon decreases the deposit is mainly formed by gypsum cyrstals. This indicates that the sulphation is dependent on the film formed by silicon (Table 5).

Table 5   Statue 15 - Microprobe analyses on sample no.5

Component	Film with treatment	Deposit above the film
	%	%
Mg	0.7	-
Al	1.9	1.2
Si	30.6	4.2
S	12.6	49.3
K	0.7	-
Ca	50.1	45.5
Fe	1.7	-
Pb	1.7	-

Over the film layer the deposit is mainly formed by gypsum crystals where Si is present in large amounts. The sulphation is depressed and it is limited only over the film surface (Table 6).

The anions contained in soluble salts are sulphates, fluorides, chlorides, nitrates and sometimes oxalates. With the exception of sulphates all the other anions are present in very low amounts.

In some samples anomalous amounts of fluorides are associated with the smaller amount of sulphates.

Table 6   Statues 35 (F.Petrarca), 36 (G.Galilei)

Sample	SO_4 %	F %	Cl %	NO_3 %	Oxalate
1 black crust	49.60	0.097	0.012	-	-
2 black crust	46.77	0.087	0.076	-	-
3 black crust	46.37	0.068	0.020	-	-
4 bl.sup. deposit	41.93	0.144	0.021	-	0.07
5 yellow layer & black crust	43.17	0.283	0.021	-	-
6 black crust	40.32	0.014	0.033	-	-
7 white sup.dep.	1.12	0.017	0.013	0.025	0.085
8 yellow layer	3.02	1.083	0.017	-	-
9 black deposit	44.40	0.295	0.015	-	-
10 black crust	48.51	0.020	-	-	0.051
11 black crust	44.55	0.075	0.015	-	-
12 scales	27.23	0.375	0.011	-	-
13 scales	29.21	0.435	0.034	-	0.051
14 scales	28.79	0.208	0.125	0.314	-
15 dechoes. powder	16.16	0.120	0.110	0.229	-

Sulphates are the main component in the analysed samples and show different amounts depending on the type of black crust (from 20% to 50%).

In the case of the surface presenting a yellow appearance, which is probably due to pest treatments, the amount of sulphate decreases sharply and correspondingly an increase of fluorides was observed.

TREATMENT OF STONE

As far as consolidation is concerned at first some people proposed the use of inorganic products which induce mineralisation of the stone thus causing structural regeneration. In this case, induced chemical reactions by use of inorganic products represent, in theory, a very good means of intervention.

These products also have very good stability over time. However, in practice, these products have a poor power of penetration, and, although their chemical nature is similar to the original stone, it is difficult to control the distribution of the mineral binding agent within the stone (1).

The development of synthetic resins has allowed new techniques of intervention to be perfected, which make possible both through consolidation without too much reduction in porosity of the stone and considerable increase in mechanical strength of the disintegrated material.

First of all it was decided to make the restoration in situ without moving the statues because they were in so bad a state of conservation that any movement, before consolidation, could have destructive effects.

The second problem was the choice of products for treatment of the stone and especially the methods of application.

As far as the consolidant is concerned we restricted our choice to acrylic resins, silicic esters and silicon reins.

Silicon ester molecules do not yield equally good results with all types of stone. They are most effective for porous, fine-grained, weak stones whose mineral constituents contain reactive-OH groups.

Limestones and marbles are not significantly strengthened by impregnation with silicon esters because the hydrolysis and condensation reactions produce silicic acid which cannot bind to the grains because these last ones do not contain any reactive-OH groups. The final result is the filling of intergranular space and the reduction of porosity without formations of bonds between silica and the grains of the stone. For this reason silicon esters were rejected.

The use of Paraloid B72 was rejected because the statues are subjected to a strong washout and an acrylic resin does not seem to have the necessary properties to resist for a long time.

In order to improve the resistance to washout it is better to use a substance which present not only consolidation action but also water-repellent properties.

For this reason the choice of methyl phenyl polysiloxane compound appear to be ideal for the requirements requested (2).

The method of application is very important for the success of consolidating treatments. We restrict our choice between slow percolation of solution on the stone surface and under vacuum treatment.

The last method was chosen because it seemed to improve the depth of penetration inside the stone.

The object was wrapped in flannelette strips attached to the stone with an adhesive.

A polyethylene tube is placed under the strips at the base of the stone; another is placed at the top and connected to a vacuum pump. The flannelette cloth is covered with a polyethylene sheet in order to obtain an impermeable coating.

The pump is switched to obtain a decrease in pressure in the space between the stone surface and the plastic sheet. The consolidating solution is then slowly introduced through the tube at the base until the top tube is reached.

CONCLUSION

The results obtained indicate that the stone decay processes are dependent on the geometry of the statue.

On sheltered areas the presence of large amounts of sulphates indicates a prevailing reaction between calcium carbonate of the statue and sulphuric acid. the rate of sulphate formation depends on some nanoclimatic condition and the final result is a different form of decay.

In addition to gypsum, large amounts of carbonaceous particles are present and they are responsible for the black appearance of the stone surface.

The black areas are characterized by different forms of decay which are dependent on their location with respect to the running water.

Black areas far from running water show 'dirt accumulation' of pollutants and the sulphate formation is not very high. The black deposits are very adherent to the substratum (Figure 6).

Figure 6 Black deposits very adherent to the stone surface

Black areas near running water show 'dirt washing' phenomenon due to the formation of dendritic crusts containing a high percentage of sulphate which is growing from the surface to outside. In this case the growth takes place by reaction of the original calcite and sulphuric acid causing an increase in the volume. Very probably the amount of water migration from the nearby washout areas cause an acceleration of sulphatation.

On the exposed areas the washout process causes a superficial erosion due to the slow dissolution of calcite and its subsequent reprecipitation (Figure 7).

The sulphate concentration is very low, about 1%, because gypsum solubility is higher with respect to the calcite one. In fact gypsum is two hundred times more soluble than calcite and consequently it is easily removed without washout. In areas exposed to running water the CO_2, reacts with $CaCO_3$ forming the bicarbonate, which is a hundred times more soluble than carbonate. The final result is a slow erosion with reprecipitation of a small part of bicarbonate into carbonate.

Very frequently very compact films are present on the stone surface especially on the base of the statue. The formation of the patina often called *scialbatura* seems to be ascribable to old treatments.

Figure 7 Superficial erosion present on the washout areas

At the SEM the patina appear to be very compact even if a spread microporosity can be observed at a higher enlargement.

X-ray diffraction show the presence of whewellite and weddellite (calcium oxalate dihydrate), gypsum and calcite from the substratum.

When the oxalate films are present the process of sulphatation is strongly reduced due probably to the protective effect of calcium oxalate (Figure 8).

Figure 8 Where calcium oxalate film is present the process of sulphatation is strongly reduced

Until now the presence of oxalate could be ascribed to past organic treatments generating oxalic acid. The presence of a high amount of lead could be ascribed to past treatments perhaps by fluosilicates. This is a treatment which was introduced in Italy in the 1950s.

The presence of a large amount of silica could also be ascribed to past treatments perhaps by potassium or sodium silicates carried out at the end of the 19th century and at the beginning of the present century (Figures 9, 10, 11).

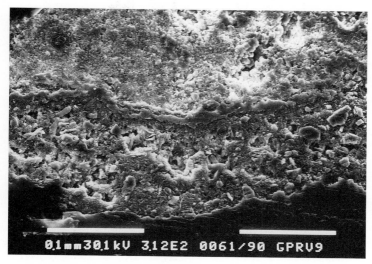

Figure 9 Thin section presenting a thin alteration layer on stone

Figure 10 X-ray distribution of silica showing spot areas at high concentration

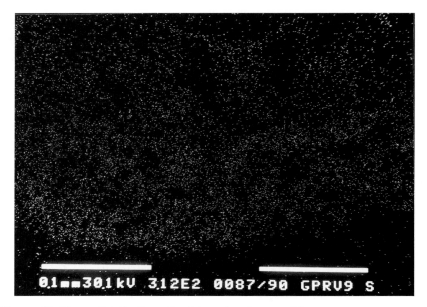

Figure 11 X-ray distribution of sulphur showing a uniform
distribution

Let us describe the different forms of alteration observed.

An example of treatment probably ascribing to past silicate treatments is reported in the thin section (Figure 9). The SEM observations indicate a layer of different nature on the stone. The X-ray analysis shows a uniform distribution for sulphur and a spot distribution for silicium. This indicates that silicium coming from a treatment can concentrate in small areas, while the sulphur which is coming from the atmosphere is uniformly distributed.

Erosion

This phenomenon is ascribed to the abrasion and the physical action of rain water due to the acidity of acid gases present on exposed areas causing a differential deterioration of the fine calcareous binder which is more soluble than the bioclasts. The damage due to migration of salts transported by water is more evident in the corners.

In fact the evaporation of water and consequently the salt crystallisation is larger in the corners and the edges and on the protrusion thus causing extensive cracks where the speed of water evaporation is higher.

Black areas

The black crusts have a different thickness and generally they are formed by thin gray-black deposits or black incrustation very thick like the dendritic crusts very commonly found on compact limestone.

Very often the crusts appear to grow over yellow patina which is generally in a good state of conservation.

The stratification of black crusts over yellow patina is mainly present on areas in which running water is absent, so we can observe a good conservation of the yellow patina. On the contrary the same patina was completely removed by washout, notwithstanding the insolubility of calcium oxalate which is the constituent of the yellow patina.

Black crusts directly in contact with limestone show exfoliation and scaling phenomena.

From X-ray diffraction the black crusts are mainly formed by gypsum, calcite (very probably of reprecipitation), quartz, feldspars from wind deposition. The extensive presence of gypsum is evident from SEM analysis showing a network of crystals homogeneously distributed all over the surface and differently crystallized inside microcracks. Sometimes whewellite and weddellite were found, probably formed by the organic decomposition of previous treatments producing oxalic acid which then transforms into the very stable calcium oxalate.

On the running water calcium oxalate does not resist indefinitely probably because at the interface between washout and sheltered areas the formation of gypsum cryustals can cause blistering of the previous oxalate films causing the detachment in the exposed areas.

Exfoliation and scaling are very often associated with the rhythmic contraction and pressure on the walls of the pores by salts which are alternatively crystallizing and dissolving. This type of alteration is mainly present in black areas and under the scales we have a powder formation due to the presence of gypsum.

The main damage observed on statues is caused by the transformation of calcium carbonate into calcium sulphate. This transformation is due to the action of sulphuric acid which can be generated:

i)   in the atmospheric droplets of oxidation of sulphur dioxide by strongly oxidising agents (hydrogen peroxide, ozone) or by oxygen in the presence of catalysts (Fe^{3+} and Mn^{2+}) (3);

ii)   on the stone surface by oxidation of sulphur dioxide absorbed on limestone in the presence of catalysts (metal oxides and carbonaceous particles) and moisture.

From these considerations it appears that the decay process is efficient when the different factors involved in the oxidation are contemporaneously present.

Polluted atmospheres containing high concentrations of sulphur dioxide, metal oxides and carbonaceous particles represent the ideal conditions but they are not sufficient if moisture is absent. For this reason urban fog conditions represent better conditions for sulphur dioxide oxidation and consequently enhance the rate of stone decay. The action of acid sulphur gases on calcareous materials causes the formation of a hard surface skin which tends to blister and exfoliate (1).

References

1. Amoroso, G.G. and Fassina, V. (1983). 'Stone Decay and Conservation' (Elsevier, Amsterdam).
2. Fassina, V. (1990). Considerazioni sui criteri di scelta del consolidante e la relativa metodologia di applicazione. Proceedings of the Symposium 'Il Prato della Valle e le opere in pietra calcarea collocate all 'aperto'. Padova 6 aprile 1990. Libreria progetto 131-145.
3. Fassina, V. (1978). A survey on air pollution and deterioration of stonework in Venice. *Atmos. Environ.* 12:2205-2211.
4. Fassina, V. (1988). Stone decay of Venetian monuments in relation to air pollution. Proceedings of the International Symposium 'The Engineering geology of Ancient Works Monuments and Historical Sites', Athens, 19-23 September 1988. P.G.Marinos and G.C. Koukis, A.A. Balkema, Rotterdam 1988, 787-796.
    Fassina, V. and Zanella, D. (1990). processi di degrado del complesso architecttonico e monumentale del Prato della Valle, in relazione alle interazioni con l'ambiente. Proceedings of the Symposium 'Il Prato della Valle e le opere in pietra calcarea collocate all 'aperto'. Padova 6 aprile 1990. Libreria Progetto 83-130.

29 Weathering as a controllable phenomenon

FRANK HAWES
DipArch RIBA

INTRODUCTION

This paper discusses the possibility of designing buildings so that they do not need cleaning. This is not intended as an attack on all those firms that do excellent work saving old buildings from the ravages of time but as a way of showing how a designer's contribution to the architectural scene can reduce the need for such help for some time to come.

Changes in appearance

Limestones, sandstones, many of the most attractive bricks and of course, concrete, will change appearance fairly quickly and none of them is the worse for that. But the architect ought to be able to predict and control those changes, so they are not left to mar our buildings. Prediction and control will be discussed later but first we ought to consider very briefly these natural processes of change.

NATURAL CHANGES

Building stones take some time to settle down after quarrying and in that time they seem to be particularly susceptible to soiling. The formation of the hardened calcium carbonate skin on the surface of calcareous stones is neither instantaneous nor uniform and there is plenty of sulphur dioxide in our polluted atmospheres to react with it to form calcium sulphate.

Both of these calcium salts can combine with dirt particles either to encourage their adhesion to the surface or, especially in the case of the more soluble calcium sulphate, to facilitate their removal from exposed parts of the surface and their re-deposition elsewhere.

Dirt deposition

The larger of the dirt particles in the atmosphere – that is those bigger than one micron or so, settle under the influence of gravity on the upward facing parts of a facade, from where they will normally be washed by rain or, in dry weather, be blown by the wind. The tiniest parts, however, form a more permanent part of the aerosol because the friction forces when they fall through the atmosphere are greater than the gravitational forces on such tiny particles (1). As a result, they are available to be attracted to and to adhere to any surface, whichever way it is facing – north or south, up or down. Their initial adhesion to any surface is the result of a complex of physico-chemical reactions, often involving moisture which in most climates is normally present in sufficient quantities from condensation even when there has been no rain. Once in contact with a building surface the dirt particles seem to become bound to the salts mentioned above if they are present.

Biological colonization

In our polluted environments it does not take long for the surface of calcareous materials to become neutralized. Any porous surface with an alkalinity below pH8 will be capable of supporting biological life – algae first, and later lichens and mosses. Lichens can be very attractive on stone – but if they are unevenly distributed due to variations in the surface or in the way that water is allowed to affect it, they can be an eyesore. If surfaces remain damp for long periods they may support areas of green or black algae rather than attractive lichens.

THE WEATHERING SYSTEM

All these processes – the production of salts, the deposition of dirt and the development of biological colonization together with the action of the elements in washing and eroding surfaces and re-distributing dirt – combine in the process called in English, 'weathering'.

In most foreign languages one can say only 'ageing' or 'dirtying', but the English terminology permits the concept of weathering as an acceptable or attractive change of appearance. It is a natural phenomenon which ought not to be regarded as a problem but rather as a challenge to architects and builders. An architect should accept responsibility for the appearance of his building throughout its life.

DESIGNING TO CONTROL WEATHERING

If it were possible to specify only materials to which dirt would not adhere, moreover, materials on which algae and lichens should not grow, then all an architect would have to do would be to contrive a flow of water over these surfaces and he would have discovered the secret of eternal youth for his building!

The solution to designing for the control of weathering ought then to be simple. All buildings should be pyramids clad entirely in so-called self cleansing materials. But the new glass pyramid in the centre of the great courtyard of the Louvre in Paris is just that and it has to be very regularly cleaned.

The designer's task

If glass pyramids do not stay clean, we must accept that any building is going to get dirty and that our real task as designers is going to be one of controlling the dirt so that it does not spoil the appearance of our buildings. Parts of any building will get dirty and other parts will remain clean. We have to predict which these will be, detail boldly to ensure that our predictions come true and choose surfaces and finishes - not necessarily the same surfaces and finishes – which will look good when clean and acceptable when dirty.

PREDICTION

Predicting the likely weathering of a building can vary from a fairly obvious assessment of known facts to an impossible juggling with imponderables. In many cases an architect will be working within a well understood vocabulary and will need only to adjust his decisions to the site in question. On the other hand he may be breaking new ground in which he has little experience. In the latter case he must gather all the information he can but he will find there is no substitute for direct observation.

Meteorological information

Meteorological records will give some help but must be studied with care. There are many places with much higher annual rainfall than Britain where the rainfall pattern and consequently the resultant weathering systems are quite different. Britain's annual rainfall is indeed not very high, especially in the south east, but it is spread over a great many days. Many continental and Mediterranean places have higher totals but most of the rain comes in a few summer storms.

The significance of this is twofold: in a thunderstorm the wind can blow from any direction so the importance of the prevailing wind on weathering patterns may be less and secondly, the propensity for surfaces to support algal growth seems to be related more to the chances that they get to dry out thoroughly than to their likelihood of getting wet.

Site studies

It is always best to get as much information as possible from observation of plants and buildings on or around the site itself. From such observations it will be possible to determine the two basic essentials: is the site in question going to prove difficult because of high levels of pollution, or is its atmosphere fairly clean? Secondly, is it likely to prove difficult because its microclimate is particularly wet or very strongly directional?

Pollution levels

If the site is heavily polluted the architect must decide whether this is from industrial sources some distance away or from local dirt and dust due to its proximity to an adjacent road, railway or other isolated source. This can be significant because, in the latter case, there is often a noticeable gradation of dirt from ground level upwards, and also because the sticky black emissions from diesel exhausts can be a particular problem.

Microclimate

If there is a noticeable directionality to the microclimate of the site, either as a result of exposure to the prevailing wind of the region or as a result of funnelling of wind by adjacent existing buildings or natural features, this too must be taken into account. Unless extremely bold design decisions are taken the exposed sides of the building are bound to perform differently from the others.

There are, of course, cases where it does not matter that although different parts of a building have been designed to be identical, time has made them completely different. Where the building is very large on plan or the elevations cannot be easily related one to another such changes may be acceptable but if the architect's intention is to create a symmetrical pavilion he will find his symmetry short-lived on such a site.

CONTROL

For some sites, however, the problems are much less. Indeed in dry continental climates buildings sometimes seem to defy time altogether. For the majority of cases even in Britain's more difficult climate careful attention to the fundamentals of good design for the control of weathering should suffice to keep the natural changes subservient to the architecture. It is when the dirt and algae are the most prominent features of a building that the public objects.

Fundamentals

We can perhaps reduce these fundamentals down to two:

1. Except in the most benign of situations a building should be subdivided in its height;
2. Each part of each elevation of a building should be designed to control any water to which it is subjected without detriment to areas below.

The benign situations referred to above would include very dry climates, exceptionally clean environments and most small scale buildings, and judgements will be influenced by the materials to be used. The more benign the conditions, the wider the choice of materials.

The second fundamental 'control' means, above all, that water must never be allowed to run off an upward facing surface on to adjacent vertical faces. It is this water that is too often allowed to cause streaks on otherwise acceptable surfaces.

Vertical variations

Natural atmospheric processes invariably make a better job of keeping buildings clean at the top than at lower levels. This variation in cleanliness is more a result of the way wind-driven rain impinges on the facades than the effect of any gradation in atmospheric dirt. It is surprisingly difficult to get rain on to the lower parts of a tall building.

A first maxim for building in dirty areas ought therefore to be the subdivision of the height of the building into top, middle and bottom. Inspection of almost any of the elegant buildings from the past which we admire will reveal a similar solution though it would be wrong to assume that it was a design form adopted for the control of weathering.

Choice of materials

As the amounts of both dirt and water to be dealt with vary with the height of the building, not only different detailing but even different materials or surface treatments might be called for at different levels. For instance the part of an elevation rising straight from pavement level in a city street will be subject to such an amount of dirt that it ought to have either a material on which the dirt will not show or a material that can be cleaned easily. Most easily cleaned materials are expensive and the cost of cleaning can also be considerable, so it would seem sensible to confine this solution to the area of the facade where the dirt is likely to be most noticeable.

Controlling vertical variations

When the wind blows at a building some of the air will rise to pass at an increased velocity over the top; the rest will form a horizontal vortex and spiral away round the ends.

Figure 1 Wind movements on the windward side of a large building.

A large concentration of rain is thrown against the upper part of the elevation while very little hits lower down (2). This phenomenon is most noticeable on tall buildings clad in semi-porous materials like concrete and the most commonly used building stones.

It can be seen from many classical buildings that a deep cornice can effectively divide the washed area at high level from the unwashed main area of the wall. It appears from observation of such buildings that there is considerable latitude in the size and positioning of such a feature without detriment to its effectiveness.

Where such features do not exist walls facing the prevailing wind develop three or four clearly visible zones. The lower part, perhaps two thirds of the height, is likely to be dirty from the deposition and adhesion of the finer dirt particles in the atmosphere. The upper part will be washed by the driven rain which will quickly saturate the surface and then commence to flow downwards taking with it any dirt deposited since the last shower. When this water reaches the area of wall which is protected from driven rain by the horizontal vortex it will be absorbed into the surface causing a typical zigzag dirt line.

The level at which the jagged line of dirt forms will be governed by a combination of the height of the vortex and the absorbency of the facing material of the wall. The height of the vortex above the ground is determined by the height of adjacent buildings or other obstructions over which the wind has passed.

Figure 2 Part of the south wall of St Paul's Cathedral showing effect of cornice.

DESIGNING FOR CONTROL

The designer can use the rain to keep as much of the surface as possible clean but on those parts of the building where there is insufficient rain for that purpose the aim should be to keep all water off the surfaces. If rain is allowed to run off on to otherwise protected areas it is unlikely to be sufficient to wash it all clean. It will either clean only the top half leaving a jagged dirt line similar to

Figure 3 Typical dirt pattern on a semi-porous windward facing wall.

those described above or it will make clean streaks through the dirt which are every bit as ugly as dirty streaks on clean surfaces.

Designing buildings that will weather well is therefore a matter of prediction and control – predicting how the environment will affect the building and then designing and detailing to control these effects. The weapons of control are the massing and detailing of the building and the colour, texture and quality of the finishes.

Details

Well designed details might be copies of traditional mouldings or they may be modern forms made to control water in a similar manner. A classical cornice after all was developed to throw crisp shadows in Mediterranean sunshine not to throw off water from a multi-storey tower. However, provided that a bold separation is made between areas that have sufficient water to keep them clean and those which do not, and provided also that the water that is intercepted is either thrown well clear of the face or is collected and led away elsewhere, the form of the division is immaterial.

Figure 4 Typical partial washing of a wall on the leeside of a building

Drip grooves

To throw the water clear of the face this bold horizontal feature must have a minimum projection of 250-300mm (3) but in many cases in order to be in scale with the building it will be much more. It must also have a drip groove on the underside to prevent water from running back across the soffite.

There are still buildings being produced with ledges and soffites without drip grooves. Such omissions will produce ugly weathering patterns whatever material is being used. The groove protects the soffite from being stained but more importantly it prevents random staining on the wall below. Grooves should be a minimum of 20mm wide and should form an angle of at least 40-45°with the soffite at the front arris (4).

Water collected by drip grooves is often blown towards one end or the other before its surface tension is overcome by the accumulated weight and it drops. If the soffite is contained between vertical faces there is a danger of causing unsightly stains on the abutting wall. In such a position the groove is normally stopped approximately 50mm from the wall. An alternative is to have a groove rather larger than the drip groove in a corresponding position on the jamb to contain and guide the water and conceal any staining it may cause.

Collecting water

Water collected at horizontal details must be taken to a place where it can be conducted down the facade without causing unsightly streaks.

Vertical flows on facades can be guided and controlled by quite subtle grooves and rebates if their sizes and positions are well judged but the most effective way of controlling such water is to collect it into a properly conceived system of gutters and down pipes.

CONCLUSION

Examples can be found of modern buildings which are still looking good after several years in spite of poor detailing, and of others where good detailing has kept difficult surfaces in an acceptable condition, but there are far too many new buildings for which the only hope of success is frequent rescue by the cleaning cavalry.

References

1. Carrie, C. and Morel, D. 'Salissures de facades'. Paris, Editions Eyrolles, 1975. 140pp.
2. Beijer, O.F. 'Weathering on External Walls of Concrete'. Stockholm, Swedish Cement & Concrete Institute, 1980. 70pp. CIB Report 11:80.
3. Herbert, M.R.M. 'Some Observations on the Behaviour of Weather Protective features on External Walls'. London DoE Building Research Establishment, 1974. 17pp BRE Current Paper CP81/74.
4. Law, N. 'Assessment of Performance of Drip Grooves'. North Ryde,NSW Australia, Experimental Building Station Department of Construction, 1978. 15pp Technical Record 442.

30 Cleaning or proper detailing to prevent cleaning?

LEO VERHOEF
Department of Architecture, Technical University, Delft,
The Netherlands

FOREWORD

In the Netherlands research is currently being
undertaken within the framework of BRIK (Brick
research innovation transfer of knowledge), funded
by the KNB (The Netherlands Brick Industry) with
the support of the Ministry of Economic Affairs. One
section of this study, presented in this paper, is being
carried out by ir. Leo G.W. Verhoef and ir. Ype
Cuperus.

INTRODUCTION

Throughout their lifetime buildings change. The
ravages of time leave their traces whereby in many
instances the attractiveness of a building is only
enhanced. This is certainly true of brick-built
buildings. Some changes however are considered to
be for the worse and we then talk of 'visual soiling'.
All kinds of decay fall under this category but it also
includes chemical processes such as chalk
efflorescence. Moreover graffiti, another form of
soiling as well as measures taken to remove it or

prevent it (for example impregnation of the facade), can affect the visual aspect of the brickwork as well.

This study chiefly concerns the soiling of brickwork caused by the irregular process of dirt deposits and gives guidelines on the detailing of brick constructions to both prevent and control the effects of soiling.

THE MECHANISM OF SOILING

The mechanism that results in the soiling of facades has been adequately described by F. Hawes and for the purpose of this paper presumed to be understood. Certain aspects have also been studied by the RILEM technical committee '62, 'Soiling and Cleaning of Building Facades'.

THE DESIGN

The primary function of any building is to provide space in which the desired functions may be carried out. The programme of requirements, for example, for a four-roomed dwelling, does not prescribe the design of the building. How dwellings are connected to each other, how they are assimilated into the urban development, the infrastructure, the internal routing and the chosen building method make almost every design unique.

This study is concerned with brickwork and the measures to prevent visual soiling. The quality of the design itself determines whether visual soiling will need to be prevented. Alas, many buildings are designed purely from the economic necessity to create space. The architectural quality is so poor and does so little to enhance the building that even the surroundings are affected.

This study is based on the principle that a building should be designed so that, as far as the brickwork is concerned, certain general features are indicated in the design, for example:

− The dimensions and structure of the facades and the various components;
− The design of edges and apertures so that the facade presents a separate shell and lends character to the building;

- Selection of a certain colour and structure that not only define the individual building but also give it elements expressing its affinity to the urban surroundings;
- The design of brickwork on an integral basis. The interconnection of the brickwork and the connection between brickwork and other building components should also be considered.

Such modern requirements as insulation and ventilation represent an important difference from the past. Facades now have to be constructed in layers. The separate layers, from the outer layer to the inner layer, form the following functions:

- Visual appearance, all-weather protection;
- Insulation;
- Sometimes bearing layers, accumulation and visual.

The pre-conditions required by a building's physical construction limit bond possibilities.

Buildings of considerable height have been constructed from bearing brickwork. For instance in Buffalo in the USA a sixteen-storey office block designed by Sullivan and in Zurich, Switzerland in 1958 a seventeen-storey building with a substructure and cellar designed by Haller. Because of the aforementioned pre-conditions set by building physics the height of the outer wall surface is also limited.

Formerly it was possible to construct brick walls of almost unlimited lengths. An example is the Orange Nassau barracks in Amsterdam with a total continuous length of approximately 260 m.

Walls of such length can no longer be constructed due to the addition of cement to the mortar. Modern mortars are stronger and work faster while they are less elastic and shrink more. Wall lengths now need to be limited. Movement of joints is often required.

SOILING IN RELATION TO DETAILING

When we look at the soiling of brickwork in relation to detailing, we must first distinguish between the quality of the brickwork and that quality in relation to the building products directly or indirectly coming into contact with the brickwork.

Classification of brickwork

In order to arrive at effective guidelines, it is important to understand the principles underlying the soiling of brickwork. Practical observation has demonstrated that generally speaking soiling occurs at 'irregularities' in the construction: above and below connections, at bulges and indentations and at connections with other building materials and products. The most common irregularities can be classified and described.

1. **Closed brickwork:**
— vertical brickwork with lower, upper and side connections;

— sloping vertical brickwork with lower, upper and side connections;

— curved brickwork with lower, upper and side connections. Depending on the curve radius, wider joints result.

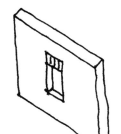

2. **Brickwork with apertures:**
— vertical brickwork with a small aperture without additional span construction. The soldier course serves to make the height of the frame independent of the dimensions of the brick courses and to

achieve a better brickwork edge than with a stretcher course.

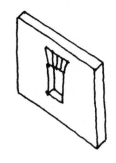

— smooth brickwork with a small aperture and a flat arch as span construction;

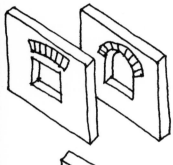

— smooth brickwork with aperture and an arch span construction;

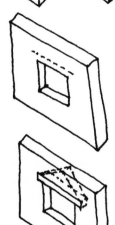

— smooth brickwork with aperture and a curved span construction;

3. **Brickwork with apertures and span constructions of another material:**
— vertical brickwork with aperture and reinforcement in the longitudinal joints as span construction;

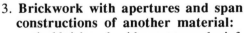

— vertical brickwork with aperture and steel lintel as span construction;

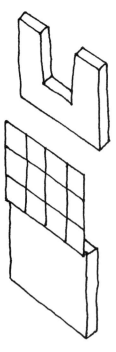

– vertical brickwork with aperture and concrete lintel as span construction;

4. Brickwork with adjoining apertures on the upper side:
– vertical brickwork in 'cut-out' facades. The aperture is spanned with a material other than brick;

5. Brickwork in combination with materials with considerably less capacity for water absorption.

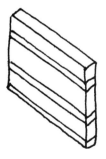

6. Brickwork with various types of bricks:
– vertical brickwork built up of different coloured brick.

The above list is not exhaustive. The aim is to reduce the principles of brickwork soiling to simple examples. For each example a soiling prognosis can be given. The aforementioned principles of brickwork soiling can then serve to analyze examples of soiling found in the field. Using the above list as reference the probable causes of soiling can be predicted and either suggestions given as to how soiling could have been prevented or solutions provided. The latter can be presented in the same simple format as the above list.

SOILING OF BRICKWORK BY RAIN FLOWING OVER OTHER MATERIALS

Rainwater flowing over brickwork causes soiling especially at 'irregularities' in the construction. Here irregularities are understood to mean: end connections, interruptions together with the addition of other materials to the brickwork. The effect of soiling increases when greater differences in absorption capacity occur. The following list indicates those connections which are more prone to soiling by rainwater.

- coping of a wall;
  roof trimming;
- open feeders and gutter spouts;
- rainwater pipes;
- lintels (brickwork, concrete, steel)
- movement joints;
- window-sill stones;
- weather cornices (synthetic or aluminium);
- non-porous materials on top of brickwork (glass, painted wood, metals etc);
- damp-proof courses;
- vent holes;
- ground level (rainwater mixed with soil splashing against building);

The above list is not exhaustive. The aim is to reduce the principles of brickwork soiling to simple examples. For each example a soiling prognosis can be given. The aforementioned principles of brickwork soiling can then serve to analyze examples of soiling found in the field. Using the above list as reference the probable causes of soiling can be signalled and either suggestions given as to how soiling could have been prevented or solutions provided. The latter can be presented in the same simple format as the above list.

GUIDELINES FOR THE PREVENTION OF VISUAL SOILING

Brickwork consists of bricks and mortar joints and is generally speaking porous and water absorbent. Although far more rain falls on the upper sides and the ribs of a building than on the other vertical brickwork surfaces, water hardly ever streams over the upper surface. In this respect brickwork is better than concrete.

The prevention of visual soiling is especially aimed at the paths taken by the water flow and is based on the following general principles:

a. Prevent a concentrated flow of water by containing and diverting the water;
b. Incorporate projections of adequate proportions to disperse the flow of water;
c. Add sufficient detailing to 'outshine' soiling.

In more detail:
1. Prevent water reaching brickwork surfaces with an upward construction. These surfaces remain damp for longer periods and form a breeding ground for biological growths. The moisture front of the water soaks into the wall and marks the surface. As the moisture evaporates released chalk and salts may be transported to the surface.
2. Water falling on to roof surfaces must not be diverted via the facade. Watch for dilatations in the roof trimming.
3. Rainwater easily flows over non-absorbent surfaces. All other materials are in principle less absorbent then brickwork and thus rainwater flows easily over them. Water flowing over the surfaces of non-absorbent facades should be contained and drained away.
4. Water flowing over smaller, non-absorbent facade surfaces such as glass in windows should be diverted from the facade. Weather cornices are required under the window. According to the dominant wind direction, water is simultaneously diverted in both an horizontal and vertical direction over the weather cornice. A barrier is necessary at the edge of the weather cornice to prevent concentrated rain run-off.
5. Additions to a facade such as the mounts for flag

poles and lamps should be adequately detailed to divert water from the facade.

6. Water which splashes against a facade at ground level leaves dirt deposits on the facade. This area of the facade demands attention.

N.B. For the purposes of this paper soiling as a result of chalk efflorescence, graffiti, impregnation as well as stains caused by cement are not discussed.

GUIDELINES FOR THE DESIGN OF NEW BUILDINGS

Based on the mechanisms described by Frank Hawes, the dominant role played by water flow in certain situations and the analyses of practical examples, this section gives simple guidelines for 'basic solutions' to prevent or contain the aforementioned types of soiling of the various connections used in a building construction.

Many examples could be described but this paper limits itself to the following:

– brickwork and aluminium roof trimming
– brickwork connections with the ground level.

Each problem is described and analyzed and a basic solution presented. Three aspects per solution are considered:

– prevention of soiling
– ensure soiling is acceptable
– ensure soiling is easy to remove.

Brickwork and aluminium roof trimming

The problem

Soiling often occurs below the connection of two roof trimming elements for the upper finish of a brickwork construction. Water that collects in/behind/on top of the roof trimming construction flows through the opening in the connection and thus over the brickwork. Dirt is carried in the flow and deposited on the brickwork.

Where the actual soiling is concerned it is noticeable that the rhythm of the scoring in relation to the roof trimming connections, differs from the rhythm of the composition of the facade.

Analysis of problem

Two problems are involved. Firstly the nature and extent of the soiling and secondly the place where soiling occurs.

In order to solve the first problem, the origin of the deposited dirt must be ascertained – is it from outside or inside the building construction ?

1. Dirt from outside
Rainwater falling on or against the aluminium will carry with it any dirt on the aluminium surface to the lower edge and from there, depending on the wind direction, to the left or right along the under edge to the end of the roof trimming. Arriving here the stream of water is blown about. If the projections are narrow the water will blow on to the facade and result in concentrated soiling. If they are wider the water will be dispersed over a wider area and soiling will be slighter and may not even form at all.

Even in the interior cavities of the roof trimming section, dirt collects from outside. Depending on the detailing of the roof edge some of the dirt may originate from the more or less horizontal part of the roof elevation.

2. Dirt from inside
Aluminium roof trimmings come in various designs – spray painted, powder coated, anodized and untreated. On the latter a finishing layer of aluminium oxide is formed, which prevents further oxidation. Where the surface layer is damaged a layer of aluminium oxide again forms as if it was untreated aluminium. Aluminium becomes corroded by cement water and by a great number of metals. Some of the products formed by this chemical process are carried along by rainwater and deposited on the brickwork construction in the same way that dirt leaves its traces.

3. Place of soiling
Aluminium has a large expansion coefficient. This means that the length of the aluminium roof trimming

has to be limited: it has to be able to expand without working loose from the underlying construction.

Regulations from the supplier prescribe aluminium roof trimmings of a maximum length of 3 m while dilatations also have to be implemented according to regulations.

Roof trimmings are fitted by a roofer. Roofing is a completely separate trade in the building world. In general the position of the roof trimming dilatations are not indicated on building plans and are left to the roofer. The latter and the architect completely differ as to the visual aspects of the facade and one finds that the formation of the roof trimming connections has no affinity with the formation of the brickwork facade.

Basic solution

1. Prevent soiling of brickwork:
    (i) Conduct water away from the brickwork of the facade. Prevent a concentrated flow of water reaching the brickwork facade under the connection points of the aluminium roof trimming components.

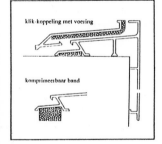

    (ii) Disperse water. A projection prevents the concentrated flow of water reaching the brickwork facade; the water has already been blown about and dispersed before it touches the underlying facade. The soiling pattern will therefore be spread evenly and thinly over the facade and not be noticeable. The wider the projection, the better the effect, which reduces the degree of soiling. A wide projection does cause a 'lee' to form underneath it, that is a horizontal zone where no rain can fall. However soiling by dry deposits will eventually form here as no rainwater will wash them away. As these deposits fall in the projection's shadow they are hardly noticeable.

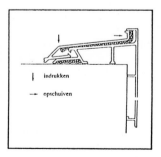

2. Ensure soiling is acceptable:
    (i) texture of facade. One sort of brick shows up soiling more easily than the other. A smooth, light brick gives a smooth facade on which traces of soiling are clearly visible. A brick with a rough surface and darker patterns

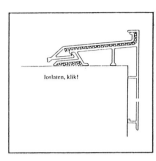

loslaten, klik!

shows less soiling.

(ii) facade relief. Practical examples demonstrate that soiling on dynamic facades is found to be acceptable. Use can be made of this fact to incorporate relieved surfaces into the facade to ensure that any soiling will be visually 'outshone'.

3. Ensure that soiling only occurs where it is least noticeable:

(i) horizontal detailing. Roof trimming connections occur at unpredictable places in the facade. The design can indicate where these connections should occur, for example coinciding with a vertical line in the facade, such as a drainpipe or a dilatation. The rhythmicity of the soiling then coincides with the rhythmicity of the facade whereby soiling is less noticeable.

(ii) vertical detailing. A few somewhat rather receding layers of brickwork could be detailed under the roof trimming construction to ensure that soiling under the roof trimming is limited to these layers. This can be done in combination with a darker coloured brick.

4. Ensure soiling is easy to remove:

(i) Install a side fascia. By installing a side board, which is easy to clean, between the roof trimming and the brickwork facade soiling can be removed. Soiling will occur on the side board and not on the brickwork facade. From time to time the side board can be cleaned and/or painted.

Brickwork connections with the ground level

Problem

Where the brickwork construction meets the ground level or street level two kinds of soiling can be distinguished. Firstly soiling from rain splashing against the facade and secondly soiling, including graffiti, wilfully caused by people. The first sort of soiling is discussed here.

Analysis of problem
Soiling caused by rain splashing against the facade depends on the horizontal surface from whence the

304

rain comes. Here, the type of surface plays a role: a gravel path is quite different from flagstones or garden soil. The soiling is different to the soiling caused by the flow of rainwater. It does not involve dry matter which has affixed itself to a building and has then been transported and deposited by rainwater. What is involved here are much larger particles such as sand or soil carried along by rainwater and splashed against the facade. Through absorption the humus-like soiling penetrates the surface of the brickwork to a certain extent and is not so easily washed away by rain.

Basic solution

1. Prevent soiling:
   The soiling of brickwork from water splashing against it at ground level cannot be prevented. However soiling can be reduced by ensuring that the building's immediate surroundings, the zone bordering on the brickwork, is of such a form and texture that rainwater has little chance to splash against it; a gravel path disperses rain and less is splashed against the facade while a flagstone path causes more rain to splash against the facade. However this rainwater is less dirty than rain splashing up from garden soil.
2. Ensuring soiling is acceptable:
   Soiling caused by rainwater splashing against the brickwork is more noticeable on a light coloured brick. If the first 50 cm of the facade was built with a darker coloured brick and possibly one with more pattern to it, soiling is less marked and thus less obnoxious. The 50 cm is more or less compatible with the trass layers to stop rising water, as seen in old brickwork constructions.
3. Ensure soiling only occurs where it is less noticeable.
4. Ensure soiling is easy to remove:
   If that part of the facade most exposed to soiling is constructed with a smooth surface, soiling is easier to remove. However in this respect two comments are called for:
   (i) as this part of the facade is prone to damage and damp, a brick type is selected based on its maintenance-free quality. There are very few smooth materials which also meet this requirement.

(ii) practical observation demonstrates that this part of the facade is not cleaned regularly. It would seem that the logic of the soiled area makes this form of soiling more acceptable.

31 The removal of graffiti

ROY BUTLIN, CLARE RUSSELL and IAIN McCAIG
Building Research Establishment, Garston, Watford, UK

(ABSTRACT)

This review discusses methods to investigate the effectiveness of graffiti removers and the use of protective surface coatings. Information regarding particular graffiti removers and anti-graffiti coatings has not been given because of the ever fluctuating market. Variations in the properties or composition of the products tested in various reports can occur at any time.

The term graffiti can be defined as a deliberate unauthorised defacement of a surface by words or drawings. Many different markers such as chalk felt tip pens, aerosol paints, lipstick and wax crayons can be used to deface many different surfaces (substrates). If the substrate is porous i.e. limestone or brick, graffiti removal is much more difficult because the marker can penetrate into the pores of the substrate and thus become harder to dislodge.

The three main ways of removing graffiti are by using:

1. Abrasive techniques;
2. Heat methods;
3. Chemical methods.

In areas where there is an incidence of graffiti, anti-graffiti coatings can be used. These coatings, which are either permanent or temporary, can be easily cleaned using chemicals specified by the manufacturer and hence can dramatically reduce the otherwise high cleaning and maintenance costs. However, it is necessary to use a coating which is permeable and resistant to weathering (e.g. UV light, pollution) to avoid cracking and discolouration of the coating and also damage to the substrate itself.